Girl/Friend Theology
God-Talk with Young People
Second edition

Girl/Friend Theology

God-Talk *with* Young People
Second edition

Dori Grinenko Baker

the pilgrim press

The Pilgrim Press, 1300 East 9th Street
Cleveland, Ohio 44114
thepilgrimpress.com

Published 2023.
Second edition. First edition *Doing Girlfriend Theology: God-Talk with Young Women* © 2005.
Scripture quotations, unless otherwise noted, are from the New Revised Standard Version of the Bible, © 1989 by the Division of Christian Education of the National Council of Churches of Christ in the United States of America. Used by permission. Changes have been made for inclusivity.

Printed on acid-free paper.

Library of Congress Cataloging-in-Publication Data on file.
LCCN: 2023932472

ISBN 978-0-8298-0046-3 (paper)
ISBN 978-0-8298-0047-0 (ebook)

Printed in The United States of America.

This book is dedicated to my daughters, Erin and Olivia Baker, and my godchildren, Indianna and Van Gillum. May you always listen to the still small voice within as you navigate your lives with love.

TABLE OF CONTENTS

FOREWORD

It is the second day of Kwanzaa 2022, Kujichagulia, which means self-determination in Kiswahili. Just two days ago on Christmas Eve, I played with, cuddled, and consoled Lauryn, the feisty three year old daughter of a friend. She embodied self-determination. She resolved not to be outdone by her talented big sister, Anna, who was already commanding the attention of Hollywood in film and video. It showed as she dominated the karaoke microphone. But Lauryn commanded the other microphone as well, singing with fearless confidence, on top of her sister, in her own language—her made-up words—to the tune of the karaoke song. Self-determination such as Lauryn's is precious, priceless, and must be heard into speech as a characteristic of girls, especially Black girls like Lauryn.

Dori Baker's *Girl/Friend Theology* offers us a process of listening for the self-determination of girls growing as adolescents in the community of other girls and their adult women partners. This second edition of her book builds on the experiences of holy listening to girls across the racial/ethnic, class, gender, and sexual orientation spectrum to offer a spiritual practice of holy listening that is more attentive and sensitive to all girls regardless of their identity as cisgender or transgender girls, or gender nonbinary individuals. Like the first edition, the second edition facilitates meaning-making and critical thinking among girls and women about the joys and sorrows of life amid a sociocultural context of mental disorders, state-sanctioned violence, and politically justified laws that demean and dehumanize girls and women. However, this edition intentionally includes Womanist, Black feminist, and Queer theory and life stories of LGBTQIA, African descended, Latinx, Asian girls, and gender nonbinary individuals alongside European descended cisgendered girls. All are invited to the center of the story-telling circle, which acknowledges the worth and importance of their lives and their voices.

Dori Baker's action of foregrounding culturally and ethnically diverse life stories concretizes an act of truth-telling and repentance about her own inheritance of and benefits from white patriarchy and white supremacy. In this edition of *Girl/Friend Theology*, she lays bare the truth about her own social location and socialization, specifically her coming to feminist consciousness as an adolescent in her Florida high school's Future Homemakers of America club. Discovering the power of her voice, facilitated by nurturing adult female teachers and church leaders, was foundational for her calling to seminary and eventually ordination as a clergywoman in the United Methodist Church. No doubt her awareness of gender oppression continued to mature as well as her consciousness about race, class, and sexual oppression. While the latter was not as forthcoming in the first edition as in the second, almost twenty years of hearing stories of women, girls, and nonbinary people has made Baker more aware of and committed to hearing to speech a diverse population life storytellers.

In addition to foregrounding diverse life stories, an attribute of the second edition is a more systematic and accessible methodology. Since the first publication in 2005, Baker offers a process captured in the acronym LIVE (Listen, Immerse, View it wider, Enact) that builds on her experience of honing the method for the past seventeen years. The four movements of the intergenerational model begin with 1) listening to a real-life story told by a participant; 2) immersing ourselves in the feelings, emotions, sights, and sounds of the story; 3) connecting the story with other stories we know from our faith traditions, scriptures, and spiritual practices; 4) exploring and enacting what we must do as a result of listening, immersing, and viewing the story wider. The method flows out of lived experience that honors the truths of the participant. This is always the starting point for God-talk—theology—that moves from beginning to end in the methodology. The willingness to immerse ourselves in the emotions of a story—feeling joy, sadness, pain, courage, and hope—is a theological exercise. What does courage that comes from God look like? Reflecting on one of the stories Baker shares in light of the LIVE movements: Is God's courage evinced in the young father who sacrificed his life to save his baby girl by covering her with his body when gang members firebomb the house where they were staying? Is a similar type of God's courage found in Old Testament scripture such as the story of David and Goliath? Or is God's courage found in New Testament scripture such as the story of young Mary, the mother of Jesus, who carried him in her womb as an unwed mother amid the ridicule of community gossipers? Is God's courage embodied in Jesus the Christ, who gave his life so that we may have access to life abundant? Is God's courage evinced in next steps that follow from the insights of the story told in step one? Is God's courage shown in acts of speaking up about injustices that poor, racial/ethnic minoritized, and LGBTQIA people experience? The four movements systematically yield theological insights about the lived experience of the storyteller that move toward actions in light of the theological activity.

The methodology is accessible to all who read the book and explore the process. Adolescents and their adult partners with little or no theological training can use the four-step method as well as theologically trained clergy and academics. All can learn and grow through the LIVE method because the language Dori Baker offers is available to everyone who venture into the theory, theology, and stories of her book.

In *Girl/Friend Theology* we find attention to diverse populations of young people and their adult conversation partners. We are engaged in a methodology that is systematic and accessible as well as provocative. We are invited to experience a spiritual practice for adolescents and their adult partners that feeds their spiritual hunger, fortifies their mental well-being, and focuses our attention on story-based meaning-making and critical thinking. Dori Baker has given us a gift to engage in all these important aspects. She offers all adolescents in our midst and those growing into adolescents to be self-determined, like little Lauryn above, and to command other attributes that include a strong voice and persistent will to be themselves in relation to God and others. Our beloved Dr. Rosemary Radford Ruether said it best in the foreword to the first edition: "The key lies in learning to listen. Dori Baker shows us how to do that." May I add that she not only shows us how to Listen, but also to Immerse, View it wider, and Explore/Enact. Dori shows us how to LIVE.

Evelyn L. Parker

FOREWORD TO THE FIRST EDITION

I first had the pleasure of reading and discussing Dori Baker's manuscript on girlfriend theology as a doctoral dissertation in the joint program in Religious and Theological Studies of Garrett-Evangelical Theological Seminary and Northwestern University, in Evanston, Illinois in the late 1990s. It has lost nothing of its freshness in being translated into a book. I felt touched and moved to read its insightful stories a second time.

Dori Baker's development of the themes and methodology of girlfriend theology is based on a poignant social reality in US–American culture. The feisty "tomboy" girl of ten gets shut down by thirteen and loses her voice. As she moves from childhood to adolescence, the girl learns to conform to the expectations of gender roles. In myriad ways, the message comes to her that she must quiet down, lower her voice, learn to make herself pleasing to others, no longer express her own feelings.

This fact reminds me of a vivid scene in my own young mothering. It is a spring day in 1969. The sounds of boys playing ball in the street rise from outside. I am standing in a second-floor bedroom in our house in Washington, DC, when I overhear an eleven-year-old friend say to my daughter of the same age, "We are becoming young ladies now. We can no longer shout and play with boys in the street." My daughter appeared to silently concur. I remember being astonished at how this socialization into gender conformity was being inculcated by one eleven-year-old girl into another.

As Dori Baker makes clear, adolescent girls pay a heavy price to learn these lessons of silence and submission. Eating disorders, self harm, depression, even suicide are some of the more extreme ways that the stresses of this process of conformity express themselves. A high level of violence affects the youth of our society. Murder and suicide are the second- and third-leading causes of death of young people from the ages of fifteen to twenty-four. Yet there is little outlet in our culture, whether in churches, in families, or in schools, for young women to share their experiences of tragedy or explore their groping efforts to make meaning in the midst of confusing messages.

Girlfriend theology is about providing the safe space for adolescent women to tell their stories and to probe the emerging horizons of hope in their lives. Girlfriend theology is about hearing young women into speech. Its methodology is one of storytelling and small-group reflection on stories. Stories that have often been bottled up inside young women find a place where they can be shared in a gathering of friends who can hold one another in grief and in joy and ask about the deeper meaning of the patterns of young lives.

Through such storytelling, young women can ask, "Where is God in this story?" Is God in the abusive father, pastor, or teacher, or rather in the friendship of two hurting young people who reach out their arms to one another? Is God in the judgmental views of adults about the young father struggling to overcome drug addiction? Or is God in that young father giving his life to save his baby girl by shielding her under his body when his gang friends firebomb the house where he and his girlfriend are living? These kinds of stories are the stuff of girlfriend theology. They have to do not with "childish things" but life-and-death matters.

A few theological principles emerge from such explorations of the hidden stories of young women. One of them is that God is mysteriously, but not omnipotently, present with us in our struggles.

Another is that God is accessible through our bodily experiences. Church is found in communities of compassion that allow us to search for meaning or sometimes simply to grieve together when meaning cannot be found.

Girlfriend theology is an invaluable contribution to reclaiming the voices of one of the most silenced groups in our society, the teenaged girl. It offers the remarkable conclusion that such girls are not only grappling with deeply serious issues. They also can be reflective theologians with much to teach the adult world that so often finds them opaque and hard to understand. The key lies in learning to listen. Dori Baker shows us how to do that.

Rosemary Radford Ruether

INTRODUCTION

God is a becoming, not a static being that
can be incarcerated in an ontology.
Bayo Akomolafe

You must learn one thing.
The world was made to be free in.
Give up all the other worlds except the
one to which you belong.
— David Whyte, *Sweet Darkness*

Welcome!

Welcome to this revised edition of *Doing Girlfriend Theology*, re-named *Girl/Friend Theology*—with a slant. Let me begin with a story.

On the day I put the finishing touches on this revision, the United States Supreme Court reversed its decision in *Roe v. Wade*. I was in quarantine, recovering from my first bout of COVID-19. I was also mourning the sudden death of a close friend, Diane, and wondering how I would get by without our almost-daily walk-and-talks that ranged from what's-for-dinner to holy listening around life's big questions.

Grieving, angry, sulking, and foggy-headed, I scrolled through Facebook and Instagram. I was in a deep funk. I projected most of these negative feelings onto my partner of thirty-seven years: yes, the one who had been faithfully feeding me, hydrating me, and checking my oxygen levels for the past four days.

1

On a whim, I suggested we take a drive on the Blue Ridge Parkway, just twenty minutes from our home. As soon as I saw trees, I began to calm. I slipped off my flip flops and stepped into Otter Creek, finding a rock to sit on. I welcomed the cool breeze. A water snake slithered between the ripples. A goldfinch swooped down: splash!

In that moment, I heard an internal voice reminding me that all will be well. Women will find ways to rise up. We will care for one another's hearts, like we always have. With allies from other genders, with friends across race, class, and creed, we will reshape the world to center on care for the most vulnerable. The next text I received reinforced this knowing through the voice of an Indigenous leader from Oklahoma who wrote: "Mothers of the earth, row your own choices and wade your own life-giving force into being."

On the way home, I texted my book club friends, inviting them to gather at the end of my quarantine. Women in the grass, barefoot, toasted Diane's transition and celebrated the life we have and the lives we choose to create.

The process of girl/friend theology begins with a story such as this one: One real-life story, told to a group of friends or strangers, begins a process of communal meaning-making that honors our bodies, trusts our lived experience, and connects us to something larger than ourselves.

The idea for this book began in 1996, when, as a doctoral student, I began to dream of a tool for adult women to help adolescent girls uproot gender oppression. Over the years, girlfriend theology happened where groups of women gathered: at lakeside retreat centers, church fellowship halls, campus ministries, counselling hubs, backyard campouts, juvenile detention centers, schools, prisons, and sleepovers. Along the way, the circle expanded to support not just those identifying as women and girls, but also boys, men, and nonbinary individuals who wanted to uproot interlocking oppressions and explore meaning-making together.

As it was adapted by people in a variety of contexts, I discovered so much more! Girl/friend theology is a delight-filled process, a way of making meaning out of life's deep pain and surprising joy. It is an invitation to critical thinking that helps us get better at choosing to side with those who've been historically silenced, unseen, or oppressed. It is a spiritual practice—one of thousands of spiritual practices that don't require belief in a particular dogma or creed—that humans steward for the good of the planet and its creatures.

Spiritual practices aid in healing of our bodies, minds, and spirits, especially when the world seems to be falling apart around us. Spiritual practices support our well-being, individually and collectively. They connect us to the Holy. They help us stay resilient. They help us cultivate joy, even in the midst of suffering. A spiritual practice helps me get out of bed in the morning, and others help me discover, repeatedly as necessary, the "why" of my existence. When spiritual practices are part of our lives, we are less likely to become depressed in the first place, less likely to suffer long depressions, and more likely to regain our mental health and sense of agency [Miller, 2021].

Girl/friend theology is a spiritual practice with the power to help us *live* better. For that reason, I came to teach the process using the acronym LIVE (Listen, Immerse, View it Wider, Enact) [Baker, 2012]. It is the lifegiving, life-sustaining, and sometimes lifesaving value of spiritual practices that calls for this revised version now.

WHY A REVISED EDITION? WHY NOW?

Creating occasions for people to discover meaning and purpose—two ingredients that make for better living, even in the midst of suffering—is especially important now, when young people are suffering an epidemic of anxiety, depression, suicidal ideation, substance abuse, and death from suicide, overdose, and addiction [Centers for Disease Control, 2022]. While professional mental health services and psychiatric medication are central in protecting against debilitating mental illness, so too are spiritual practices [Miller, 2021]. We fail our young people when we do not welcome their spiritual hunger, doubts, and questions alongside needs for professional mental health services. I hope this revised edition will find its way into the hands of caring and curious adults who know that storytelling – even about life's most painful moments – can reconnect us to beauty and help us discover our purpose. As my colleague, the joy advocate Angela Gorrell, writes: "Despair struggles to breathe where meaning resides" [Gorrell, 2021].

The original version of this book appeared in 2005. The slash in the title of this revised edition—*Girl/Friend Theology*—is new. It reflects how this work evolved over the last two decades. The slash asks us to look with a slant, to slow down, to acknowledge that many of the concepts entangled in our images of self, community, and God are not fixed and static, but are constructed by humans, and, lucky for us, are always under construction. The slash invites us to make room— and then even more room—for voices that have been erased from our histories, our prayers, and the blueprints for world-building we call progress. The slash asks us to imagine what we cannot possibly know from any one perspective and to acknowledge that all perspectives are necessary in the communal task of meaning-making. The first edition of this book centered the voices of people whose stories had been silenced, cut out, pasted over; now we make space for even more voices to enter that center in the ongoing work of girl/friend theology. Welcome to the slash!

I've spent the past two decades as an independent scholar focusing my research and writing on young adults and the search for meaning and purpose. Serving as senior fellow at the Forum for Theological Exploration (FTE) for fourteen years allowed me to listen deeply to thousands of young adults in the midst of discerning their way forward, particularly as they explored calls to lead in fields of ministry, social entrepreneurship, and social justice. With my colleagues at FTE, I helped create numerous resources for discernment.[1] Most of these are based on spiritual practices that have been stewarded by multiple religious traditions—tools that the world, especially young adults, need right now!

Revising this book gives me a chance to incorporate some of what I've learned as a scholar, writer, facilitator, and leader among leaders in the fertile space of young adult culture, spiritual activism, and vocational discernment.

In this revision, I have kept most of the original content and methodology in place, braiding together real-life stories of young women, insights from feminist theologians from around the world, and coming-of-age snapshots from women's autobiographies. This three-part braid embodies the rhythm of alternating theory and practice that is embedded in girlfriend theology. I have incorporated newer research on adolescent girls, the gender binary, and emancipatory theologies in the text and footnotes when helpful.

All of the young women's stories, voices of feminist theologians, and passages from women's autobiography that follow are from the original book. Even though some of these now seem dated, I've retained them here because they provide a thick description of girlfriend theology in action, shining a light on adults facilitating in ways that hold truths lightly, allowing new truths to emerge, tender and green. They also depict recent history: at times these stories offer a glimpse of improvement in the lives of girls and women in US cul-

---

1   Numerous books, chapters, and articles I wrote, edited, or coauthored based on research with young adults and spiritual practices while working with FTE can be found in the bibliography.

ture; others show how much has worsened because of the stubbornly reinforcing tendencies of whiteness and patriarchy. As I continue leading groups in girl/friend theology and write about those experiences, the method has evolved, and I share new stories from more diverse audiences elsewhere—in published work, in the podcast *Live to Tell*, and on my website www.doribaker.com ^{(Parker 2010) (Silverman et al.} 2017) (Baker 2012) (Baker and Reyes 2020).

Then and now, girl/friend theology makes a central claim: images of God are rooted in us, for better or worse. Some of those images are positive; they serve to uplift and free us. But many God-images become deadly tools. Together, we can uproot the damaging and deadly images and find liberating images of God that free us all. Girl/friend theology invites us to the playful, communal, life-saving work encouraged by poet David Whyte who advises us to act as if "the world was made to be free in"—free for all of us.

CONTEXT IS EVERYTHING: REBOOTING CHRISTIANITY WHERE WE LIVE

While writing the first edition, I was the mother of two young girls, then an infant and a toddler. I began each chapter with a story from my own life: navigating gender oppression as a teenager, coming to awareness of racial oppression as a young adult, and discerning my vocation as a mother and practical theologian. Becoming a theologian was my direct response to discovering oppressions of race and gender as epic obstacles to the kind of freedom David Whyte's poem evokes. Because I desired that kind of freedom for my children and all people, rebooting Christianity became a central task in my vocational unfolding.

Today, with my daughters grown and living across the continent, I am ever more aware that faith traditions have a way of becoming tools in the hands of oppressors. Christianity is often a bludgeon. I am especially aware of this because I live in Lynchburg, Virginia, the home of Liberty University, a center of religious right-wing extremism.[2] Lynchburg's early economy benefitted largely from the trade of enslaved people and its name bears connection to the word "lynching."[3]

Each morning when I step outside my bedroom door to connect with the earth beneath me, I remember that European settlers stole this very land from Indigenous Monacan Indians and, not far from my backyard, tortured Black people stolen from their African homelands, along with their descendants. Settlers habitually violated women's bodies and sold children, using a warped rendition of Christianity as a primary tool. Similar forms of Christianity continue to bludgeon my LGBTQ+[4] friends today.

Even as a white, cisgender, economically privileged, ordained clergywoman, many days I struggle to stay Christian. But I can almost always—with the help of my friends—glimpse and find hope in a historical version of the Jesus story that predates colonizing Christianity and its ongoing harm.

Lucky for me, I've been surrounded by people who follow a version of the Jesus story that is lifegiving and liberatory: That he was a young person of color, born to a mother who migrated under life-threatening conditions, that he lived on the underside of the Roman Empire

---

2   Liberty University is also home to some people I admire who do not hold the perspective of fundamentalisms or the politics of the Christian right. While the university itself attracts a wide diversity of people whose presence has enriched my life, I remain an outspoken critic of the university's policies, especially around gun laws, LGBTQ+ inclusion, sexual assault and harassment, and women's rights.

3   The word "lynch" is believed to originate from Charles Lynch, a Virginia farmer and American revolutionary who set up a system for punishing Loyalists who supported the British during the American Revolutionary War. His brother, John Lynch, was the founder of Lynchburg, Virginia.

4   LGBTQ+ refers to Lesbian, Gay, Bisexual, Transgender, and Queer or Questioning. The "plus" signifies all the gender identities not specifically covered by the other five initials.

and upturned the oppressive norms of his day.[5] Jesus, thus remembered, is the revolutionary who captivated my imagination when I was a young adult and whom I continue to glimpse among communities of other followers, seekers, and doubters such as the one where I met my friend Tyson.

Tyson identifies as nonbinary and uses the pronoun them. Tyson left organized religion after being subjected to "conversion therapy," a dangerous practice that targets LBGTQ+ youth and seeks to change their gender or sexual identities.[6] One day, I asked Tyson why they stayed connected to the fringes of Christian community. They paused for a moment, then said: "I am still chasing that feeling—you know—the feeling of belonging—not being merely tolerated or included—but being embraced wholeheartedly as one dazzling, awesomely beautiful incarnation of the divine among us . . . I still chase that feeling." Tyson experienced that feeling in a Christian youth group, and even though this form of Christianity also did great harm, Tyson still seeks the depth of beloved community discovered there.

Thanks to people like Tyson, Christianity is undergoing a massive and necessary reboot. We turn our computers off to recover from an error. When we reboot, the information is still there, but stripped of the sludge so we can get a fresher view. The sludge of Christianity that needs to be removed comes into focus when we center the experiences of people who have been systemically oppressed, marginalized, silenced, or subjugated. The work of rebooting to recover from Christianity's errors is never done. But we are not alone!

You, like me, may be discovering that it is our task to support one another as we do the hard work of growing beyond the "entrenched

---

5   I am indebted to my colleague Stephen Lewis for his regular depiction of Jesus using these descriptors.

6   Conversion Therapy is now deemed harmful by the American Association of Child and Adolescent Psychiatry (AACAP 2018).

racialized divides" that Resmaa Menakem describes [Menakem, 2017]. Menakem reminds us that this work begins in our bodies, where trauma is stored, passed down in our DNA from generation to generation. We must support each other in the work and also in the accompanying grief and lament. We must lift one another up, enjoying the lifegiving energy that can come with decentering ourselves and the myth of white superiority that wants to engulf and belittle us all. I have experienced such life-giving energy while doing girl/friend theology.

Menakem helps me remember why girl/friend theology is necessarily communal. We need others—friends who think like us and those who don't, along with those who came before us—to help us recognize what God is up to and what God may be calling us to, in our bodies and within our social contexts, right where we live.

LIBERATING COMMUNITY

Discerning a wider repertoire of images of God is lifegiving, communal work that feeds us and fuels our actions in the world. This work begins with our own bodies—where we see suffering, where we experience rage, where we find empathy, where we find joy—as we pay attention to the embodied lives of others. These "others" are, of course, people we actually know as well as those whom we must seek out. Most of us grew up in neighborhoods and learned histories that were segregated by design and so must be deliberate in learning and honoring stories very different from our own [Hannah-Jones, 2021].

Girl/friend theology is about expanding the narratives and parables we live by. It is about discovering and claiming wisdoms that were once silenced or suppressed.

I first learned about the long history of reclaiming the suppressed strains of Christian tradition that empower women and predate the gender hierarchies of the church from my mentor, Rosemary Radford Ruether, an acclaimed Roman Catholic feminist theologian and historian. Ruether, who wrote the foreword to the original version of this book, died as I was completing this revision. Years earlier, in a book honoring her long and prolific career, Ruether wrote that girlfriend theology achieves what she had in mind when she coined the term "women-church." She wrote: "Girlfriend theology goes beyond the production of ideas. It creates what the doing of authentic theology is intended to do and should do, the creation of church: church as liberating community of life together" (Silverman et al. 2012, xvi).

The phrase "liberating community of life together" was the highest praise I could have received from her. I believe the creation of "liberating community of life together" is especially important now. If we, collectively, are to discern our unique roles in healing the trauma around race and gender that threaten the lives of people of color and diminish human community, we will need liberating communities doing life together. If we are to tend adequately to the grief of species decline and the warming of oceans that will kill and displace millions of people over the next decades, we will need liberating communities doing life together.

This book is about using all that is available to us—especially the subversive, spirit-fed sparks of divine disruption—to heal and to grieve, and to keep up the good work of building a world of flourishing for all creation.

Those of us looking for better images of God today have access to the writings of Black women and the stories of Indigenous North Americans. We have queer theology in many manifestations and numerous specific cultural expressions of Christianity from women throughout the global South.[7]

---

7   This is an area of significant ongoing study for me. An updated list of the books that continue to save my life can be found at www.doribaker.com.

Alongside the flourishing of such explicitly theological works, an abundance of stories told from the perspectives of people of color and genderqueer people point to Spirit—in the name of joy, love, abundance, and suffering—without being explicitly theological. As these stories move from the margins to the center, they turn into bestselling books or Netflix binges, both stoking and quenching a thirst for truths that provide a fuller glimpse of humanity.

THEOLOGIANS, ONE AND ALL

While some of the work mentioned above offers guidance on how to tell our stories, few of them take on the task that is central to this book: inviting more people into intentional meaning-making using their own stories, dreams, and intuitions in conversation with the larger stories at play in our culture.

Girl/Friend Theology urges us to linger in the territory of meaning-making. There we discover that we are theologians, one and all! When more people from more perspectives take part in the telling of history (and the doing of theology), we hold the power to reshape not only the past but the future.

New York Times bestselling author Elizabeth Lesser, in her book *Cassandra Speaks: When Women are the Storytellers the Human Story Changes*, wonders how history would have unfolded if women had been the primary storytellers [Lesser 2020]. She writes:

> Humans love stories. We always have. We write them and read them, tell them and show them, learn from them and live by them. Throughout history, most of humankind's origin stories, hero's journey tales, novels and films have been created by men. Embedded in the stories are the values and priorities we live by, and what we believe

about women and men, power and war, sex and love [Lesser 2020].

What we believe about God, spirituality, and our human capacity for creating a world we want to live in has also been determined by men seated within dominant culture. Lesser goes on to ask: "But what if women had been the storytellers too? What story would Eve have told about picking the apple? What would Pandora have said about opening the box?" Those stories are ripe for imagining from the perspective of women, girls, and genderqueer people.

Leaning a little deeper into Lesser's premise, I ask: What if the stories we all come to know by heart include those told by Indigenous inhabitants of an occupied territory? Or genderqueer folks who experience embodied reality as more than the male/female binary? What if the stories we weave into conversations with young people included memoirs of young mystics, discovering their inner light in ways that change them forever, like this one, recounted by civil rights activist Rosemary Freeney Harding?

> I can't say exactly where the Light entered, where it started from. Suddenly, it was just there with me . . . I felt the most astonishing sense of protection, of peace. It surrounded me and I was in it, so joyfully. I don't know how long I was engulfed by this Light, this space. But when I came out of my room my family was looking at me oddly, like there was something different about me they couldn't quite name . . . The Light became a kind of touchstone in my life. It was so much love. Like an infinite compassion [Harding, 2015, 1].

Harding goes on to ask how her life might have been different if she had more access to wise elders with whom to share this experience and integrate it with a non-static view of Christianity.

> Sometimes I wish I could talk to somebody . . . who was there when Grandma Rye was questioning the Christian God, working out the transition. Figuring out what parts were useful, what parts should be ignored; and where the connections lay between what she already knew to be true of the world, true of herself and God, and what new things the struggle (to be human) in this land was teaching her [Harding 2015, 13].

Harding speaks here to the holy yearnings of young people I've met along the way. They want to figure out what parts are useful and what should be ignored. They want to hold on to what is good, to "chase the feeling" of deep belonging the Christian community can beautifully impart, while extricating and leaving behind that which harms.

Girl/friend theology is a way of replicating what might already be happening in families and communities where young people have access to elders in the process of curating a healthy spirituality. The process welcomes adults who have navigated their way to new truths about God to offer these treasures into a young person's life, in an act that sometimes amounts to throwing a lifeline.

How lifesaving might it be for a contemporary thirteen-year-old to come upon these lines, written by National Poet Laureate and member of the Muscogee Creek Nation Joy Harjo:

> Though I was blurred with fear, I could still hear and feel the knowing. The knowing was my rudder, a shimmer of intelligent light, unerring in the midst of this destructive, terrible, and beauti-

ful life. It is a strand of the divine, a pathway for
the ancestors and teachers who love us [Harjo 2012].

Harjo places these words after the story of an abusive stepfather
whose expression of Christianity she rejected. "By the time I was
thirteen," Harjo writes, "I had grown tired of the misuse of the Bible
to prove the superiority of white people, to enforce the domination
of women by men, and I didn't agree with the prohibition on dancing and the warnings against prophecy and visions."

The dissonance between Harjo's own inner knowing and the form
of Christianity to which she was subjected inspired her to read the
Bible multiple times, finding there "a great respect for dreams and
visions" and, in the Song of Solomon, a vision of God as a sensuous
beloved "rather than as a wrathful white man who was ready to de-
stroy anyone who had an imagination."[27]

Back in the 1990s, I, like Lesser, was primarily concerned with the
voices of young women. Girlfriend theology grew out of my desire
that young women had access to the life-affirming voices of their
elders— particularly Womanists, *mujeristas*, Asian feminists and
white feminists—who were rebooting theology from the ground up,
using their lived experience to dismantle dominant versions of God.

The dominant versions of God—born in white supremacy and its
colonizing visions of reality—then constituted the ever-present realities of mainstream US culture. I wanted young women to be able
to see the water of mainstream culture as polluted. I wanted them to
have access to the tools they would need to trouble that water, drain
it completely, so they could draw from their own deep wells of spirit,
ancestry, imagination, and culture, where submerged streams reflected more diverse, lifegiving images of God. I also wanted to free them
to learn from, borrow from, be in relationships of give-and-take with
the wells of others in ways that did not rob or steal, but shared in
mutuality and respect.

As a young feminist youth minister and pastor, I found that it wasn't enough simply to translate liberatory theologies to young people. They wanted to be part of the action. If they were to let more freeing images of God seep into their bones and replace the damaging, limiting, harmful stories, they needed a seat at the table. They wanted to create it, own it, mix it up in their own bespoke ways. It had to emerge from within them and reflect their own ways of knowing.

Placing their autobiographies-in-the-making alongside an ever-widening canon of written autobiographies—this, I discovered, worked magic. It invited young people to wonder about the ways they had been formed in faith. They become transformative iconoclasts who also cared about rebuilding a working faith on the other side of deconstruction.

They became theologians of their own lives.

NEW THEOLOGIES ARE YOURS TO WRITE

When my younger daughter, Olivia, was in college, she created a piece of art that now hangs in my study. In a ripple of water swirl these words: "No matter who I am, no matter where I am, no matter how I look, no matter how I speak, deep down in the deepest place, in the truest place, in the quietest place, and the loudest notion, I am Divine Love. You can feel me in the grass when your toes crunch in green and when birdwings whistle over your forehead and when sun and moon dance on your face." Finding better images of God—or Spirit, Divine, Creation, Universe, however you choose to name the whisper of love "deep down in the deepest place"—can be a grounding, centering, lifegiving force in our lives. Better images of God can help us grow into people who survive and thrive in our own personal realms and return excess loving energy back to our communities.

In their podcast and book *Truth's Table: Black Women's Musings on Life, Love and Liberation*, the authors make the claim that theology is biography. I agree. It is in telling our stories that we surface images of God and practices of soul that can help us survive and thrive [Uwan et al. 2022]. Perhaps you know people who have stories to tell. Perhaps it is a story about a sparkling day when everything felt right with the world, or a day when you discovered your path to activism. Maybe it is a story of deep grief, the death of a person, the growing awareness of a trauma, or the loss of an identity, like so many of us suffered during the pandemic. Girl/friend theology is not about pasting shiny rainbows on suffering. It's about sitting together in the suffering. It is about those times that God shows up in unexpected ways, both in the stories people tell and in the shared meaning-making that happens as we walk through the steps of girl/friend theology together. It is an art, a practice, a sometimes hard-edged, and sometimes playful tool for pushing against the constructs we live within. It provides space for people to consider the role of God in welcoming their identity and loving their very existence. It seeks to revise the stories that limit, oppress, and squeeze people into boxes, replacing them with theologies designed for our flourishing.

These new theologies are yours to write.

WHAT YOU WILL FIND HERE

THE LIVE METHOD

The most significant update in this revised edition is the acronym LIVE, which guides the four-step method of theological reflection central to girl/friend theology.

LIVE is an acronym for: Listen; Immerse; View it Wider; Explore and Enact

This four-step method guides group theological reflection around one person's story. It's simple, adaptable, and repeatable. If practiced together over time, it can become a default path for wholehearted meaning-making that lives in our whole bodies, not just our heads. I provide nuanced examples of groups using these four steps, showing exactly how new images of God arose when we thought critically together about inherited interpretations of scripture and tradition, alongside our own lives and the larger stories emerging from non-dominant voices around the globe. This encounter with girls and their stories in conversation with larger bodies of feminist work gave birth to a set of beliefs that challenge white, patriarchal norms about God. That list of seven assertions of girlfriend theology is particular, situated in time and place with those who participated in my original research. But I hope they serve as an example of affirmations that you might hear arising as you lead girl/friend theology with new groups of young people.

THEORY HOLDING HANDS WITH PRACTICE

If you are a practitioner, such as a youth worker, a pastoral leader, campus minister, or other kind of caregiver, you will find in this edition resources to help you adapt the method to your setting. The appendix includes guidelines to facilitating girl/friend theology using the LIVE method, tips for eliciting a story, and a graphic to help others follow along with the process. You can find examples of people engaging the process in the podcast *LIVE to Tell* and other resources at www.doribaker.com

If you are a scholar, you will find descriptions of my original research methodology intact, and other places where I update the research. My original conversation partners—researchers who described race and gender oppression in United States culture during the last decades of the twentieth century—remain alongside newer voices.

The back-and-forth rhythm of practice and theory reflects my refusal to create a binary between the two, and I trust you will pick and choose the portions that are useful for you.

AN OVERVIEW

Chapter 1 begins in a tent near a lake under the full moon. It tells the origin story of girlfriend theology as a research project that sought to create a positive intervention for adolescent girls coming of age at a particular time in history, when some girls experienced "silencing" and girls, by and large, had been left out of the conversation of white feminists. I describe the LIVE process that grounds the following chapters.

In Chapter 2, I tell a story from my own adolescence, out of which grew my convictions regarding theology, education, and research. I describe two key feminist theological metaphors guiding my method. I then introduce my collaborators, tell how they came to participate in the project, and share the seven theological assertions I heard. The necessity of being able to share across faith traditions and the centrality of stories about violence and death emerged as two significant themes.

Chapter 3 brings the voices of the girls in the form of two stories. These stories show the value of encouraging theological conversation across religions and about our bodies. As these girls engaged their life stories with persons of varying faith traditions, theological imaginations broadened and a reshaping of Christian tradition regarding female bodies took place. This chapter begins a thick description of the practice of girl/friend theology.

Chapter 4 relates experiences of deeply ingrained misogyny in US culture. Fashioning a response to such a culture is an act of practical theology informed by key sources within feminism's usable past: women's autobiographical literature and women's emancipatory theologies. I share stories from women's autobiographies that provide examples of women mentoring adolescent girls with attention to race, ethnicity, and class.

Chapter 5 delves back into the worlds of contemporary girls, engaging again in the practice of girl/friend theology. The two stories here relate to death and violence, issues of overwhelming import in adolescent lives today. When girls are given the opportunity to tell a story from their lives in a safe space, tales of violence and death often spill forth. Making meaning of the Christian tradition in light of tragic loss, the girls echoed motifs inherent in theologies emerging from non-Abrahamic, Indigenous, and non-Western contexts.

Chapter 6 explores these contexts, bringing girl/friend theology into dialogue with three key movements in contemporary theological literature: *Mujerista* theology, Womanist theology, and Asian-feminist theology. Here I name key theological sources that inform my practice of girl/friend theology.

Chapter 7 turns to bodies. As I concluded my research, I realized that "the female body" was not one theme among many for the girls and women in my groups; rather, body issues surfaced continuously. In this chapter, I argue that girl/friend theology is an embodied pedagogy, a term I use to describe ways of teaching and learning that engage bodies as a primary source of knowing. Using the postmodern critique of education advanced by scholars of cultural studies and critical pedagogy, I describe the girl/friend theology classroom as one in which bodies matter.

Chapter 8 brings this focused conversation between girls and women's stories, feminist theologies, and spiritual practices to a conclusion. I construct a model of God in relationship to humanity that grows out of the theory and practice of girl/friend theology. I call this a meeting at the crossroads of souls.

SENDING FORTH

I hope you will dive in and be encouraged to help people tell the stories of their lives out loud to one another in a communal process of meaning-making. This process can retrieve those stories from the abyss of Instagram and Facebook, surfacing them as sources for growth and freedom.

Spiritual practices that empower young people are now more necessary than ever because we stand at a cultural crossroads. Margaret Atwood's *The Handmaid's Tale* often feels like the daily news. As the novel and television depiction shows, oppressive norms do not arrive by accident: these structures are by design. Incrementally, these forces seek to keep power structures weighted towards those who've historically held power. Those of us with hopes of upsetting the dominant norms must equip ourselves with all tools possible, particularly spiritual tools that metabolize hate and scarcity into love and abundance.

While girl/friend theology is decidedly *not* therapy, I've learned that it can support people who are undergoing therapeutic interventions. It can be healing for people who've been harmed by church teachings. It can also be healing for those responsible for being part of that harm. It can create a desire to learn about stories told by people whose journeys collided with dominant powers and did not survive that encounter intact. It can create a common ground for coming together, no matter our points of departure.

While I originally designed this tool to revise oppressive forms of Christianity and reform the church from within, I learned along the way that girl/friend theology also feeds a hunger in wider circles. It is a spiritual technology that can be used by anyone eager to tease out the meanings of their life, anyone doubting a religious tradition, anyone looking for better ways to live into a sense of meaning and purpose.

You don't have to identify as a Christian to engage in revising the underlying harm Christianity has done in shaping cultural norms that persist within and around us. Any of us can use this story-sharing process to animate the work of excavating harmful culture-shaping images, while uncovering and illuminating images that liberate us.

The slash in this revised edition is no small thing. It is a celebration. The slash is an invitation to listen to, elevate, and support the realities of all people coming into their embodied identities and asking big questions, such as "Why am I here? "What do I long for?" "Who is God for me?" "Why does that matter?" and, perhaps most significantly, "*Do I matter?*"

Girl/Friend Theology (the book) and girl/friend theology (the process) both insist that *you do matter*—but even more, they show a path toward creating a community of peers and elders to remind you that you matter, deeply. Fervent love creates and holds you—as you are and as you are evolving. I invite you to the hard, life-affirming work of finding new stories to live by, beginning with the stories that already live within us.

Dori Baker
June 24, 2022

CHAPTER ONE

VESPERS WHISPERED UNDER A FULL MOON

THE FEMINIST THEOLOGICAL EDUCATION OF ADOLESCENT GIRLS

> What would it mean for a girl—against the stories read, chanted, or murmured to her—to choose to tell the truth of her life aloud to another person at the very point when she is invited into the larger cultural story of womanhood—that is, at... adolescence?
>
> — Lyn Mikel Brown, *Telling a Girl's Life*

Our tent stood a mere three feet from the lake's edge. The gentle lapping of the waves upon the shore bathed us in a comforting rhythm as we snuggled in our sleeping bags and began our evening whispers. During the course of a week in the remote Minnesota wilderness, my tentmates and I had fallen into this ritual. Bedtime became a time to reflect on what that particular day of portaging canoes over muddy trails and paddling through winding rivers might mean for ourselves and our relationships.

This night, as we debriefed our day, one of us happened to look out the open window of the tent. What we saw took us by surprise. The moon, rising gently over the tree-lined horizon, shone full and bright, reflecting perfectly on the water below. Throughout the next few hours, our conversation carried us toward morning in contented wakefulness. We spoke of the joys of being seven women ages fourteen to forty, confronting the challenges of canoeing and camping in a wilderness with no phones, no motors, and no male gaze upon us. We spoke of the mystical moose whose eyes had met our own during an early-morning walk to the latrine. We spoke of the wholeness—body, mind, and spirit—that emerged as we communed in creation, surrounded by sisters who were there to help when the mud grew too deep or the canoes became too heavy. That night, as our conversation lingered on unusually late, we watched the progress of the steadily journeying moon as it drew its reflection on the calm skin of the water.

That night I was reminded—nestled as I was in the comfort of my friends and the wideness of the universe—of the ever-changing, yet constant nature of the moon. It became for me a symbol of my Creator—always changing face, always revealing a new aspect, but always also present. I can, as Mary Chapin Carpenter sings, "rely upon the moon."

For centuries, women have relied upon the moon. Our physical cycles are tied to its changing phases. Our bodily tides move in sync with its rhythms. The moon symbolizes the bond that connects women today with women of centuries past: women who walked to the deep well each morning to draw sustaining water for the day; women who struggled against the overwhelming odds of white, wealthy male power structures to claim their strength and voice; women who found ways to name their personhood and pursue their callings.

That night in the moon's full glow, my tentmates and I were telling new stories, but speaking an old, old language. We were joining our particular voices with a chorus of women that began long ago. Joining this chorus is the beginning of a process central to girl/friend theology. Girl/friend theology begins with the

24

bold act of adding new voices to the strong chorus of those who have gone before us. It is adults meeting younger women and girls in the light of a full moon. It requires the creation of safe spaces within faith communities for the stories of young adults to be told, heard, honored, and reflected upon. It views those stories in light of the stories of the canon of scripture, the long tradition of faithful mystics and saints, the legends of people whose stories have been only scantily recorded, and the wider corpus of texts from all of the ancient wisdom traditions that shape the reality of a postmodern world in which gender is not fixed but fluid.[1]

In this way, girl/friend theology addresses three problems I noticed as a young pastor: the missing voices of youth in youthwork, the psychological effects of being silenced, and the fact that attention to girls was largely missing from white, feminist theology and practice.

THE PROBLEM: MISSING VOICES OF YOUTH, SILENCED SELVES, AND GIRLS IN THE FOOTNOTES

MISSING VOICES OF YOUTH

The three teenagers in the tent that night came from a predominantly white United Methodist church in a middle-class suburb of Chicago. At the time they were still in the midst of forming their identities, but now more than one of them consider themselves as a part of the LGBTQ+ community. This church, the first place I served following seminary, was not a place that readily invited

---

1   For helpful definitions and recent research on gender and gender fluidity, see https://www.health.harvard.edu/blog/gender-fluidity-what-it-means-and-why-support-matters-2020120321544. The original research related here involved young women; however, many of the themes apply similarly to other gender-related oppressions, such as those experienced by young people who identify as gender nonbinary.

adolescents to tell their stories, explore their sexual orientation, or question troubling aspects of their faith.

Church was something their parents required, and the rite of confirmation was the ticket out. Once confirmed, they could decide for themselves whether they wanted to continue participating in the Christian faith. As the confirmation teacher, I took on the challenge of creating a community that might flip this dynamic. Maybe, I hoped, they would fall in love with each other and keep coming back!

I ordered the curriculum and entered the confirmation classroom with high expectations. I imagined relationships forming, questions getting tossed about, minds opening wide, and hearts expanding. All of these things happened over the course of our yearlong confirmation quest and beyond as those teens formed the core of an active youth ministry (that still keeps in touch via social media today). More often than not, the truest teaching and learning happened in moments of frustration when we tossed the curriculum aside and proceeded spontaneously. In those moments, I would weave into my leadership the lifegiving expressions of theology I had experienced in seminary. These expressions did not appear in any youth ministry curriculum I could find. So, I figured out creative ways to translate to my students the God I had come to know through the writings of feminists, activists, and scholars of varying racial backgrounds. Listening to those voices—particularly those of people struggling for emancipation from various types of oppression—revealed to me that something was missing in resources guiding youth work.

Across my theological education, I had been struck by the way emancipatory theologies begin with concrete life experience. They reflect on that experience in the context of the Bible and society. They encourage people to practice faith and engage in action. But without that crucial first step of valuing lived experience, these writings would not have transformed so much of the landscape of contemporary theology. I became convinced that the first step in youth ministry should be hearing the voices of the youth themselves. This became a deeply rooted conviction for me, shaping my research into the faith lives of young people.

As I workshopped the original form of girlfriend theology at churches, women's groups, and campus ministries across the country, I became attuned to the issues facing boys and nonbinary folks. Parents who appreciated my work on behalf of girls frequently asked, "But what about our boys?" A culture of violence, access to guns, and rigid gender expectations combined to form combustible environments for boys struggling to reach adulthood. Malicious forms of toxic masculinity persist and can lead to misogyny, LGBTQ+-phobia, gender-based violence, and severe mental health issues.[2] In the wake of these issues, I expanded my vision of girl/friend theology, sharing in my seminary classrooms and later writings the ways it could be helpful beyond girls and women. Two of these, in particular, stand out. First, the process models the formation of robust emotional lives and the capacity for intimacy for young people, a skill set reported to be lacking in the formation of boys, but one that is equally valuable for people of all genders. Secondly, the process is valuable for college and seminary courses for helping people integrate academic study of God and gender into their own unfolding identities related to race, gender, and sexual orientation. But originally, my feminist passion required that I started where I live, in this female

---

2   Michael Kimmel defines toxic masculinity using the idea of the *good man* versus the *real man*. *Real men* in US culture are expected to uphold principles and ideals that may conflict with their perception of *good men*. Strength, dominance, and emotional suppression are just a few norms that *real men* are encouraged to uphold. These can be internalized and taken to the extreme until they become toxic to themselves, those around them and culture at large.

body, addressing the particular issues that society, culture, and the church bequeath to women. As I grew close to young women in the 1990s, I found their life stories echoing the then contemporary research in the field of women's psychological development [Gilligan and Brown 1992]. Not only were some girls being silenced in early adolescence, but they were also having difficulty regaining their voices and shaping their identities well into adulthood. Since then, researchers have widened their view to focus on intersecting oppressions of gender, race, class, sexuality, ability, and ethnicity that limit options around identity formation. Similarly, they have widened their lens on adolescents, acknowledging a period of emerging adulthood that lasts well into the second decade of life [Johnson and Roberts 1999] [Arnett 2004].

While some young activists use social media as a platform to advocate for the dismantling of structural oppression, social media simultaneously reinforces a number of harmful norms that contribute to high levels of anxiety and depression among young people. Research shows the effects of social media, particularly Instagram, are worse for girls than boys.[3] The authors of *Behind Their Screens: What Teens Are Facing (and Adult Are Missing)* surveyed and interviewed more than 3500 middle and high school students for their report on the experiences of teens with technology. Using young people as co-researchers, they surface the complexities of teen's experiences of social media, including social comparison and performance commenting [Weinstein and James 2022]. The effects of social media, while nuanced and diverse, make it ever more crucial that young people develop skills for critical thinking. The ability to sort, analyze, and chose one's responses is a skillset that can be supported by parents and other caring adults.

---

3   Social psychologist Jonathon Haidt provides an excellent summary of this research here: https://www.theatlantic.com/ideas/archive/2021/11/facebooks-dangerous-experiment-teen-girls/620767/.

The most visible expressions of Christianity in the United States continue to embody white, patriarchal narratives. Thankfully, many other forms of Christianity exist! Creative theologians in our midst are mixing and borrowing, crafting theologies that speak to the realities of our day. Girl/friend theology offers a process for noticing negative, harmful images of God, self, and others. It lifts up expressions of Christianity, deeply rooted in history and tradition, that celebrate the diversity of creation and the wide embrace of God's love. It simultaneously lifts up the voices of young people themselves, putting them at the center of ongoing conversation with feminist and other emancipatory worldviews.

SILENCED SELVES

On the way to adulthood, some girls in contemporary US culture experience a dramatic loss. Researchers describe the vivacious, feisty ten-year-old who is unafraid to stand up for herself going underground; while a tempered, silenced thirteen-year-old emerges with a veneer of "nice and kind" that covers turbulent feelings churning within [Gilligan and Brown 1992, 41]. As adolescence unfolds, some girls shed previous identities-in-the-making—ones that allowed for complex and relatively unfixed expressions of selfhood—absorbing instead dominant cultural norms of what it means to be female.

Loss of voice is one primary psychological marker of the move into junior high school and beyond. This is shorthand for a series of transitions that sometimes occur as girls begin to belie an inner sense of knowing, internalizing voices that run counter to their own experience. Voices from social media, consumer culture, or adults in their lives can lead to internalizing cultural cues. Girls begin to "not know" and to behave in ways deemed "nice and kind" [Gilligan 1982]. Conventional gender stereotypes seem to creep into the mind of the early-adolescent girl, catching her unaware. Descriptors such as "vivacious," "spunky," and "willful" give way to adjectives such as "non-confrontational" and "pleasing" (AAUW 1996; Pipher 1994). Social aggression—portrayed in popular culture as the "mean girls" phenomenon—can also shape girl's behavior and cause them to outwardly belie their own inner voice (Underwood, 2003).

The silence of adolescent female selves, however, is not a universal experience. To some Black and Asian American women, conclusions about "silencing" and "losing voice" appear askew, bearing little resemblance to the life they knew. As Beverly Jean Smith writes, much psychological research on women leaves out the experiences she had as a young African American woman, which taught her not to be passive but to resist. "Raised as a resister, I am able to question these paradigms. I see spaces that need filling, so that a more complete picture of women's development emerges"(Smith, 1991, 137). When researchers make central the experiences of girls from varying class, racial, and ethnic backgrounds and with differing sexual and gender identities, psychological wounds bear testimony to added oppressive forces of dominant culture. Thus, while mindful that the silencing of girls still exists in many forms, we also see evidence of girls resisting: It surfaces in descriptors such as smart, sassy, gentle, and unbossed (Parker 2003; Peck McClain 2018; Stevens 2002; Adam 2020, 2022; Percy 2022).

Clearly, when young women use their voices, culture can change. Greta Thunberg rallied the world's attention around climate change at age eight and continued to be an international leader throughout her teens. X Gonzalez, previously known as Emily, used their experience as a survivor of the Parkland, Florida Marjorie Stone Douglas High School shooting to bring attention to gun violence. Amanda Gorman became a household name and spurred a resurgent love of poetry and spoken word after her 2021 reading at the presidential inauguration. Billie Eilish, first famous at age thirteen, became a vocal leader of the body positivity movement. These young people—at least as we can know them through media representations—seem to be quite the opposite of "silenced selves."

I celebrate these examples, even as I mourn the fact that many young people internalize voices that limit their potential to be active agents forming and transforming their world. This has not only psychological, emotional, and political implications, but spiritual ones as well. As Carol Lee Flinders notes, a secular framework alone is not adequate to "strengthen girls enough so they can look patriarchy in the eye and keep walking." Like Flinders, I believe faith traditions, reformed and reclaimed from patriarchy, can bring vital resources to the task of getting girls across that threshold so that they "stand a good chance of remaining whole and safe"[(Flinders 1998, 277)].

GIRLS IN THE FOOTNOTES VS. GIRLS AT THE CENTER

White liberal feminists have a long history of critiquing dominant Western theological models. Alongside them, but often unacknowledged by them, women of color constructed their own models of theology and ethics based on the truths of their embodied lives and their critiques of racism, sexism, and classism. This discipline, known as Womanist theology, is grounded in the experiences of Black women and offers critical insight to broader theological and ethical discourse.[4] Within *white liberal feminist* theology, the lives of adolescent girls were largely ignored. Within *Womanist and Black feminist* literature, however, young girls are pervasive. Comparing these two approaches highlights white feminism's lack of attentiveness to younger generations , especially in its earlier expressions.

As I began to notice the issues facing the teenagers I knew, I realized that my white liberal feminist foremothers in theology focused almost exclusively on adult issues. Teenagers, if they appear at all, show up as footnotes. An example of such a footnote appears in Nelle Morton's book, *The Journey Is Home*. In acknowledging the political voice she inherited from her mother, Morton writes, "When she was young, she wrote a prize-winning oration, 'The Woman I Want to Be.' It anticipated the women's movement today. When I was in my teen years, she gave it to me to use in an oration contest. I, too, won a prize with it" (Morton 1985). That brief story, which contains seeds for a tradition of educating girls into feminist consciousness, is an anomaly. More frequently, white feminists of the mid-twentieth century failed to turn an intentional eye towards the feminist socialization of younger generations.[5]

---

4   In using the term "womanism," I refer to a body of literature by contemporary African American scholars—especially the foundational works by Katie Geneva Cannon, Jacqueline Grant, Delores Williams, and Emilie Townes—who challenge interlocking systems of oppression including racism, classism, homophobia, and ecological abuse. The womanist movement traces its roots to the black feminist movement of the nineteenth century, when women such as Maria Stewart, Sojourner Truth, and Anna Julia Cooper voiced the multiple oppressions of black female life (Baker-Fletcher 1996, 316 –17).

5   A few notable exceptions include the works of Maria Harris, *Women and Teaching: Themes for a Spirituality of Pedagogy* (New York: Paulist Press, 1988); Bonnie Miller-McLemore, *Also a Mother: Work and Family as Theological Dilemma* (Nashville: Abingdon Press, 1994); Carol Lakey Hess, *Caretakers of Our Common House: Women's Development in Communities of Faith* (Nashville: Abingdon Press, 1997); and Rosemary Radford Ruether, *Women-Church: Theology and Practice of Feminist Liturgical Communities* (San Francisco: Harper & Row, 1985), which includes rituals for girls at puberty, persons leaving home for the first time, and women coming out.

I wondered about the possible reasons for this. Perhaps juggling the demands of professional life and the still-imbalanced burden of women's familial responsibilities left little attention to turn toward girls coming into womanhood. Perhaps the struggle for ordination, tenure, and publication left little time to attend to the practical application of feminist theology in the lives of adolescents. Perhaps as they acclimated to the rewards of academia, they forgot the painful memories of their own adolescent years. And, for certain, early feminist theologians gravitated away from practical theology (including religious education) because nurturing the next generation had been traditionally relegated to women and deemed less prestigious work.

Whatever the reasons, I noticed the gap. I could find few resources for spiritual formation that sought to translate the work of white liberal feminists for young people sitting in the pew, walking to class through the crowded hallway, hiding away in the safety of their bedroom, preparing an evening meal for siblings, or learning to care for a new infant of their own.

Womanist thought provides a corrective to this. From its very inception, Womanist thought has made girls not only visible, but prominent. Alice Walker's classic definition of the term "Womanist" points to the existence of precocious girls. It includes these often-quoted words:

> From the Black folk expression of mothers to female children, "You acting womanish," i.e. like a woman. Usually referring to outrageous, audacious, courageous, or willful behavior. Wanting to know more and in greater depth than is considered "good" for one. Interested in grown-up doings. Acting grown up. Being grown up. Interchangeable with another Black folk expres-

sion: "You trying to be grown." Responsible. In charge. Serious ^(Walker 1983, xi–xii).

Although Womanists are thus defined as being "not girls," inherent in the definition is a sideways glance of affirmation to girls who act womanish. Although audaciousness may bring rebuke from a Black mother, it may also, as in this definition, be highlighted as a virtue in the same breath. In two other stories told in her definition of "Womanist," Walker refers to conversations between "Mama" and a child. Thus, the very definition of Womanist has its roots in the education provided by a mother to her female offspring.

Beyond this definitional acknowledgment of adolescent girls, Womanists have a tradition of interpreting domestic life as a place of power, power that emanates from instilling values in new generations.

Womanist sources retrieve evidence of Black women cultivating "homeplace" as a site of resistance out of which emerge women with high self-esteem [hooks 1990, 41]. Within this view, "[t]he common understanding of women's psychological state as rooted in her powerless existence as homemaker and child-rearer, or a pedestal queen, carries little weight"[Smith 1991]. In the concept of homeplace, attention is given to adolescent girls and sometimes results in the ability to "observe the social world critically and to oppose those ideas and ways of being that are disempowering to the self"[Smith 1991, 143]. However, because systemic and structural forms of racism and sexism continue to limit Black girls' access to the future they desire, high self-esteem alone does not always translate into self-fulfillment, agency, or empowerment [Robinson and Ward 1991].

Practices addressing the spiritual and psychological health of all people would encourage feminists to learn from Womanist practices of cultivating healthy resistance in adolescents, while also working to dismantle structural oppression. They might also support Black girls in integrating what Katie Geneva Cannon called the "sass, unctuousness," and healthy resistance they have inherited into their identities-in-process [Cannon 1995, 91–100]. Girl/friend theology welcomes the voices of all people who are making meaning out of their lives, incorporating their own experience of oppression into forms of resistance and liberation.

GIRL/FRIEND THEOLOGY DEFINED

Girl/friend theology attempts to address the problems of silenced selves, missing voices, and girls in the footnotes. It does so through a spiritual practice that begins with the voices and life stories of young people. It engages those stories with the stories of adult women who have found voice and translates the resources of women's theological thought into the context of female adolescence and young adulthood. It is a meeting at the crossroads between adolescence and adulthood. It is a relational model of producing meaning. It moves from making meaning to taking action, as girls and adults emerge changed, able to identify new callings, and to take steps toward unfolding vocation. It is a process designed to bring young women's development as feminist theologians into central focus.

Girl/friend theology is shorthand for a method of eliciting girl's autobiographical stories and reflecting theologically upon them. It is a method that grows out of research in the fields of women's emancipatory theologies, critical ethnography, religious education, and critical pedagogy. Literature from these fields will enter this conversation to provide a theoretical basis for the practical theological act I am describing, but first I want to make clear my use of two words: "girl" and "theology."

During my own feminist awakening in my early twenties, I learned to stop referring to myself and other adult women as "girls." My ears grew sensitive to that word's derogatory nuance. When used by someone in a position of authority, "girl" vs. "woman" carries negative connotations. I reclaim that word here, just as many adult women have found power in reacquainting themselves with the "girl within"[Hancock 1989]. We may grow up and gain power, voice, and authority, but at some level we remain girls, and that deserves to be celebrated. Girls need girlfriends—those special bonds that form when females of any age develop deep and abiding, playful, and creative relationships of respect and nurture with each other. Black girls influenced the English language with their use of the term "girl," as in "You go, girl!" I am indebted to them, as well as to the Black, Asian-American and Latinx women who *embraced me* as a girlfriend for helping me shed the negativism white liberal feminism attached to the word.

"Theology" is the second word I reclaim, rescuing it from the exclusive domain of the professionally trained and naming it more broadly as the process of making meaning of our lives in relation to God [Seymour, Crain, and Crockett 1993]. Theologians in mosques, seminaries, and synagogues do theology; so do people in pews, workers walking home at sunset, and women nestled in moon-drenched tents. In the words of Rebecca Chopp, "Theology no longer uncovers unchangeable foundations, or hands down the cognitive truths of tradition, or discloses the classics, or even figures out the rules of faith. Rather, theological work is a communal process of bringing scraps of materials used elsewhere and joining them in new ways"[Chopp 1995, 73].

Sometimes we do theology on purpose, intentionally setting out to create rituals or write songs articulating our encounters with the divine. Sometimes we stumble into it accidentally, as my tentmates and I did on that moonlit night. Naming those conversations as vespers, an ancient term for prayers recited at the end of the day, blesses them with theological authority, claiming traces of the sacred in the midst of the everyday. When we lead others into the act of making meaning, intentionally creating spaces where new theological awareness emerges, we are doing religious education and spiritual formation.

Girl/friend theology, then, is not a new set of ideas systematized and categorized, but rather part of the ongoing evolution of religious education and spiritual formation as these practices change to meet emerging needs. When we bring to voice the "God-talk" between female adolescents and adults, we do what psychologists Carol Gilligan and Lyn Mikel Brown advocate for as one powerful way to combat the loss of voice that adolescent girls sometimes experience [Gilligan and Brown 1997]. Women, however, often feel ill-equipped to bridge the chasm separating themselves from young people. Girl/friend theology is what *could* happen if a group of faithful, feminist, adults—those of us who have painstakingly constructed a "usable past" that reconciles our spirituality and our feminism—decide it is time to pass those tradition on to a new generation of young people.

Naming the content and practices of feminist theology as a tradition that transforms Christian community is in keeping with Mary Elizabeth Moore's definition of a "traditioning" model of religious education [Moore1983]. Carol Lakey Hess also acknowledges the importance of transforming Christian community so that it might aid in the moral development of women. She writes, "Rather than being a place that colludes with our sexist culture, [the community of faith] can be a place that holds on to women in affirmation, appropriately challenges and let's go of women as they grow, and stays put as these supported women celebrate their distinctiveness and exercise their voice [Hess 1983, 74]. As adult women retrieve the "hidden texts" of faith traditions, it is the task of the religious educator to develop methods by which those hidden texts become part of our ongoing, living curricula, enabling Hess's vision of faithful communities as "holding environments" to take shape [1997].

THE RESEARCH

The research for this project involved eliciting autobiographical stories and engaging in conversation around them in three small-group settings in Chicago and Atlanta. We told stories in groups of five to eight people, meeting in a home, a church, and a church-related institution. After hearing the story, we listened to our feelings, our emotions, and our memories of similar moments in our own lives. Then we plumbed the depths of the larger stories available to us—stories from scripture, from our particular cultures, and from history and tradition—seeking to name the connections and discontinuities between our lives and the stories embedded in our psyches.

For each of the sessions, I solicited the participation of an adult woman with a graduate-level theological education and a feminist commitment. In addition to bringing a story from her own life to begin the series, the woman joined me in the role of a participant-observer who engaged in conversational give-and-take.

Themes emerged. Often these themes resonated with themes appearing in the world of contemporary, professional, Christian theology. Echoes of feminist theology, liberation theology, and process theology drifted to the surface, to be teased out and heard by the trained ear of the professional theologians listening and participating. With the participants' permission, I audio-record-ed and later transcribed each of the ninety-minute sessions.

This research is a type of ethnography that proceeds in awareness of the interventions taking place. I acknowledge that the adults and adolescents are in ministry with one anoth-er, reflecting ethnographic knowing as connected and mutuality constructed [Crain and Seymour 1996]. In this light, the ethnographer is a minister. This passionate scholarship is echoed in the feminist stance of intersubjectivity, which seeks to break down hierarchi-cal and potentially exploitative relationships between research-ers and collaborators. This kind of scholarship acknowledges desired outcomes, which in this case, is the ability of girls to lead more fulfilling lives because of a connection to their feminist inheritance.

ADOLESCENCE AS THE "FIELD," AUTO/ETHNOGRAPHY AS THE METHOD

To speak of adolescence as a stage of life is to engage in dia-logue with developmental theory, the discipline in which Gilligan trained and which her body of work critiques for its lack of gen-der inclusiveness. In 1904, G. Stanley Hall first coined the term "adolescent." In doing so, he shaped underlying assumptions about this time of life as one fraught with "storm and stress" and full of unique emotional upheaval, mood swings, and psycholog-ical crises [Hall 1904]. Setting off decades of conversation and debate about this period of transition from childhood to adulthood, Hall was a precursor to the clinical observations of Jean Piaget, Erik Erikson, and Lawrence Kohlberg, whose work supports the view of adolescence as a time when converging biological, emotion-al, and cognitive transitions cause unparalleled developmental difficulties [Torney-Purta 1990]. To speak of essential characteristics of adolescence that transcend cultural boundaries or to understand maturation as an unvarying sequence of developmental stages overlooks differences based on race, class, sexuality, gender identity, ability, and culture. In light of this critique, scholars have turned their attention away from stage theory in recent decades and toward narrative as a key to understanding moral development (Csikszentmihalyi and Freeman 1986; Vitz 1990; Tappan and Packer 1991). Throughout this project, I frequently adapt key concepts from developmental theory to analyze my ethnographic research. However, like Gilligan, I see developmental stage theory models as social constructs that are thoroughly imbued with modernist assumptions. These models present possible windows through which to view reality, but are just as likely to limit our view to alternate realities. Qualitative research, particularly critical ethnography, supports a turn toward narrative as a means of understanding the ways in which adolescents mature and develop (Denzin and Lincoln 1994).

Critical ethnography, an area of scholarship emerging from the discipline of anthropology, informs my work in two ways: first, as I turn to the "field" of adolescent girlhood, and second, as I interrogate my own connection to that field through memories of my own adolescence.

As I turn to adolescent girls to elicit their autobiographical stories and theological reflection, I resemble an anthropologist entering a "foreign" land. I enter that land steeped in the political agenda of feminism and aware of a power dynamic at play between my collaborators and myself. I am older, more educated, and the designated interpreter of events. Although committed to sharing my interpretations with my participants, I have the final say in the way they are represented. Critical ethnography supports the acknowledgment of these dynamics. As opposed to older models of anthropology, critical ethnographers do not pretend to be invisible, detached observers collecting neutral data [Behar 1993; Behar 1996; Lowenhaupt Tsing 1993; Lancaster 1994]. By situating myself in the research space, I name myself as a player. Along with my recording device and notebook, I bring my empathic person-hood. The result of such qualitative research does not pretend to be scientific or universal. Rather, it seeks to be about "particular and specific embodiment." The result of this is "situated knowledge" [Harraway 1988].

As a person who once lived in this foreign land of female adolescence, I am both an insider and an outsider. Kamala Visweswaran writes that "fieldwork" becomes "homework" as we, through auto/ethnography, expose our own entanglements of race, gender, and power. This kind of scholarship explicitly addresses the tensions between the self and other, and between the personal and the political, allowing those connections to become visible [Visweswaran 1994; Reed-Danahay 1997]. It sees the researcher's own engagement with another culture as part of the story, rather than an invisible fact read only between the lines, as traditionally has been the case. In adopting auto/ethnography as my method, I introduce myself into the lives of my subjects and introduce my subjects into my theorizing. Auto/ethnography challenges researchers to "interrogate our reasons" for immersion in a particular "field" [Visweswaran 1994, 105]. I do this throughout my project by weaving autobiographical fragments of my own adolescence into my discussion of the theory and practice of girl/friend theology. This is in keeping with feminist objectivity, which is defined by Diane Wolf as being about limited location and situated knowledge, which allows for a multiplicity of viewpoints. This perspective not only allows and encourages feminist researchers to bring their own particular location and position into the research, to acknowledge and build on their partial perspective, but makes it imperative for them to do so before any discussion of another's reality can be introduced [Wolf 1996, 14].

Throughout this project, my ethical and theological commitment is toward helping girls come into ownership of voice and moral agency. I adopt this reflexive practice in line with a long list of scholars who have chosen to break from the anthropological tradition of the unbiased observer. In acknowledging my desire to create meaningful change as part of my research and to do research for and with women, I follow the lead of scholars who adopt participatory and action research. The research model I use is action-oriented because it allows participants to define the agenda, creating a reciprocal event in which there is greater potential for the research subjects to become empowered by the process [Wolf 1996; Middleton 1993]. Although I bear responsibility for the finished product, subjects of my research become authors of their own meaning, entering into a cooperative venture with me in which they are more collaborators than informants [Geertz 1989; Limon 1991]. The result of this collaboration is a practical, constructive theology. In this way, girl/friend theology moves from research to adult/adolescent encounters that become a guide for the creation of such relationships.

Many of the girls and women who assisted in this project remained part of the process of interpretation. As I transcribed sessions, coded them for theological themes, and wrote my analyses, I turned to them as conversation partners both formally and informally.[6] The girls, most of whom were high school juniors at the time of our meetings, were college freshmen during the months I was writing. They kept me posted on dorm life and campus feminist movements. The women, most

---

6   I followed the model of "meta-ethnography" outlined by Ada María Isasi-Díaz in *"Mujerista Theology's Method: A Liberative Praxis, a Way of Life,"* in *Mestizo Christianity: Theology from the Latino Perspective*, ed. Arturo J. Bañuelas (Maryknoll, NY: Orbis Books, 1995).

of whom were former students of my youth ministry courses, were engaged in the frontlines of local parish ministry during the months I was writing. They constantly reminded me of the pressing issues facing their youth, especially in the wake of the killings at Columbine High School in Littleton, Colorado, and the ripple effects of such violence. They also reminded me of the need for the translation of emancipatory theologies into youth ministry curriculum.

Since publication of the first edition of this book, events have unfolded that profoundly impact young adult development. Mass shootings in schools. The ongoing police shootings of unarmed Black men and women. The prevalence of gun violence. Species demise. Climate despair. The emboldening of white supremacist terror movements.

As a result, we've seen movements for change, many of them led by young people. The Black Lives Matter movement. The #MeToo movement. Sunrise, a youth-led climate justice movement.

As I updated *Girl/friend Theology* in 2022, young adults struggled to make sense of the spiritual as it relates to the political in the aftermath of a global pandemic, a racial reckoning, and widespread awareness of climate warming. The Springtide Research Institute's post-pandemic research with adolescents and young adults between thirteen and twenty-five notes that more than half of young people say they have experienced trauma. Thirty-four percent of young people report that they are not flourishing in relation to their mental health (Springtide 2022).

Now more than ever, young people need practices that welcome their spiritual hunger, support their mental well-being, and prevent reliance solely on crisis response tools. Girl/friend theology, an intergenerational model that elevates critical thinking and story-based meaning making, is a resource for people who want to replace outdated, used up, oppressive theologies and mental models that cause real harm.

THE LIVE METHOD

As described in the introduction, the process of girl/friend theology is a four-step method that uses the acronym **LIVE**:

L = Listen: we listen to a story of a real-life experience told by a group member.

I = Immerse: we immerse ourselves in the feelings the story arouses in us.

V = View it wider: we connect the story before us with other stories we know from faith traditions, scriptures, and soulful practices.

E = Explore/Enact: we explore and enact next steps that follow from new insights about ourselves in relation to God, self, and others.

Throughout this book, I will point out the steps in the method as a group encounters it. I follow a similar rhythm in the structure of the book. I reflect autobiographically, situating myself historically and culturally—especially in regard to race, gender, sexuality, class, and age. This mirrors first step of the method. I then move to larger discourses, bringing my life experience into conversation with the wider culture's texts, especially those of academic theological discourse. This follows the second and third steps of the method. Finally, at this intersection of lived experience and intellectual encounter, I construct theory and theology, which affects future actions by providing a framework for the next lived experience, reflecting the fourth move of LIVE. Thus, I move in my writing from story to theory, theology, and action. I return to story, all the while making and discovering meaning in a process more akin to a spiral than a straight line.

GUIDELINES FOR FACILITATING LIVE

Over decades of facilitating this and similar processes, I've honed my skills for creative and emergent facilitation. I pull from a toolbox of facilitation techniques I've learned from the work of Priya Parker, Adrienne Marie Brown, The Art of Hosting, and World Café, among others [(Parker 2018; Ter Kuile 2020; Kaner 2014)].

As you facilitate this process, I hope you will adapt it to your particular context. Additional tips for leading and frequently asked questions appear in the appendix.

I begin by explicitly creating a set of group norms, or Covenants of Presence, that create safe-enough space to welcome vulnerability and confidentiality. I refer back to these agreements regularly, so they truly become the groups' default setting.[7]

The best facilitators for this process are versed in feminist theology and trauma-informed learning. I always review and select the story in advance, and I am always prepared to alert participants if sensitive subject matter, such as sexual assault, suicide, or other forms of violence appears in the story. I discuss trigger warnings in chapter 2.

I recommend having two adult facilitators when possible. Both facilitators participate in the process, offering moments of insight that come from their adult perspective, keeping the method moving through the four steps, and making sure everyone's voice is invited. We keep each other accountable to focusing most of the time on the voices of young adult participants. And we tend to any pastoral care or mental health needs that arise. It is absolutely necessary that the group have access to emergency mental health care in case a story triggers a mental health emergency.

I welcome the storyteller to take part in the conversation, but I ask that they refrain from speaking first. When the storyteller is

---

7   For a description of this process and a sample of group norms, see Lewis, Williams, and Baker 2020, 37–40.

done telling their story, we move into discussion of feelings and associations. Often groups will need to be gently reminded to stay in this step. The tendency is to move on to thought and interpretation without dwelling for a few long moments at the level of embodied feeling.

Once the storyteller finishes reading, the story belongs to us all. We are not trying to figure out the meaning for the storyteller, but rather for us all. Sometimes a participant needs to ask a question for clarification, but participants should refrain from questions unless they are necessary. Questions such as "what happened next?" or "do you still feel that way?" are not helpful to the process.

When possible, I share a written version of the story with participants. I ask them not to look at it while the storyteller is speaking, but it sometimes comes in handy to look back at as the conversation unfolds, especially for visual learners.

As I share the facilitated sessions in the chapters that follow, I highlight moments when the facilitator's role became significant. I also occasionally share a decision made while facilitating. Sometimes I look back and wish I had listened more intently, held back on guiding the conversation, or offered an insight that stayed locked up inside.[8] While it is important to reflect and learn from our mistakes in facilitating, it's also important to remember not to be too critical of ourselves. Modelling self-compassion as we facilitate soulful practices is a gift we can offer ourselves and others.

In that moonlit tent all those years ago, I witnessed girls and women falling into a rhythm of reflection. We looked back over our day, experiencing the emotional highs and lows. We wondered about the day's challenges in light of the larger challenges in our lives. We weaved into our wonderings the ways our ideas about God, self, and

---

8   For best practices in facilitation, see also https://couragerenewal.org; https://artofhosting. org; https://www.chriscorrigan.com/parkinglot/facilitation-resources/.

others were evolving. We made a few promises about what we might do differently tomorrow.

This process of reflection—which occurred to us quite naturally—is a soulful practice that we can teach and learn together intentionally; but it also simply happens as part of who we are as humans. We are meaning-making beings who gather in moonlight and starlight to question our existence and ponder the worlds we are creating.

Out of this moonlit encounter grew the seed of girl/friend theology. The process of LIVE (Listen, Immerse, View it Wider, and Enact/Explore Next Steps) will show up repeatedly in the chapters that follow.

CHAPTER TWO

FUTURE HOMEMAKERS AND FEMINIST AWAKENINGS

METHODS OF THEOLOGY, EDUCATION, AND RESEARCH

> You heard me. You heard me all the way.
> I have a strange feeling you heard me before I started.
> You heard me to my own story. You heard me to my own speech.
> — Nelle Morton, *The Journey Is Home*

When I entered Turkey Creek Junior High in 1976, women were participating in consciousness-raising groups all across the country and were experiencing liberation from the idea that life held no more than marriage and motherhood. But my cohorts and I knew nothing of that. Cindy, Donna, Kay, Tavia, and I joined an organization called Future Homemakers of America (FHA). We were drawn by the promise of an annual weekend trip to Orlando—a ticket away from our families—even if it was only a two-hour jaunt. Being a Future Homemaker held zero status, especially compared to being a Future Farmer, which meant you could make thousands of dollars selling prize-winning steer at the county fair. But subtly, subversive acts transpired under cover of "homemaking."

In FHA, we learned to sew. We learned to cook. We dressed in club colors of red and white. But that is not what I remember most about my years in FHA. I remember Kay learning Robert's Rules of Order and presiding over large gatherings. I remember Cindy creating subcommittees, Donna organizing phone trees, and Tavia learning to account for the money we raised selling calendars and stationery. I remember Mrs. Margaret Ann Doak, our adviser, recognizing a potential in me on one particular occasion. She provided the text. I memorized it, and, to the awe of my friends who feared public speaking, I delivered the morning devotion to a room of a thousand people at the state convention. In FHA, I learned something fundamental about myself: I have a voice that carries and feel empowered when using it.

Whether or not she did it purposefully, Mrs. Doak was planting seeds of feminist consciousness. In a fashion similar to that of generations of women organizers and activists before her, she gave us the basic skills of political involvement. Packaged in a club ostensibly devoted to gender-based roles of unpaid domestic labor, Mrs. Doak helped us discover our voice and agency, laying groundwork so that we might be "heard into speech" (Morton 1985).

When we reached Plant City High School, we tried our best to become savvy. We ditched the FHA and branched out into different areas of expertise, still encircled by the community of care created by Mrs. Doak. In high school, Mrs. Suzette Thompson—a Spanish teacher motivated by her own adolescent journey—noticed my gifts and encouraged me to enter a contest. She provided the next words for my fledgling voice to speak: "Córdoba. Lejana y sola. Jaca negra, luna grande." These words, by Spanish poet Federico Garcia Lorca, tell of a man journeying on horseback through the Andalusian town of Córdoba.

I would speak these words loudly into the wind as I performed the chore of mowing and disking my family's orange grove. I won first prize reciting that poem at an event celebrating Tampa's Cuban heritage, even though I have no Cuban ancestry. While learning the nuances of Spanish inflection, I caught a glimpse of myself traveling someday to places far beyond my family's small farm. Having encountered wanderlust, I began collecting the many words I might need to describe the world I would find, the feelings Córdoba's full moon might evoke in me.

It would be years after graduating from high school before I would come into fullness of voice as a political being equipped with tools of critical thinking, a social conscience, and a feminist commitment to resisting patriarchal Christianity. With a Midwestern seminary degree and ordination papers to gird me, I returned to the South, accepting an invitation to preach one Sunday at my in-law's church in the town where I grew up. I naively assumed the invitation was a commonplace courtesy, extended routinely to homegrown seminary graduates. Much later I learned that my invitation had been hard-won. It came only after months of persistence by none other than Mrs. Thompson. My high school Spanish teacher wielded the power of her United Methodist Women's presidency to ensure that I would be the first ordained woman to preach from the pulpit in that male-dominated bastion of Southern religiosity. Having helped me find voice as a teenager, a decade later she fought the reigning patriarchy in our corner of the world to ensure an audience for my more mature voice.[1]

---

1   I use the word "voice" in keeping with the multi-layered usage of the term in the works of Carol Gilligan and Lyn Mikel Brown. Voice refers first to literal utterances, grounded in the body. Voice also refers to the psychological capacity to "say what we know" in a relationship, rather than to silence true feelings in an effort to conform to social norms. When women's and girls' voices are silenced, they go underground and can be related to various degrees of depression (Gilligan and Brown 1992, 19 –23).

In my journey from adolescence to adulthood, I was fortunate. My privilege as a white, middle-class person who aspired to fit norms of academic and social success made me a visible and rewarding project to teachers and mentors. People threw lifelines that pulled me in and helped me to continually add the pieces of myself I would need to survive and flourish, to find a life of meaning and purpose.[2]

To paraphrase Nelle Morton, my mentors "heard me all the way." It happened, however, in fits and starts. A teacher here, a powerful peer there. Cumulatively, they mentored my thriving.

Looking back as an adult, I am grateful. Looking ahead, I hope for more for the young people I see coming of age today. I especially want more for the young people who live on the underside of privilege. Poverty, systemic racism, and gender-based oppression multiply to create a gap of resources for young people learning to survive, thrive, and make meaning of their lives today.

THEOLOGICAL METHOD: HEARING TO SPEECH AND SAVING WORK

In the intervening decades since my feminist awakening, attention toward and activism around the lives of teenagers has increased dramatically. The compounding tragedies of multiple school shootings and increasing teen suicide rates have attracted resources to address the often-deadly effects of bullying culture. Black Lives Matter emerged in part because an activist pastor nurtured young people in resisting state-based violence against unarmed Black men and

---

2   In I *Know Why the Caged Bird Sings*, Angelou uses the image of one who throws a lifeline to describe one of her early mentors, describing her as a "lifeline." The importance of mentors in the lives of young people cannot be underemphasized (Angelou 1969). As Mary Pipher writes, "Many women tell stories of what saved them from the precipice . . . Girls can be saved by a good school, a good teacher, or a meaningful activity. Many women report that when they were in adolescence, they had someone they could really talk to, who encouraged them to stay true to who they really were" (Pipher 1994, 18).

women [Gunning Francis, 2015]. Meanwhile, the internet provided new platforms for young activists such as Greta Thunberg and Malala Yousafzai to exercise their voices in world-shaping ways. Thanks to the support of grassroots, national, and global organizations, young feminists and activists are more likely to encounter networks of support and affirmation for their emerging public selves.

Despite these hopeful signs, the journey through adolescence in the US remains remarkably riddled with inequities caused by structural racism, patriarchy, and gender-based oppression that limit the flourishing of Black and Brown individuals.

Progressive faith communities are an important additional sphere in which to nurture the public voices of adolescents. In ancient times, the church operated in such a way. In the fourteenth century, a teenager named Catherine used her power to change the world through the church in Siena, Italy, by creating hospitals. Another teenager named Teresa found her path to politics through a convent in Ávila, Spain. Motivated by the young lives of saints like these, I envision contemporary Teresa's and Catherine's finding support as they learned to transform their communities.

I envision spaces in which young people could question and critique dominant cultural norms, choosing for themselves the possibility of resistance. I began to imagine adults, committed to the holistic well-being of young people, helping to create such spaces in ways that were culturally sensitive and attuned to all that we are learning about adverse childhood experiences, trauma, and healing. I imagine the creation of zones of safety in which young people could be "heard into speech." Perhaps churches could play a prophetic role in nurturing the power and sense of agency of young people as they come of age. This method would do consistently and self-consciously what my beloved teachers did spontaneously and sporadically.[3] I knew the key was not in *providing* the texts, as Mrs. Doak and Mrs. Thompson had done for me, but in *evoking* the texts already present in contemporary lives.

Story is the opposite of silence. Girl/friend theology is story theology. Two feminist theologians provided guiding metaphors for me in support of this method: Nelle Morton's concept of "hearing to speech" and Rebecca Chopp's concept of "saving work" help articulate the foundations of such a story-based method of spiritual practice [(Morton 1985) (Chopp 1995)].

HEARING TO SPEECH

Nelle Morton describes a moment in her educational career when a student brought her to a new understanding of hearing. Several days into a week-long workshop, a reserved woman began to speak, relating a painful story. "No one interrupted her. No one rushed to comfort her. No one cut her experience short. We simply sat. We sat in powerful silence. The women clustered about the weeping one went with her to the deepest part of her life as if something so sacred was taking place they [dared] not withdraw their presence or mar its visibility." Afterward, when the woman described this experience, she said, "You heard me to my own story. You heard me to my own speech." Morton relates the recurrence of such liminal moments on different occasions where women gathered to accompany one an-

---

3   This reflects an institutionalization of feminist consciousness, a process Gerda Lerner traces as fundamental to women's emancipation throughout history. Without such institutionalization, individual women deprived of a female tradition do not share the male advantage of standing "on the shoulders of giants." See Gerda Lerner, *The Creation of Feminist Consciousness: From the Middle Ages to Eighteen-seventy* (New York: Oxford University Press, 1993). The intersection between this dynamic and girl/friend theology will receive fuller treatment in chapter 8. Although I initially envisioned my audience as churches only, I came to adopt the term "communities of faith" to include a wider set of faith traditions. Women within church, synagogue, mosque, and other faith spaces hold the power to institutionalize feminist consciousness, especially as it relates to theology.

other "into the depths . . . where sound is born." She tells of a "depth hearing that takes place before speaking—a hearing that is more than acute listening. A hearing that is a direct transitive verb that evokes speech—new speech that has never been spoken before. The woman . . . had indeed been heard to her own speech" (Morton, 205).

Morton goes on to affirm that: "Hearing to speech is political. Hearing to speech is never one-sided. Once a person is heard to speech, she becomes a hearing person."[4] A commitment to this kind of depth hearing, whenever it is possible, is foundational to girl/friend theology. When we gather as a circle to hear each other's stories, we enter a space where we learn to sit in powerful silence and listen in ways that evoke new speech. Naming this as sacred space affirms God's presence in the act of holy listening. Being called forth into speech is not a solitary act of personal devotion, but a political one; it names a new reality and creates a community with the potential to effect change.

This resembles a "community of resistance" described by Sharon D. Welch. Being grounded in a community of resistance, Welch writes, enables and sustains transcendence of the multiple oppressions that cripple human life. Stories of renewal and transformation written to "save ourselves" emerge from such communities of resistance (Welch 1990, 18). In girl/friend theology, we tell stories and hear one another to speech. These stories and this speech offer transformation to both the speaker and the listeners. I witnessed such a community of resistance emerging while facilitating girl/friend theology at a college retreat in Oklahoma in 2019.

A retreat participant, Liz, who is of Native American ancestry, shared a story about the intricate snake tattoo on her arm, the anger

---

4   Morton acknowledges her indebtedness to Paulo Freire, who makes a similar point from the perspective of Latin American peasants in *Pedagogy of the Oppressed* (New York: Herder & Herder, 1970).

it sparked in her adoptive parents, and its redemptive meaning within her own Indigenous worldview. After Liz's story, a groundswell of voices rose up to give witness to the power of tattooing—both the lasting image itself and the temporal ritual of receiving the tattoo alone or with friends—as a spiritual practice of naming and claiming body and identity. Three Native American women in a room filled with mostly white women spoke up to affirm Liz's rejection of a normative Christian interpretations of the serpent as evil, harkening to the temptation of Eve in the Garden of Eden. One person flipped that interpretation to name the connection between the way a snake sheds its old skin and the Christian concept of becoming a new person.

In this session of girl/friend theology, I perceived a momentary decentering of white normative interpretations Christianity. Others in the room confirmed my perception when they gave thanks out loud for the moment in which the group centered the snake as a symbol of empowerment. The celebrated collective meaning-making through the lens of an Indigenous person's ways of knowing. Although these moments of decentering often occur only in glimpses, they can develop an appetite for creating more of them. This, I believe, is the important incremental work of cultural change happening collectively in moments when we risk becoming communities of resistance for and with one another.

SAVING WORK

From Rebecca Chopp, I borrow the metaphor of "saving work" to highlight a second foundation of this theological method. For many of us, "salvation" brings to mind the vocabulary of Protestant evangelicalism, in which "being saved" is an individual objective, an exchange between self and God. Especially within fundamentalist interpretations of Christianity, "being saved" connotes a particular set of understandings. For me, growing up in the Southern

Baptist Bible Belt, "being saved" meant making a personal confession of Jesus Christ as Lord and Savior. This limited understanding of salvation cuts us off from more relational understandings. Chopp reclaims this word. For her, to participate in "saving work" is to join the communal process of continually reshaping the Christian tradition [Chopp 1995, 85]. This understanding of "saving work" allows us to reclaim the theological motif of salvation in a way that makes sense in a postmodern world.

By "saving" our stories, I refer to the intentional recounting of the life experiences that shape and form us. The existential philosopher Martin Heidegger reminds us that to be human is to experience an essential "thrownness." This thrownness is a seemingly arbitrary set of particulars: an abusive parent, an attentive older sibling, or a violent neighborhood. It diverges into an ever more intricate web of specific events, surroundings, and interactions that combine to make up an individual life. This thrownness is the raw material out of which all of our interactions with the world are shaped. Psychologists name it as the stuff out of which we endeavor to construct a self [Heidegger 1962]. [5]

To be human is to give meaning to these raw materials. Experiences lead us to "address basic questions about the nature of the world, of God, of relationships, of the presence of evil, and of our life commitments." This task, whether it takes place within a religious community, inside an individual's thoughts, or in dialogue with family, friends, and professionals, can be called theology. Each of us theologizes as we filter our experiences through our "temples of meaning"—unfinished buildings that house our ongoing processes of meaning-making [Seymour, Crain, and Crockett 1993, 23].

---

5 For a discussion of shifting views of the self in modernity and postmodernity, see Dan McAdams, *The Stories We Live By: Personal Myths and the Making of the Self* (New York: William Morrow, 1993), and Anthony Giddens, *Modernity and Self-Identity: Self and Society in the Late Modern Age* (Stanford, Calif.: Stanford University Press, 1991).

By telling our stories and enlisting the help of others in making sense of our stories—especially as they relate to the larger stories of our sociocultural and religious contexts—we save our stories from the oblivion of isolation within our own referential boundaries. When we engage in the sharing of stories, we engage in a communal, saving work of reinterpreting our inherited traditions into forms and shapes that make sense in an emerging landscape. By saving our stories, we participate in saving our selves, connecting our lives to evolving religious and spiritual traditions, and, to use explicitly Christian language, engaging in the ongoing incarnation of God's word in the world.

This act is especially important in youth culture today. Young people who harbor deep distrust of institutions, especially the church, need spaces in which to make sense of inherited traditions as they intersect the horizons of a postmodern world [Beaudoin 1998]. Inviting young people to examine what their stories have to say to the story of their faith tradition holds promise as one way for the church to remain relevant to this generation, especially if these methods allow youth to "produce their own representations, narrate their own stories, and engage in respectful dialogue with others" [Giroux 1996, 50].

Such spiritual practices benefit young people in other significant ways, providing protection against depression. The brain research of Lisa Miller at Columbia University's Spirit Mind Body Institute shows that the spiritual practices can help mitigate the severity of depression, length of depression, and outcome of depression as suicide, suicidal ideation, and accidental drug overdose [Miller 2021]. When I encountered Miller's work in 2021, I immediately sensed a clarity about why practices such as girl/friend theology matter. The "so what" of girl/friend theology is this: it is a spiritual practice that can be used inside or outside of faith communities to help young people become more resilient in the face of multiple daily affronts on their mental well-being. These multiple daily affronts are not hard to imagine. On a recent Zoom call with thirty religious educators and spiritual directors who work with young people, I asked participants to list in the chat box the urgencies they see arising within young people. The list populated quickly: fear of mass shootings, anxiety about career, climate despair, trauma from the pandemic.

Storied theological reflection is a narrative spiritual practice. Written between the lines is the theological conviction that we help save one another' s lives when we slow down to hear one another into speech.

LIVE AND THE STORY THEOLOGY METHOD

LIVE grows out of what I first experienced as Story Theology. It begins with a person telling a story from her life to a group of others, one of whom is a designated facilitator. In advance of each session, one participant agrees to prepare, in writing, a story to read aloud. When time allows, we distribute copies of the story to each partic-ipant to refer to after the reading. The group then reflects upon the story in two ways: "experience near" and "experience distant."

The first half of the session is "experience near." During this time, the listeners share feelings and associations that the story evokes. Related stories and memories surface, and group members respond. Participants tease out of the story the range of emotions and asso-ciations it suggests. The storyteller participates in the conversation, but I suggest they let others speak first. Central symbols, themes, or messages may arise; but we hold for them for the next step of the method. This first half of the method relates to the L and I (Listen and Immerse) steps of the acronym LIVE.

The second half of the session is "experience distant." During this time, conversation turns to themes, theological concepts, and issues embodied in the story. Participants may voice related stories from scripture or myth, or they might respond to the question "How is God present (or absent) in this story?" This second half of the method relates to V and E (View it Wider and Enact/Explore) in the acronym LIVE.

The original designer of this method wanted to create a way to reflect on lived experience that would allow for interfaith theological dialogue in a religiously diverse setting. It attempts to cast the broadest net possible in order to include the most varied interpretations of that tradition. As a theologian committed to encouraging ecumenical and interfaith dialogue, I intentionally recruited girls from different Christian denominations and from outside the Christian church. I was especially interested in finding people who identified themselves as religious seekers, those who come to faith critiquing or questioning their affiliations with organized religion, yet self-consciously on a spiritual journey. Such seeking is both a developmentally appropriate step for adolescents and a culturally appropriate response to postmodernity. Because of the interplay between my beliefs and those of my collaborators, I alternate between the terms "church" and "faith community," depending upon the religious mix of the group.

"Going forth" is the final step in the process. Here we ask the question, "How might this story and our conversation around it change any future action?" The aim of this process is not to end with grand conclusions, but to have each participant leave the storytelling space with her own awareness or set of conclusions, some of which may be communally agreed upon and some of which may be individual. The final step of naming a potential change completes an action/reflection educational model and helps reinforce portions of the story/conversation that stood out as particularly meaningful. Going forth aligns with E: Explore Aha! Moments and Enact Next Steps.

I first encountered Story Theology through the leadership of Beth Burbank, a supervisor in a Clinical Pastoral Education program (CPE) at Rush-Presbyterian-St. Luke's Medical Center in Chicago. She conceived it as a way for seminary-trained persons involved in clinical training as hospital chaplains to engage in theological reflection as a group. The groups using this method are working, learning, and reflecting together in a variety of didactic and clinical settings. The CPE method relies heavily on an action/reflection model of learning, in which experience is the basis for critical thinking. Learning, in this method, is a result of that reflection guided by individual supervision and group interaction. The story theology method reflects this educational philosophy I encountered student at Rush-Presbyterian-St. Luke's Medical Center in 1990 and 1991.

At the time, I was a resident in the pediatric unit, helping young oncology patients and their parents deal with issues of grief and loss. My colleagues were part of an intensive year-long residency focused on the needs of people diagnosed with HIV/AIDS in its still early years. As I used the method with my peers, I was able to articulate new theological understandings, growing spiritually while also maturing in my capacity to provide pastoral care in a clinical setting. As I moved from the crisis-driven ministry of chaplaincy to the more varied ministry of a suburban parish, I realized that the practice of story theology had changed fundamentally my views of theology.

Theology once meant reading other people's work and integrating it into my own thinking: it became a process that started in my own life experience, moved out to the intersecting worlds of scripture, reason, and tradition, and ended with action in the world. I began to use the method with groups I led—first, with a group of adults in their late twenties and later with a group of adolescents. When I began teaching youth ministry at the seminary level, I introduced this method to my students as a way of teaching young people to engage in the spiritual practice of theological reflection.

Having lived with this method for more than three decades, I have liberally adapted it and encouraged others to adapt it for their contexts. I also have discerned connections between story theology—as Burbank conceived it and practiced it with her colleagues—and the writings of several religious educators. As a model of religious education, girl/friend theology finds much in common with Anne Streaty Wimberly's method in its use of life stories as a primary source of group theological conversation [Wimberly 1994]. It shares with Wimberly's method a bias toward centering lived stories and connecting them to biblical stories and faith traditions. It also resonates with Wimberly's emphasis on inviting participants to break silences to which they have been relegated. An important difference between Wimberly's method and mine is the role of facilitator. In Wimberly's method, the leader strategically brings stories from African American heritage and from scripture into conversation with everyday stories. In girl/friend theology, the introduction of the story, themes, tradition, and related stories from scripture or culture arise from the conversation itself, in real time. The larger canon of stories from women's history, other subjugated histories, literature, tradition, and scripture flow in and out of the discussion and may be introduced by anyone in the group, as the connections arise, rather than planned in advance by the facilitator.

Girl/friend theology also echoes the movements of Patricia O'Connell Killen's work of theological reflection. Imagine a Venn diagram. In one circle is a person's lived experience. In the other circle is the person's faith—its scripture, tradition, community, and history of interpretation. The space in the middle is where we do the work of theological reflection, critically selecting what parts of tradition we choose to keep, and which parts we choose to leave behind [O'Connell Killen and de Beer 1994]. Thomas Groome's "shared Christian praxis" model similarly provides a process for leading communities through an action/reflection educational method. We name a present action and move to critical reflection on that action. Then, we draw on scripture and tradition to evaluate the present action and to guide future actions. Next, we converse with our traditions, discerning a response in the form of future action. The goal is that "participants appropriate the faith Story/Vision to their own lives and contexts, to know for themselves through judgment," and to thereby make that story their own [Groome 1991, 147]. Girl/friend theology shares similar trajectories with these two models of theological reflection, as well as a similar goal of reinvesting scriptural traditions with new meaning.

Zora Neale Hurston, a writer who crosses the disciplines of literature, anthropology, and ethnography, writes, "There is no agony like an untold story inside you" [Hurston 1996, 15]. As participants in my research groups moved through the steps of this method, they often shared stories they had never told before. In releasing those untold stories, they were heard to speech by the sheer presence of safe-enough space. Participants in my research groups often reported leaving the space with a new sense of ownership of their religious tradition. Having saved their own stories from obscurity within their individual frames of reference and having made powerful connections to the larger stories of their faith traditions, they felt emboldened to claim their rightful place as ongoing interpreters, engaged in the saving work of making old, old stories relevant to a new day.

MY RESEARCH PARTNERS

At the heart of this book are the voices of fifteen participants—eleven teenagers and four adults. The research began in May 1997 after a student in one of my youth ministry courses expressed an interest in learning how to use story theology with the youth group she was serving in an upper-middle-class suburb of Chicago. Lisa introduced the idea to three girls, two of whom agreed to take part in a series of two-hour sessions over the course of a month. Leila and Maggie, two young, middle-class women nearing the end of their junior year in high school, both agreed to participate in three sessions. Lisa, twenty-three, and I, thirty-four, joined Leila and Maggie during the following weeks. Although both Leila and Maggie were confirmed members of the Lutheran church where we met, neither of them attended church or youth groups regularly. They both expressed doubt about Christianity and described themselves as "spiritually seeking."

The second group formed in the home of my neighbor, Elaine. A gregarious and politically active sixteen-year-old, Elaine heard about my research and offered to take part. She was interested in the conversations that might take place with her colleagues in Future Leaders Chicago (FLC), a leadership development program funded by the Community Trust. Through a competitive selection process, thirty high school juniors from the Chicago area were selected annually to take part in monthly immersion learning events related to public life. Elaine told me that often during their animated conversations, questions of spirituality and religious conviction surfaced. We sent invitations to the fifteen female members of the FLC, asking them to come to a weekend retreat at Elaine's home. Of the seven colleagues who responded with interest, four were able to commit to the entire weekend. Emma, Katie, Hannah, and Elaine joined me and Peg—a twenty-four-year-old seminary student I recruited to be a part of our conversations—for two days of story theology sessions on June 28–29, 1997. Katie, Hannah, and Elaine, all seventeen, were preparing to enter their senior years of high school. Emma, also seventeen, was preparing to move away to college.

The third group took place in Atlanta, Georgia, in July 1998. Every summer, sixty rising high school seniors gathered at Emory University for a program called Youth Theology Institute (YTI). Funded by a Lilly Foundation Grant and the Candler School of Theology, this four-week intensive learning event provides theological education for a select group of youth already steeped in religious thought and language. The five girls who participated in our group did so voluntarily, giving up their free time in the afternoon. Cathy, Mary, Holly, Tina, and Kaitlin were all sixteen or seventeen years old. I recruited Sarah, twenty-six, from the staff of YTI to take part in the conversations. Our meetings were part of YTI's officially approved research component.

These three groups are in no way representative of teenagers in general. Participants' identities varied ethnically, religiously, economically, and in sexual orientation, but most participants were from backgrounds of economic and white privilege.

Much of the research documenting loss of voice in girls points to early adolescence as a particularly ripe moment for intervention. Although I intend for this method to be a potential intervention tool aimed at helping girls find and maintain their voice, I was also interested in documenting the God/human relationship from an adolescent perspective. I chose an older population to ensure a wider breadth of life experience from which to draw. Although a younger population might have allowed me to better test this method as an intervention, the literature documenting the phenomenon of silencing describes it as beginning in early adolescence and often continuing well into adulthood. My choice of an older population also reflects a simple truth of fieldwork: I sought teens with whom I had some connection, assuring easier and more authentic access into their worlds.

In alternating the time element of the groups—weekly, weekend, and weeklong—I was attempting to determine which format would best provide an environment for thinking that was "lithe and beautiful and immensely generative" [Bruner 1969, 121]. Thus, I engineered three different educational environments, hoping to compare the success of the method among environments [Brown 1992]. Although I have ideas about which environment was the most fruitful, in the end, the generative capacity of each session depended more on the individual makeup of the group rather than the type of setting. While I was facilitating a spiritual practice and designing a learning moment, I was simultaneously creating a space where I would also be a participant. The method was thus simultaneously an ethnographic research method, in which data was recorded for later analysis, and an innovative educational method, which I was testing for its ability to generate theological thought.

All the participants and their parents completed consent forms. I recorded and transcribed the sessions, with particular attention to the subtleties of adolescent conversation, including body language, overall mood, and facial expressions. I changed the names of participants to protect their anonymity. I paid their travel expenses and a small stipend for taking part.

THEOLOGICAL ASSERTIONS OF GIRLFRIEND THEOLOGY

In interpreting the text of the thirteen story sessions, I chose four of them for careful analysis. Within those four sessions, I identified seven theological assertions I heard my collaborators making.

In many situations, they articulated these assertions on their own, bringing their implicit and explicit religious learning into conversation with their life stories. At other points, one of the two adults made the assertion and received a resounding "aha" from a younger participant.

Each of these assertions grew out of my analysis of one or more of the story sessions and will appear in later chapters, when the accompanying story session is related. For ease in tracking these assertions, I have included the number of the story session out of which each assertion grew. The seven theological assertions are as follows:

God is mysteriously omnipresent, but not magically omnipotent. Although we cannot explain it, God *is* at work within human tragedies to create healing potential. God may not fix things, but neither does God abandon us (story #3 and story #4).

God feels our pain and cries with us (story #3 and story #4).

We have direct access to God through our bodies (story #1 and story #2).

Our lives are like "fifth gospels." Our life stories are sacred texts where God continues to reveal God's self (story #1 and story #2).

We go to church to "*share* God, not find God." Religious institutions affirm our hunches about God but do not usually introduce us to God for the first time (story #1 and story #2). God is most fully alive (incarnated) in us when our eyes are open to the pain of others (story #4).

Church, at its best, is a community of compassion, a resource in our healing, and a potential agent of change in the world (story #1 and story #4).

I see these seven assertions as the beginning of an inclusive list that will grow and mutate. The list is heuristic and is in no way static. Often a theme or assertion voiced in one group setting was echoed by a different group of girls in another time and place. The ensuing chapters will examine these themes in detail, using the stories and accompanying conversations to illuminate the method by which the girls "heard to speech" their emerging theological understandings and by which adult feminist theologians provided support at the crossroads of female adolescence.

In recounting these sessions, I make every attempt to stay as close as possible to the actual words spoken by my adolescent collaborators, so that their theological voices might be claimed and heard. However, their words were constantly co-mingling with words and images offered by the adult women. What emerges is a thick description, a richly nuanced portrait of the meaning-making moment, both its content and its method. My hope is that this detailed snapshot will enable not precise duplication of the teaching/learning event, but creative adaptation of the method.

CHAPTER THREE

GOD-TALK ACROSS RELIGIOUS BORDERS

> God's story is revealed in our story in myriad
> and mysterious ways. Each of us is the pen with
> which God writes a fifth gospel.
> — Judith Siqueira, *In God's Image*

The two stories in this chapter stand in stark contrast to one another. The first, "Will You Be My Friend?", is a seventeen-year-old's story about the death by suicide of her childhood friend. The second, "Tomorrow, Then," is a sixteen-year-old's story about one of those shining moments when all is right with the world and God feels as close as the next breath

These two stories and the accompanying conversations show teens doing theology out of tragic pain and ineffable beauty— themes that surface frequently in adolescent lives. In both of these stories, the conversations about God transcend the boundaries of a single religious tradition, landing "someplace between religion and spirituality, at a crossroads where tradition, tolerance, and universality intersect" (Shandler 1999, 258).

Awareness alert: The references to suicide in this first story are intense and may be triggering to some readers. Please take the necessary care for yourself and others as you engage this material or lead a group using it.[1]

STORY #1: WILL YOU BE MY FRIEND?

Emma, a seventeen-year-old girl from a suburb of Chicago, told the following story. Also present in the session were myself, an adult collaborator, and two young people, Hannah and Elaine. Hannah was a seventeen-year-old Roman Catholic who joined the church as a third-grader after "succumbing to the pressure" of nuns at a parochial school to which she had been sent by her Baptist mother and Jewish father. Elaine, also seventeen, was an active member of her Conservative Jewish synagogue and takes part in national Jewish youth organizations. Emma, whose extended family is Roman Catholic, was not raised in the church. She described her beliefs as outside of organized religion but having affinity with Indigenous belief systems. The adult collaborator, Peg, and I are both ordained United Methodist clergywomen. We were gathered at the home of Elaine, who was my neighbor at the time.

Elaine and I frequently enjoyed theological conversations over the back fence. After hearing about my dissertation project, Elaine volunteered her home for a weekend retreat. We met on Friday and Saturday and were joined by three other young women for portions of the retreat. We worked around job schedules, figure skating practice, and a Shabbat dinner, meaning the makeup of our group occasionally changed. The core group of girls knew each other through

---

1   For guidelines on best practices with using trigger warnings, see https://sites.lsa.umich.edu/inclusive-teaching-sandbox/wp-content/uploads/sites/853/2021/02/An-Introduction-to-Content-Warnings-and-Trigger-Warnings-Draft.pdf. For specific guidelines about how to address the topic of suicide when it arises, see https://www.samaritans.org/about-samaritans/research-policy/internet-suicide/online-safety-resources/how-talk-about-suicide-safely-online/.

an urban leadership program from the previous school year. Emma was a friend of Elaine's who did not know the others but was interested in our project and decided to take part.

Before gathering, I asked each participant to prepare a story from her life to share with the group. I asked them to choose an event or moment in their life about which they were curious and not necessarily a pivotal or life-changing moment.[2] In later iterations, I sometimes ask participants to record a story on their phones and send it to me, if writing it down seemed less welcoming. I also change the story prompt if I am hoping to hone in on theological reflection around a particular issue. For example, in the wake of the Covid pandemic, I began asking participants to "tell me a story about a difficult challenge you went through." Purposefully welcoming stories about the hard parts of life can surface stories that may need telling. From these stories might surface spiritual practices that foster resilience. Similarly, they offer opportunity to question inherited narratives such as "God doesn't give us more than we can handle." These moments allow us to weave in the wisdom of contemporary authors like Kate Bowler, whose bestselling book *Everything Happens for a Reason: And Other Lies I've Loved* offers helpful follow up for participants who want more [(Bowler 2019)].

I review the stories in advance, select the one we would use for a given session, and check in with the storyteller ahead of time to make sure they were willing to share the story. I set up the space by creating or reminding the group of the Covenants of Presence or group norms we are holding, and I briefly share the four-step method we would be using to engage with Emma's story. Emma told the following story.

---

2   See the appendix Guidelines for Facilitating Girl/Friend Theology and a sample invitation to write a story.

WILL YOU BE MY FRIEND?

My story begins back in first grade. I met this girl named Rachel, and she was the first person that I ever met in first grade. The first friend that I ever really had.

She came up to me on the playground and she said, "Hi, who are you? I'm Rachel. Will you be my friend?" I said, "Okay." And we were friends from then on. From forever. For twelve years we were friends. She moved to the city a year ago, and she got her own apartment. We kind of lost touch a little bit this past year, but we were still really good friends. We've been best friends for so many years that to lose touch, like one, maybe two years didn't really matter. Every time we saw each other it was like—click—we were friends again.

So, this was about a month ago. It was about one-thirty in the morning. The phone rang, and I didn't really pay any attention to it. My mom answered it apparently, because it stopped ringing. I went back to sleep. Then, my mom comes in and wakes me up. She tells me I had a phone call. I was disturbed a little bit. I picked up the phone, and it was my other friend Lori, who was the second friend that I met, right after Rachel, in the first grade. The three of us had been friends for twelve years. She was crying. I asked her what was wrong, and she said, "Rachel's dead." I didn't believe her. Rachel had hung herself.

A few hours before, she had been in a play. She was an actress, and she went to a school for acting and visual arts, a school where you have to audition to get in. She was a theater major. She was a senior. She was just about to graduate. It happened right after a performance, the last performance of the play she was in. She was still in her costume. There were people still filing out of the theater. Someone found her right after the play in a costume room. She had hung herself from a pole in the costume room. There were still hundreds of people there when this happened, when they found her. So, Lori is friends with her roommate. And her roommate called Lori, and Lori called me. And then Lori came over. It was about two in the morning at that point. And we just sat there the whole night.

We didn't sleep. We just kind of held each other the whole night. We had that support.

The story doesn't really have an end. It's like day by day we have to deal with the fact that we never got to say goodbye. We never got a chance to say anything to her. That night I went through about four stages. It was interesting, almost all the stages. The first was just hysteria. I cried and cried and cried for hours. And the second stage was denial. Like, I recognized all this afterward. I was just like—"No." I blocked it out of my mind for the next few hours, "just go eat something." Nothing happened. And then the third stage was just anger at her—for doing that. This was like continuing on to the next day. I didn't sleep for two days. I'd throw pillows at the wall and punch the wall and just scream. I have pictures of my friends, a wall of pictures. And I would just talk to the picture of her I have on the wall and just scream at her in anger. And then the next stage, I was just depressed. It was like, you know, I'll never get over it.

So, then I went to her service. Her parents had a service. She wanted to be cremated. She told me that beforehand. Her parents had a service for her at her grand-parents' church. I went to that. I guess this is where the story ends.

It was a very frustrating service. She was not a religious person at all. She didn't believe in God at all. Yet, they had this service for her at this church where they passed out a program for her saying that "Rachel is now with God." The whole service was like, "She is now in heaven with God, where she belongs." Blah, blah, blah. The preacher was saying all these wonderful things about her, but he didn't know her at all. I felt bad because I didn't even really cry at the service. It angered me a lot, thinking that this was how people were going to remember her.

I don't believe she is in heaven. Because for her, there wasn't a heaven. So, I don't believe that she's in a place that she didn't even believe in. It just totally angered me.

Later on, we found out different clues that kind of brought everything together. She hadn't told anybody this. Not me or Lori or her roommate or any of her friends, but she had been diagnosed with clinical depression and had been on medication and going to therapy for six months. She kept all of that a secret from everyone but her parents. She kept everything inside.

She was beautiful. She looked like she was straight out of a magazine. She was gorgeous. She was talented. She had a boyfriend. She seemed to be so happy, and then this happened. I don't know. It made me question. It made me thankful that I don't feel how she did, that I can see through my problems. Whatever problems she had, she kept inside her. I know she could have worked through them, but I guess she didn't feel like she had the strength to do that. The whole experience made me thankful that I'm able to work through my personal problems.

DOING LIVE WITH "WILL YOU BE MY FRIEND?"

L: LISTEN DEEPLY

The first step of LIVE is L: Listen deeply to the storyteller.

We are sitting in a circle with a beautiful cloth in the center. I invite everyone to take a few deep breaths, ground themselves, and prepare to be fully present to the storytellers. I light a candle and signal that it is time for the storyteller to begin. If copies of the story have been circulated, I ask them to be put aside so we can focus on the voice and presence of the storyteller. I invite people to: "Listen deeply as the story is read aloud. Listen with the ears of God / Spirit / Creator / Source. Listen with your whole body, without an agenda, paying attention to the feelings the story stirs in you. Listen, as if you are listening to scripture, as if you expect the Holy to show up."

I: IMMERSE IN FEELINGS

The second step is to I: Immerse yourself in the feelings. I invite people to: "Share the full range of emotions you felt as you listened. Surface feelings that showed up in your body: tense shoulders, change of breathing, tears, etc. Share briefly any stories from your own life that this story called to mind."

Often the initial moments after the storyteller finishes are filled with silence. It sometimes takes a few minutes to move from the immediacy of our feelings to the ability to formulate speech around them. It can be a vulnerable moment for the storyteller, who perhaps has just shared intimate details of their life. I told the group ahead of time that this silence is okay, maybe even sacred. "We don't have to jump in right away and fill up the silence," I said. "We can just hold the silence until someone begins to speak."

At the end of Emma's story, everyone was silent, and some were tearful. One participant reached out and touched Emma's hand. After a few moments, people started sharing their feelings, beginning with sadness, and moving on to anger. At one point early on, a participant asked how long ago this had happened, and Emma clarified the timeline of the death and the memorial service. Questions for clarification, although not explicitly part of the process, are often necessary during the initial part of the conversation. Also, this is a time when participants (especially those who are visual, rather than auditory, learners) often refer back to a written copy of the story, if it is available.

A moment later, a participant introduced the question of why God allows bad things to happen. I noted the comment, then gently interrupted that chain of thought by asking them to name the feelings behind that question. "I want to remind you to try to stay on feelings for now. We'll come back to that as we move further into the process." This is an example of the facilitator gently helping the group honor the LIVE method, without being too formal or heavy-handed. In this moment, the feelings expressed were those of sadness for Rachel, for Rachel's family, and for Emma in her loss. Several people connected with Emma's anger about the service. Two people shared associations of funerals that had left them feeling angry or empty.

V: VIEW IT WIDER

The third step of the method is V: View it Wider. Here I invite: Let this story speak to the stories you know by heart. Where does scripture, your faith tradition, or another faith tradition show up in this story? How might this story unearth a new interpretation or invert a familiar passage for you? Whose voice is missing from the story or from our conversation around it? Where does power, inequity, or systemic evil show up in the story?

In this session, the third move happened quite naturally, as the talk flowed away from the immediacy of our feelings to the level of thoughts, symbols, and larger connections. When that happened, I drew attention to it by saying, "We've moved on to the next step in the method now. I want to remind you to open your mind up to the wider traditions, scripture, and stories that are part of us. Let's bring them into the conversation now."

A metaphor emerged that was later incorporated into conversation about the nature of the church. The metaphor was that of life as a stage or a play, where a girl diagnosed with clinical depression could temporarily live out an alternative existence. The Rachel whom people saw on the outside—a gorgeous, talented actress—hid a deeply troubled and closely guarded interior life.

> *Emma:* One of the last times I saw her, she was complaining about how she was "a big, fat pig." She weighed ninety-eight pounds. I'm not blaming the media, but something had her convinced she wasn't good enough, that she wasn't pretty enough, that she needed to be better than she was. I mean, she was straight out of a magazine. She wore plastic miniskirts.

> *Elaine:* The play was another world where she could be. It's a place where, when you change your costume, you change yourself. She could totally step out of this life, wanting to step into a whole other setting. When I play the character, I am the character. It's not the story of Rachel.

> *Emma:* People could watch her—

Elaine: And she was the star—

Emma: She could be a completely different person in a completely different world. I think she had a re-alization that this was the only place people could watch her and praise her and love her.

Elaine: And when it's over, she can't go back to where the problems are…

Peg: And, following the metaphor of the actor, peo-ple who are mentally unwell are not themselves. It's not the Rachel you met on the playground in the first grade.

God-Talk: A Covenant, a Minyan, an Icon

God-talk emerged straightforwardly as we moved into "V: View it Wider" step of the method. We discussed the disjunction between the official religious ceremony and the gathering of friends and family immediately after the tragedy. In the process, three images—a covenant, a *minyan*, and an icon—surfaced, bringing motifs from Jewish and Christian traditions into the conversation.

To Emma, the church service felt like a betrayal of Rachel's truest self, the self hidden behind the beautiful actress facade. The service angered Rachel's closest friends and alienated them at a time when they longed for closure. A more faithful representation of church—to the participants in this conversation—was the group of friends who sought each other out, instinctively knowing their need to be togeth-er. They made a promise to each other regarding their own future acts, becoming a covenant community in the wake of this tragedy. Emma recounted: "My friends and I all got together. We didn't go to school, obviously, the next day. So, they all came over to my house and I made everyone promise. It was a dumb promise, well, not a dumb promise. I made them promise never to do anything like this. To always find a way of working through our problems."

Emma received overwhelming support from the other girls present that this was no "dumb promise," even though it reminded them of teachings from junior-high health class they disregarded at the time. Elaine said, "It's the kind of thing you think will never happen, until it hits home."

Building on the image of promise-making, I pointed to the covenant as a predominant theme in the Hebrew Bible. Often, at pivotal moments or in the wake of tragedy, people make covenants with each other and with God. I also focused on Emma's description of friends and parents who gathered at Rachel's home two days after her death to comfort, console, and covenant together. "That's an incredible image," I said.

Elaine gave a theological name to this image, bringing her Jewish heritage into conversation with the Christian context of Emma's story. "This is like a *minyan*, the community gathered," she said. She explained that a *minyan* is the quorum of ten men traditionally necessary for a ritual of celebration or mourning to take place in Judaism. In Reform Judaism, women worshipers are included in the number to form a *minyan*. In Conservative Judaism, individual congregations decide for themselves whether to include women in the quorum.

Elaine took the word out of those contexts, freeing it for a non-Jewish, non-gender exclusive adaptation: people need a community of support in a time of loss. Emma and her friends created a *minyan* that moved in and out of the grief-filled days following Rachel's death. Perhaps, Elaine conjectured, it would continue to function in the months and years to follow because "in Judaism, it's important for us to remember that there's no set grieving period. You can never say someone's time of mourning is up." Here the image of the play and the God-talk about a *minyan* converged, leading to a conversation about religious icons.

> *Dori:* So in your story, there's the "play" community—the church and all the people gathered there—and there's the "real" community. And if I were to say where the church is, in my best image of the church, it's everybody coming together afterwards. If there's a God, and God wants church to look like something, that would be it. Flexible and moving, human and alive.

> *Elaine:* Yeah, in Judaism, we believe you can pray anywhere. It's what you're saying to each other, rather than the church or the pastor. It was being there with each other.

> *Emma:* Yeah, that was so important. To be with everyone was the most important thing.

> *Peg:* If we wanted to move with the church being in your home, especially in your room, the symbols don't have to be a cross we hang up. They could be the pictures you have on the wall.

We talked about the fact that in ancient times, fragments of saints' bodies were saved and are, to this day, kept and revered. Relics such as these are visible reminders of an invisible God. We also talked about the cross as being like a photograph of the scene of Jesus's crucifixion, and thus a type of icon. The community of the first Christians, gathered together for support at a time of grief, held onto the symbol of the cross as a reminder of the friend and rabbi they had lost.

The symbol took on meaning beyond loss, as resurrection became part of the ongoing story. Emma appreciated the connections.

> *Emma:* I like what Peg said about the picture and all the little scraps of paper we save after someone we love has died. Because I kind of did that, too. I have a little clay jar she made me. I keep that. I actually have a lot of her clothes. I didn't think of this when I got up; I'm wearing her shoes right now. They're little things, but they're important.

> *Dori:* They have sacred significance?

> *Emma:* It's a way I have of taking her with me.

As the church has icons—ways of taking God with us—so Emma has Rachel's shoes on her feet. Like a religious icon, they are a visible reminder of a relationship—this one begun on a playground—that yearns to express itself even beyond death.

E: EXPLORE AHA! MOMENTS AND ENACT NEXT STEPS

The final step of the method is to underline any "aha-moments" and name any actions that the story and conversation might cause. Here, I invite questions such as: What surfaced for you that you might keep pondering? What idea had heat or energy for you? What do you want to say out loud so we can help each other hold onto it? What action, or Next Most Faithful Step, is emerging for you here? I also might ask what title they would give the story or if they agree with a title I have given it.

Peg spoke first. She said her professional life as a minister would be shaped by Emma's story. "I will always have this image of you if a family comes to me and says that their son or daughter died of suicide," she said. Reflecting the mutuality of this teaching model, Peg said this image would remind her to avoid the insensitivity of the priest whose service did not reflect Rachel's life.

Elaine said the story reminds her to appreciate her own mental health. "The fact that we have the support of each other and that we can work through the bad times." Emma agreed. "I have this extra little bit of strength now. I know that I will never do what she did."

Finally, I asked permission to call this story "Will You Be My Friend?" because of a Godlike image that had stayed with me throughout our conversation.

> *Dori:* I saw God in one place especially in your story. I saw God on the playground, when Rachel came up to you and said, "Will you be my friend?" For me, that's a beautiful image of the holy or the divine because here, she's her genuine self. Rachel was a role in the play, on stage, but here is the real Rachel on the playground, and you have that particular memory.

> *Emma:* It was so honest. I didn't even question it. "Will you be my friend?" My answer was yes.

ECHOES OF FEMINIST THEOLOGY AND ASSERTIONS OF GIRL/FRIEND THEOLOGY

The concept of *minyan* voiced by Elaine reflects a prominent theme in feminist theology. Rosemary Radford Ruether wrote about the nurturing exodus community she called "women-church" [Ruether 1985]. In women-church, women step outside male-dominated institutions and experience redemptive community. In such communities, cultural critique takes shape.

One goal of women-church is to deconstruct "symbols in their alienating form and reconstruct them in a form that reconnects with original blessing and authentic life"(Ruether 1985, 58–61). In naming "church" as the group of friends gathered for genuine support and in redefining *minyan* to fit their own understanding, the participants were taking part in the creative reconstruction of symbols such as that which Ruether describes. Living a moment of women-church, they freed a symbol from its patriarchal roots, giving it new, redemptive meaning. Rebecca Chopp writes about a new *ecclesia* that allows women to name the holy in ways that fit their experiences. The creative adaptation of tradition practiced by my collaborators reflects Chopp's underlying assumption that tradition is a "living object liable to growth and change." In this example, girl/friend theology becomes a grief-infused *and* playful space where "symbols and narratives . . . change and continually transform themselves if they are to be meaningful"(Chopp 1995, 14). This echoes Godly Play, Jerome Berryman's method of religious education with children, in that it provides a place of "spontaneity where one does not need to be compliant or acquiesce"(Berryman 1991, 11).

As the participants played with the images of covenant, *minyan*, and icon, they were doing the "saving work" of theology that Chopp advocates. This is work that enlists skills of critical thinking that allow for naming the dichotomies between tradition and experience. Chopp writes, "women challenge the church as to whether or not it is really true to the Christian message and credible to contemporary human experience"(Chopp 1995, 46). In naming church as the ad-hoc community of faithful who gathered after the tragedy to console each other and make a promise, the participants were acknowledging new definitions of church and synagogue that critique long-standing tradition. Their assertions reflect Alice Walker's words:

> Have you ever found God in Church? I never did. I just found a bunch of folks hoping for him to show. Any God I ever found in church I brought with me. And I think all the other folks did, too.

Out of this session emerged two of the seven preliminary assertions of girl/friend theology: (5) We go to church to "*share* God, but not find God." Religious institutions can affirm our hunches about God, but do not usually introduce us to God for the first time. (7) Church, at its best, is a community of compassion, a resource in our healing and a potential agent of change in the world.

A final connection between "Will You Be My Friend?" and feminist theology is the issue of Rachel's body image. Emma referred to Rachel feeling like a "big, fat pig" when she weighed in at ninety-eight pounds. Rachel's negative body image could have spurred a lengthy reflection, but it didn't. It was dropped in favor of another line of thinking.

Unfortunately, those lost moments occur during girl/friend theology.

As the facilitator, I mourned this lost opportunity to listen to young women talk about their bodies and to integrate their ideas with the wealth of mature feminist thinking on the topic of female bodies. At the same time, I remembered that the topic probably will surface again. I made a mental note to refer back to Emma's comments about Rachel's body image if the topic arose in a later session. In this instance, I never got the chance to revisit the issue with this group of girls. However, girls' bodies do become central in the next story under analysis.

The issues surfaced by Rachel's unfortunate death and the ripple effect it caused among her friends remains salient thirty years later, as I revise the original edition. In the early decades of the twenty-first century, social media creates additional burdens on the psyches of young people, especially young women, pressuring them to perform a more perfect version of themselves while hiding away their perceived imperfections. The ongoing work of girl/friend theology could be one helpful antidote to the culture of despair created by the pressures of social media and social isolation on young people today.

In sharing this story with a group, I would use a trigger warning, similar to the "awareness alert" found at the beginning of this chapter. I extend such warnings as an act of hospitality that invites people to exercise their own agency in taking care of their own needs as they choose if and how to participate. This also becomes a place to remind people of the norms or covenants established by the group to create safe enough space to explore difficult topics together (Stephens and Ott 2020).

The next story reflects the first of the two assertions named above, while introducing two others: (3) We have direct access to God through our bodies; and (4) our lives are like "fifth gospels." Our life stories are sacred texts, where God continues to reveal God's self.

STORY #2: TOMORROW, THEN

Cathy, a sixteen-year-old girl from a small town in the Southeast, told the next story to a group consisting of myself, an adult collaborator, and four other sixteen and seventeen-year-old girls: Kim, Mary, Holly, and Tina. They were from Roman Catholic, Eastern Orthodox, and Protestant faith communities. The girls, who were from the South and Midwest, had gathered at a university campus as part of an intensive summer institute about theology. They volunteered to take part in these sessions during their free time in the afternoon on five consecutive days. Sarah, my adult collaborator, was raised in a fundamentalist Christian home and trained in a United

Methodist seminary. At the time of this session, she described herself as "in between" religious affiliations.

Again, I had asked all of the participants to be prepared to share a story. On the previous day, we heard a story about a friendship between a girl with an eating disorder and a boy who had been physically abused. The conversation focused on the pervasiveness of evil and produced an image of God as "the eyes which see the pain of the world." The sadness of the previous day's session was still with us as we gathered. For our second session, Cathy read aloud this story, which she had written the night before in her spiral notebook.

TOMORROW, THEN

We rode our bikes down the crunchy, sunbaked path. I was in the lead, and I didn't prefer to be, because I was feeling out of control, but I led anyway. Leah was close behind me and I could hear her breathing fast and unsteady.

"Leah, you okay?"

She did not answer, and in my obliviousness, it did not occur to me that maybe she wasn't as used to traveling along these overgrown paths as I was.

We stopped our bikes at the dusty shore of Lake Jackson. Wow.

The trees encircled us. Before us lay a crystal lake. Looking into the shallow part, I could even see the polished stones at the bottom. The air seemed clearer—sweetened with the freshness of summer. There was a magic around me I couldn't quite put my finger on. Looking into Leah's eyes, I knew she saw it too.

"Here, you can blow these up." Leah handed me two inflatable rafts. One was blue, the other red. I sat upon the shore and began to heave out what little air was left in my lungs.

"You know, we're not supposed to swim here."

I was still breathing, my cheeks puffed out like a blowfish, but I questioned her with my eyes.

"Lake Jackson is where our drinking water comes from."

I paused for a moment, taking a breath that seemed to make my whole body float.

"Well, would it be totally weird if I peed in our town's drinking water? Because I'm about to burst."

She made a face. "I guess not. I don't want to think about it." She flipped her straw-colored hair from her eyes. "I need sunscreen."

I looked at the rough, sandy bank stretching around us. "You know, these are the types of places where Bigfoot is sighted."

Leah's eyes widened. "Yeah, I can see it now: Two girls abducted by Bigfoot in the deep woods of Mississippi."

"Eek," I squirmed. "Let's talk about something else." But a part of me would have been very happy to see Bigfoot.

We sailed across the water, enjoying the thought that those flimsy Super D rafts could take us anywhere. The cool shade of the tulip poplar trees mixed with the light breeze to make an unsummer-like pleasantness. I laid on my back and locked eyes with the big cloudless sky. Spreading out my arms and legs, I offered myself to whoever might be watching me up there.

"You know what would make this perfect?" Leah interrupted my trailing thoughts, and I successfully managed to roll on my side and look at her.

"What?" "Margaritas."

I thought for a moment, chewing on my thumbnail. "No, blue margaritas." "But don't you have to go to Mexico to get those?"

"Maybe." The wheels in my cooped-up summer mind began to turn. "Hey, we could go there!"

Leah jumped right in. "Yeah! We could take the Greyhound bus and fly over the border. I've got money in my bank account."

"Me, too. And we could sit on the beach and watch the sunset like they do in the movies—"

"—and listen to a guy with a big gut and a sombrero play one of those little guitars."

"Wow, we really could do it."

"I know. We could." Maybe we were reassuring ourselves. "Let's do it." I bit my lip in excitement.

"All right." Leah wistfully dangled her hand in the glossy water. "But hey, Cathy?"

"Mmm?" My mind was with the guy and his little guitar. "Why don't we wait?"

I bent my eyebrow in thought, staring at the stripes on Leah's swimsuit. "Okay. I actually think I'm pretty happy right here, too."

"Yeah, we'll go tomorrow." "Okay. Tomorrow, then."

DOING LIVE WITH "TOMORROW, THEN"

L: LISTEN DEEPLY

As described above, I invited participants to gather, breathe, and center down before lighting a candle and asking Cathy to begin reading her story.

I: IMMERSE IN FEELINGS

As Cathy concluded her story, smiles spread across all of our faces. During her story, there were several nods and laughs. All of the participants jumped in to share feelings, emotions, and associations ranging from fear to joy.

> *Mary:* You're riding your bike, and the sun is behind you, and Leah's breathing that way and, okay, some big tragedy is going to happen. I'm expecting an asthma attack or something. But then it turns out that it's just one little moment in life when you're reassured that everything is okay.

> *Holly:* I love those kind of moments. You can always look back at them and say, even though I have the most hectic life, I do have these moments. As you get older, you may not be able to have those moments as much.

Often, during this part of the discussion, a participant will ask the storyteller to clarify or provide additional detail. However, Cathy provided more detail on her own accord, spurring another participant to share an associated memory and raising what would become a prominent theme:

Cathy: That's two years ago. I don't know, I guess you probably noticed the voice is young in that story. That was my voice then. But, like, we still talk about that day. We knew it was a good day, you know. It was a pretty perfect moment.

Mary: It reminds me of the time when, it was like spring break. In Minnesota, that's a time when there's still snow on the ground. My friends and I went to the beach and, of course, the lake was frozen over. There was a park bench out there, and the snow was up to the seat. We just walked out and sat there on the bench. And everything was fine, you know. We still talk about it.

Throughout this part of the discussion, participants expressed memories of feeling directly connected to God through their bodies and memories of naive innocence. They juxtaposed those with feelings of fear. Bigfoot lurked in the woods, and all-too-prevalent news accounts of real-life abductions lurked in our minds.

V: VIEW IT WIDER

Kim turned the conversation toward images:

Kim: To me, everything in the story was shiny. The rocks, the water, the sky, the eyes, and the raft—it was all like glistening back on you and reflecting the joy of the moment.

Cathy: It's like, the world is so imperfect, but that doesn't mean there's not perfection. It's very important to have eyes that see the imperfection, but there are also so many wonderful things.

Then, as the facilitator, I shared some comments about the process, so the participants would be mindful of the way the conversation had shifted.

> *Dori:* We've moved toward images naturally, so let's carry the conversation away from feelings to name those images. We've talked about shining, reflective light, and also the image of beauty—the beauty which is the flip side of the pain of life. God sees terrible sadness, but at the same time, God is seeing these shiny, glorious moments. God's with you lying there with your beautiful body, sprawled out.

> *Kim:* I thought of that when you said, "I locked eyes with the cloudless sky." I thought that was the coolest image. That was like a connection with God right there. You're seeing each other there and keeping it.

> *Cathy:* That is God. Being in church is godly, but it's not God. Here are these beautiful, beautiful trees and not a single white cloud in this blue, blue sky. That's what makes me believe. Not being in a church where someone's telling me this story about some woman at a well, which is a good story, but that's not what makes me believe. It's the true witness of this wonderful moment.

After Cathy introduced the biblical story of the woman at the well, I jumped in to affirm Cathy's earlier statement, connecting the bright, shiny image of epiphany with the refrain, "And we still talk about it."

Dori: There's a metaphor I like. Our lives are like a "fifth gospel."

I went on to briefly explain the concept of a fifth gospel, as developed by Judith Siqueira, the editor of the journal *In God's Image.* She uses the metaphor to describe the contextualization of feminist theologies, particularly those from the Global South [(Siqueira, 1994)].

> *Dori:* So, when I think about the story of the woman at the well, I think how it's been handed down through the tradition through the centuries with layer upon layer of interpretation. I think it must have been something like this that happened at the well that day—some inbreaking of the holy into the ordinary. She must have had feelings like yours, feelings that made that story be one worth telling again and again. Somebody made the story of the woman at the well the community's story. And this moment for you is like your own personal scripture. Your fifth gospel. It's how you know, in a deep, despairing moment, that God exists. You go back to that snapshot in your mind. You hold that. Just like we hold those scriptural stories as a community.

God-Talk: Water, Bigfoot, and Breathing

The theological language spilled forth in this conversation, which was typical of the sessions with this group. Sometimes participants focused on a single image of God and explored its depths. Instead, in this session, a wide-ranging free flow of images ensued. Eventually, a shared concern regarding bodies emerged, but only after quite a bit of fluid, meandering God-talk.

The participants loved the image of our lives as fifth gospels and added to this interpretation, remembering and sharing stories that need telling again and again among the communities of which they are a part.

We talked about "floating on the raft" moments as little epiphanies and Sabbath time. We talked about the times, such as the gospel account of the Transfiguration, where we see glimpses of what heaven might be like. We receive "foretastes of glory divine."

We also talked about the significance of water in many different religions. After sharing a story about a family ritual that takes place on a lake, Kim focused on the image of water. Just as the nameless woman in John's Gospel experienced Holy presence at an ancient well, Cathy and her friend tasted the Holy at a reservoir, the modern equivalent of a well.

> *Kim:* It's weird how much of it often has to do with water.

> *Cathy:* The image of water . . . I forget, there's something somewhere in my brain. Someone somewhere told me that the image of water had something to do with rebirth and being clean. But I'm not sure what. I'm wanting to say it's the Buddhist tradition that says that water is the source of pureness that cleans people.

> *Kim:* In the Hindu religion, they wash so many times a day.

> *Dori:* Like baptism?

> *Cathy:* Right! Right!

> *Kim:* Oh, that's it! Baptism! (Laughter.)

Dori: The United Methodists have a prayer in our hymnal before the baptism. It's my favorite prayer because it talks about the waters of the womb as being connected to the waters of the flood and the waters that baptized Jesus. All of the places that water shows up in our lives and in scripture are pulled together in this moment right before we use water as an acknowledgment of coming into a community of faith.

The conversation eventually returned and stayed focused on Bigfoot and the danger lurking in the woods. The girls voiced anger about the struggles they encounter as they balance their parents' (and more seldom their own) fear over the safety of their bodies with their need to be free "to float on a raft on a crystal clear lake in the middle of the wood" without fear.

Holly: My mom's always like, "Don't do this, because you'll get hurt here. Don't do that, because you'll do this." It's like, if every time I have to think about all the terrible, horrible things that could happen. Sometimes I want to put all those bad things behind me and just do, just do what I want to do.

Kim: I run in the morning. And my dad's always like, you know, "Don't run alone, you're gonna get mugged, you're gonna get raped while you're running." But to run for forty minutes within the view of this dorm? You'd be like a rat, just going around. So, this morning, my jogging partner forgot to wake up. I was like, "Hey, forget this, I'm just gonna go." And so I just went all around campus. It was so liberating.

I got to look at people's faces. There are people who are smiling, and some frowning, on their way to work.

Here, using voice inflection and body language, Kim interjected a bit of sarcasm:

Kim: In my moment, I had forgotten that I was going to be assaulted, (laughter) and I was breathing. When you can break out of that, that's when it's the good times.

Cathy: It's really dangerous to have this feeling, because when you do, it weighs so much more than the chance of getting assaulted. That's good and dangerous. My mom thinks it's dangerous, and I think it's good.

Kim: (Laughter.)

Cathy: We cross a lot on that.

Kim: Me and my dad do, too.

Dori: And you know that risk is incredibly exciting and fulfilling and thrilling and liberating—

Holly: Not to your parents—

Dori: God is not in the parental moment there, I don't think. I think God is in that—

Sarah: God is in that risk.

Dori: God is in that jogging moment, breathing. You said it all when you said "breathing." That encapsulated the crux of five of the world's great religions in one. Breathe. Breathe. Be connected to the holy.

E: EXPLORE AHA! MOMENTS AND ENACT NEXT STEPS

The final step of the method is to name any changes that the story and conversation might cause. In facilitating this session, I noticed it was time to ask that question while the God-talk was still going strong. I opted to introduce it later, with only a few moments left, rather than interrupt an energized conversation. I did this, not because I deem the final step of less importance, but rather I knew this group would have other occasions to talk about the future actions inspired by this story and conversation. Sarah, who on the previous day had shared the story about a girl with an eating disorder and a boy who had been physically abused, expressed this final thought.

> *Sarah:* I'm reminded, with your story, that a lot of us spend so much of our lives trying to get to those kinds of moments and we often use so many other things to try to get there, whether it's addictions or other relationships. But it's really not about the substances. It's about those moments. And they're free. The lake was free. It's incredibly hard to get there, but it's also incredibly simple. You just got on your bike and went there. I wish I could take that story and tell it to some of my friends who are trying to sober up.

ECHOES OF FEMINIST THEOLOGY AND ASSERTIONS OF GIRL/FRIEND THEOLOGY

Three assertions of girl/friend theology surfaced in this session. First, participants directly echoed Alice Walker's character Shug in *The Color Purple*, stating the belief that we *bring* God to church. Cathy's story and the ensuing conversation underline this assertion, which also arose during discussion of the previous story, "Will You

Be My Friend?" Our experiences of God, according to these adolescent girls, most often originate outside religion's official institutions. We look to the church to affirm these original visions of God.

Two other assertions of girl/friend theology—our life stories as fifth gospels and our bodies as sites of access to the divine—emerged in this session. Both of these echo in feminist and emancipatory theologies.

In introducing the image of fifth gospels, I was directly translating a piece of emancipatory theology I encountered in my study of transnational feminist theology. Kwok Pui Lan, a Chinese feminist theologian, critiques traditional Western theology for its focus on a narrow and mystified view of the Bible. While acknowledging the power and authority of the stories found there, she asserts that "our religious imagination cannot be based on the Bible alone, which often excludes women's experiences" (Kwok 1994, 153).

Confining religious imagination to the narrow cultural boundaries of the stories of scripture excludes the metaphors, traditions, and life realities that arise from the many cultures into which Christianity was adopted or forcibly imposed. In order for Christianity to take root in a new setting, it got reshaped and transformed by the cultural soil in which it now grows. This entails widening of attention from the Bible and the tradition of people in the Ancient Near East two thousand years ago to also include contemporary people's stories, which likewise embody culturally conditioned images and metaphors.

Sadly, the image of Bigfoot lurking in the woods—interpreted more starkly as the real fear of sexual assault or abduction—is written into the cultural script of what it means to be an adolescent girl, a person of color, or a member of the LGBTQ+ community in the United States today. To experience a transcendent moment of connection to God even in the midst of that pervasive reality constitutes a story worth retelling. In this moment, the participants were connecting their experiences of oppression with a particular glimpse of potential liberation. Remembering and retelling this story, and others like it, is a powerful act of cultural critique that, to echo Kwok, includes the stories, metaphors, cultural traditions, and life realities of a unique substrata of American culture—namely, adolescence.

Kwok's perspective is given the metaphor of the fifth gospel by Judith Siqueira, who writes: "God's story is revealed in our story in myriad and mysterious ways, in content and in form. Each of us is the pen with which God writes a fifth gospel. God's self-revelation to each of us through daily life and experience are our faith stories as fifth gospels. Hence, there are innumerable fifth gospels all over the world"[(Siqueira 1994, 2–4)].

By introducing this idea, I entered an explicit teaching moment. It differed vastly from a didactic lecture on postcolonial feminism because its springboard was Cathy's story and the common chord it struck with her peers. In this way, experienced facilitators can gently offer religious reframing. Girl/friend theology allows for embodied teaching moments to be offered as suggestions, which can be accepted, rebuffed, adapted, discarded, or owned. As a method of theological reflection, it is conversational and democratic, encouraging a shift in the power dynamics of the adult/young person relationship. It is a kind of "real talk" that reflects a constructivist way of knowing and draws on the analytical abilities of each participant[(Belenky et al. 1986)].

Connected to the assertions that "we bring God to church" and "our lives are like fifth gospels" is the assertion that our bodies provide us direct access to God. Feminist theologian Carter Heyward expresses this theme. She argues that traditional Christian spirituality trivializes and denies "bodyselves," thus damaging the self-image of those who are shaped within it. She offers an alternative: embodied spirituality. After telling a story rich with sensual details, she writes:

If we learn to trust our senses, our capacities to touch, taste, smell, hear, see, and thereby know, they can teach us what is good and what is bad, what is real and what is false, for us in relation to one another and to the earth and cosmos. I say to myself, as I return to campus from my outing with my dogs, that sensuality is a foundation for our authority [Heyward 1980].

Cathy, an exceptional writer adept with nuances of the language, beautifully imbues her story with sensual details. We hear about full bladders, chewed thumbnails, heavy breathing, straw-colored hair, and striped bathing suits in a fashion consistent with Heyward's notions of embodied spirituality:

Our feelings are evoked and strengthened sensually by touching, tasting, hearing, seeing, and smelling with one another. Our senses and the feelings that are generated by them become primary spiritual resources. In knowing one another through our senses, feelings, and intelligence—and intuition is a form of intelligence—we come to know God [Heyward 1980].

Cathy and her companion—along with the participants in this session who resoundingly recalled similar moments in their own lives—confronted dominant culture notions that diminish our bodies as a source of knowledge. Here we see bodies portrayed as central to a way of knowing God. Naming this embodied knowing is an act that resists dominant norms and contributes to a refashioning of the Christian tradition.

In their final moments of Viewing it Wider, the participants echoed strains of feminist theologies, while carrying them a step further into the unique particularities of their young adult world. Bigfoot lurking in the woods became a metaphor for a specific type of oppression permeating their everyday lives. An act as simple as choosing a jogging path can be, for some young people, imbued with the fear that women's bodies, Brown and Black bodies, or trans bodies are often objectified, sexualized, and abused when merely occupying space.

The metaphor of breathing, relaxing into the jog, and "forgetting I was about to be abducted," reveals a liberatory moment—a fully sensual connection to an alternative reality—that does not exist rationally, within the structures of the here-and-now. Indeed, it is a "foretaste of glory divine."

GOD-TALK ACROSS RELIGIOUS BORDERS

In this chapter, I've given thick descriptions of two girlfriend theology sessions that occurred in the early 1990s. The voices of the girls spoke first through their stories, then through their group conversations, and finally through my analysis of the sessions. In that analysis, I connected the images, metaphors, and recurring themes I heard participants voicing with the images, metaphors, and recurring themes in contemporary theology. The result is a meeting place—a site where emancipatory theologies may inform and may potentially be informed by the voices of adolescents.

I chose to group these two sessions together because they shared one thing in common: interfaith dialogue. In both of these sessions, the story theology model threw a wide net, creating an atmosphere that provided entrée to God-talk across religious borders.

Explicit interreligious dialogue took place in the first story session. The religious diversity of the group, which included a practicing Jew, three practicing Christians, and an open-minded and curious religious seeker, offered resources for expanding theological imagination. The interfaith group claimed ownership of the concepts of covenant, *minyan*, and icon as they engaged in reciprocal dialogue around their respective traditions.

In the second story session, the ecumenical group brought to the table questions about water symbolism in Hinduism, Buddhism, and Christianity. Had this been an interfaith context, this moment could have opened into deeper discussion of the differences and particularities of water symbolism across the cultural and religious spheres represented by the three traditions.

As a theologian, I focus primarily on my own faith community. However, ministry in a postmodern era invites—perhaps even requires—dialogue across religions. This is especially important in ministering to young people—especially those who, for both developmental and cultural reasons, may be testing or adapting inherited faith traditions. Developmental psychologists hold that a primary marker of adolescence—formal operational thinking—makes it a prime time for religious seeking. Young people often try on different identities, testing their parents' beliefs against those of their peers in an effort to come to ownership of their own unique identity. Scholars of contemporary youth culture hold that tolerance of religious diversity is a hallmark of the generations born after the Baby Boomers. Generation X, Millennials, and Gen Zers show an openness to religious diversity and questioning that differs from generations before. Generation X and the postmoderns—those born after the late 1960s—are multi-religious generations whose distrust for universal narratives encourages questioning of faith traditions. In this milieu, writes Tom Beaudoin, "people of various religious traditions (or none at all!) need each other in a dialogue about the religious"[1998, 34]. The playfulness and open-endedness of the story theology model invites this crucial border crossing.

Girl/friend theology requires more than interfaith dialogue. In order to understand the world of young people, adult women must be open and willing to empathize with those who hold different identities and experiences. I have identified two key sources that provide us with the tools and perspectives necessary to step outside of our own experience: women's autobiographies and women's emancipatory theologies.

In the next two chapters, we turn to these sources, continuing the process of unveiling the biases and commitments that inform the practice of girl/friend theology. The next chapter also will begin autobiographically. Experiencing the misogyny of contemporary culture reminds me of the importance of celebrating women whose voices—be it in the form of political action or creative expression—have survived. Collecting and sharing these voices becomes central to a model by which adults might mentor young people in crafting life-giving spiritual practices.

CHAPTER FOUR

COLLECTING SEA GLASS

BUILDING AND SHARING THE USABLE PAST

Someone in her life, or at least, very
powerfully, in her imaginative life, must give her
reason to rejoice that she is a woman.
— Carol Lee Flinders, *At the Root of This Longing:
Reconciling a Spiritual Hunger and a Feminist Thirst*

I am not a football fan. I just happened to be in the room with
my two young daughters one Saturday afternoon in the fall of
1999 as my husband, sister, and brother-in-law sat deeply en-
grossed in the University of Florida vs. University of Tennessee
game. During a break in the action, my eyes and the eyes of my
four-year-old daughter drifted toward the television. What we
saw appalled us both. A young woman, bound and gagged, lay
tied to railroad tracks in the snow-covered Colorado Rockies.
Her assailant stepped away from the tracks, smiling to himself as
a train approached.

"Mommy, why did that boy do that?" asked Erin, her eyes riv-
eted to the screen as she walked over to share my lap with her
baby sister. I couldn't formulate a response, so I opened my arms
to encircle her. In a state of shock, I watched the drama progress

through the eyes of my daughter. The engineer, seeing the woman, brought the train to a screeching halt.

I breathed a sigh of relief, and so did Erin. Then, the engineer peered out the window of his train at the bundle of woman and rope lying on the tracks in front of him. Making eye contact with the assailant, he smiled and said, "Nice knot." Someone popped open a Coors Light, and the commercial was over.

Adrenaline surged through my veins in a visceral reaction to that thirty-second segment of mainstream American culture, a flashback to the silent film era, and a perfect, if dated, example of the objectification women's and girls' bodies. Every once in a while, I still get caught off guard by what I see in the media. I forget momentarily how very poisonous this culture is to young people, girls yes, but also anyone in the midst of forming a gender identity. During adolescence, people experience a time of sorting out what's going on in their bodies/selves in relation to cultural norms. This appropriate developmental phase that includes creating a healthy sexuality and coming home to one's gender identity is unnecessarily complicated by cultural messaging that enforces various binaries and structural oppressions. Regularly occurring developmental explorations often get pathologized, rather than being welcomed as part of growing up. Sex education classes often do not include presentations of LGBTQ+ related topics and often fail to discuss such topics as consent, communication between partners, gender dysmorphia, trans identity, or the role of sexual pleasure for all parties [Gutacher 2015]. Widespread media images of sexual encounters that fetishize, objectify, and demean often stand in for insufficient or missing sex education in schools and other youth-serving institution.

Porn becomes the de facto sex educator. The most accessible forms of porn continue to portray coercive, non-consensual, and violent sexual encounters. All of this can negatively influence perceptions of sexuality and gender roles, limiting young people's imagination around healthy, consensual sex.

Decades after the television commercial I witnessed with my young daughters, I remain dismayed by how underlying cultural assumptions about gender remain in full swing across newer platforms of popular culture. When the football game resumed that afternoon so many years ago, Erin's questions persisted. "Why was that boy being mean to that girl?" I didn't try to explain away what we had just witnessed. The only response I knew how to make in that moment was to endorse her instinct that something was terribly wrong. I let Erin know it was very right to be angry. At the same time, I found myself sadly wishing Erin could share a little longer in her baby sister's obliviousness.

I was similarly caught off guard during my early parenting years when watching a late-night sports broadcast in Chicago. In bed with a book, my husband was catching the last of the news; we were both half-listening in that state of sleepiness just before turning the lights out. "The Bears acted like a bunch of *women* out there on that field today," sportscaster Mark Giangreco said to one of his colleagues in the newsroom. Needless to say, he was not complimenting them on their decisive conquest of the Green Bay Packers. For days, in an angry fog of disbelief, I told this story to everyone I knew. In private moments, I alternately whispered and shouted the mantra, "Woman *is not* a derogatory term."

Regardless of my efforts to convince myself otherwise, the word "woman" and its synonyms are often used in derogatory ways. A history of the English language shows this "semantic derogation" (Haegele 2000). Positive or neutral terms for the female gender accrue negative connotations over time. Historically the words

"harlot," "hussy," "spinster," "prude," "tart," "wench," and "trol-
lop" all degenerated from neutral or positive connotations to
decidedly negative ones. Contemporary examples include words
such as "cunt," "bitch," "slut," "whore," "fag," "queer," and "queen,"
all of which have multiple possible meanings depending on who
is using them and in what context. Some words that were once
considered hateful epithets have been reclaimed by the very people they hurt; however, they may still be harmful. Even though
LGBTQ+ people may gain a sense of power through reclaiming
the word "queer," its usage may still cause pain in certain contexts.

Strong feelings similarly surround the word "feminist." At the
time of this book's first publication, I wanted to use the word
in the subtitle, but was persuaded that negative perceptions of
the word would keep readers away. Thankfully, new generations
embraced the term, widening its once narrow connotations. It
is a refreshing and welcome experience to more regularly hear a
man or nonbinary gender person identify as feminist. The word
no longer calls to mind predominately white, liberal, middle-class
ideologies as it once did, although it includes wide diversity, such
as TERFS, a cohort of feminists who self-identify as radical
and are unwilling to recognize trans women as sisters, like the
majority of feminists do.[1]

People sometimes ask how something called girl/friend theology can be open to other genders. Having regularly practiced
the method with mixed gender groups and having heard from
numerous colleagues who have done the same, we know it works.
What matters is that we mindfully create the conditions in which
each person can be heard. When we do so, those who do not regularly hold structural power—nonbinary, women, girls, people of
color, Indigenous people—are free to discover and claim images

---

1   TERF is an acronym that stands for trans exclusionary radical feminists.

of God/Spirit that arise from their lived experience. When that happens in the presence of those who hold nuanced differences in traditional forms of power, culture can potentially shift. Even if this shift is small or almost imperceptible, it can create an opening for change. When it happens outside the gaze of those who have traditionally held the power, new ways of naming reality happens. In both cases, we widen the possibility of new realities emerging. These new realities are poised to more fully reflect the broad diversity of human experience. This is necessary work if we hope to see cultural shifts toward greater equity.

One of my favorite stories of girl/friend theology in practice comes from my friend Audrey, a recent college graduate. Audrey learned about girl/friend theology, reached out to me via email, and asked for guidance. Could they begin gathering a group around their dinner table in Texas? "Yes," I replied. "Let me know how it goes!" Audrey told me about regular gatherings that ensued: young adults who were not all female, white, cisgender, straight, or of the same economic class got together once a month to hear one other into speech. Such spaces reflect what Rosemary Radford Ruether described as "liberating communities of life together"[(Silverman et al. 2012, xvi)].

Spiritual practices that support gender equity can make space in us for the anger spurred by experiences of oppression, even as they connect us to our deep wells of hope. Whether the anger is activated by a micro-aggression during an everyday encounter or as we consume popular media, our anger is a priceless resource. It can incite us to action, but only if it is also connected to those deep wells of hope. In order for this hope to be reliable, it must be grounded in reality and in the possibility of a different future.

Looking to our "usable past" can provide substance for this kind of reliable hope. The term "usable past" refers to the ever-growing body of texts that provide alternatives to predominant patriarchal and white-normative worldviews [Flinders 1998, 97]. Building and sharing our usable past is a necessary step in the feminist formation of adolescents.

In the three stories that follow, we see adults reminding young people of their inherent value and worth as they come of age. After each story, I will reflect on ways in which the interplay between the individual and collective stories of our usable pasts can enter the process of girl/friend theology. Before relating the stories, however, I invite us to consider the concept of organic formation, an idea that grows out of my critique and appreciation of "natural education" within developmental theory [Kegan 1982].

ORGANIC FORMATION AS A MODEL FOR FEMINIST EDUCATION

Organic formation points to potential moments in a young person's life, such as the moment when Erin looked at me and asked "Mommy, why did that boy do that?" These are moments when one of the myriad influences organic to a young person's life—ranging from the small circle of family members to ever-widening circles that include neighborhood, school, church, the media, etc.—function to remind them that they are a person worthy of dignity and respect. When a question like Erin's is treated with respect by an adult caregiver, the young person learns to value their innate sense of moral outrage and build a sense of agency. I call this organic formation because it happens as we go about our lives, in organically occurring conversations between friends, loved ones, teachers and caregivers.

If we can observe such moments happening in real time, we might learn how to emulate them intentionally in our feminist models of spiritual formation and religious education. Constructive-developmental psychologist Robert Kegan maintains that the best therapeutic processes are rooted not in theory but in naturally occurring habitats. Often, a therapist's best guide in nurturing a client toward psychological health is a careful simulation of what occurs in families with "good enough" parenting [(Kegan 1982) (Winnicott 2005)].[2] These therapies mirror "those relations and human contexts that spontaneously support people through the sometimes difficult process of growth and change." Exposing the details of those interactions is the key to building successful therapeutic models. Those details include the presence of "holding environments," which function to "keep buoyant the life project" of their guest. For the infant, the holding environment is quite literally the "mothering one," or, to make Kegan's term more gender inclusive, a "parenting one." For the adolescent or young adult, the holding environment may exist in the school, the family, the peer group, or the faith community [(Kegan 1982, 255–60)].

I look for examples of organic formation in the stories found in autobiography, history, and art, because the developmental models often lack them. Narrative examples of a young person learning to love themselves and see their identity as valuable is an especially useful tool in understanding female and genderqueer lives, because, as Gilligan and others have shown, broad-scope developmental models reflect male, heteronormative, and cisgender lives almost exclusively (Gilligan 1982). Female and genderqueer patterns of moving across the life span differ from those male "norms." Mary Catherine Bateson describes the differences in female adult development using the metaphor of improvisation, pointing out that women's lives were traditionally interrupted by patriarchy's demands. Pursuing

---

2 Kegan's theories of development have undergone significant critique and subsequent revision. A particular critique is the term "natural" which can often elide cultural and contextual differences. I am using the term organic, rather than natural, to point out my conviction that there are multiple expressions of healthy formation that differ vastly depending on culture and context.

one's meaning and purpose—for women and gender nonconforming people—often took second or third place to domestic labor and external responsibilities, rather than following a seemingly linear path. Memoirs with a focus on gender identity, such as Janet Mock's *Redefining Realness: My Path to Womanhood, Identity, Love and So Much More*, and Samantha Allen's *M to (WT)F* provide glimpses into moments when organic formation supports more exploratory and experiential form of identity formation [Mock 2014; Allen 2020].

Rather than seeing some lives as deviating from a norm, Bateson reframes the goal, stating that we traditionally saw achievement as "purposeful and monolithic, like the sculpting of a massive tree trunk that has first to be brought from the forest and then shaped by long labor to assert the artist's vision, rather than something crafted from odds and ends, like a patchwork quilt, and lovingly used to warm different nights and bodies" [Bateson 1990, 4].

Life stories we gather up from memoir and autobiography can create a patchwork quilt of memories, providing examples we can draw from to guide and affirm our own improvisational life journeys. We can point to these life stories as part of our usable past, lifting them up as possible models of healthy development.

In perusing my usable past, I looked for evidence of organic formation—moments in which a young person gains a sense of self-worth, a sense of moral agency, and possession of a voice with which to enter public discourse. Moments like this include memories of resisting the dominant culture's norms regarding gender roles and expectations. These are moments in which young people coming of age experience "holding environments that keep buoyant their life projects" [Kegan 1982]. With the goal of glimpsing moments of organic formation, I turn to autobiography, a key source in constructing a collective feminist usable past.

THE USABLE PAST AND DANGEROUS MEMORY

Carol Flinders writes that, as an indirect response to her awareness of deeply ingrained misogyny, she began to pull together for herself a "body of evidence and imagery" to support a belief in women's strength and dignity [1998, 45]. This process echoes my life experience and the experience of many of my peers. Like Flinders, we devoured books in an effort to sustain our belief in ourselves, despite the negative voices we heard around us. This process borders on a religious quest, as young people deprived of relevant faith traditions find in literature an "adequate substitute for religion" [Norris 1996, xvii]. Flinders writes:

> This reading was not just for myself at all, but on behalf of the young girl I had been once, who would have given anything for these narratives of feminine courage and creativity, and, yes, unabashed feminine sensuality—a girl who might well have found the courage to speak and write her own truths much sooner if she'd had them [Flinders 1998, 45].

This act of gleaning stories—from written autobiography, memoir, poetry, podcast and Instagram videos—accumulates to provide an individual's usable past. As individual people, we have our own usable pasts; as communities of feminists in solidarity with one another, we have a collective usable past.

The concept of a usable past intersects with the term "dangerous memory," which Sharon Welch uses to describe acts of resistance found within communities practicing liberation theology. According to Welch, oppressed communities can move toward acts of resistance only after recovering their dangerous memory. Dangerous memory has two dimensions: the memory of suffering, conflict, and exclusion—and the memory of hope, freedom, and resistance [Welch 1985, 35–42]. Scholars have adapted dangerous memory from liberation theology to feminist theologies [Kang 1998]. Dangerous memory refers to the moments when we recognize how our culture continues to be poisonous to female identifying and genderqueer people; naming dangerous memories as such helps us regain power over our feelings of exclusion and oppression.

In recounting at the opening of this chapter the disturbing television commercial and the sportscaster's gender slur, and in naming the phenomena of semantic derogation, I shared a connection to an anger-inducing part of my dangerous memory. In collecting and celebrating our usable past, we recall the hope, freedom, and resistance that forms the other half of dangerous memory.

Each of us has a usable past that can be used in the development of critical consciousness within ourselves and in our sphere of influence. Some of our usable past is individual and particular, and some of it is shared among communities of mutuality and support. Our collective usable past is a body of evidence and imagery, gleaned from poetry, fiction, theater, painting, quilts, dance, and other sources. It is this body of evidence that girl/friend theology invites now into the conversation with young adults.

The first half of the girl/friend theology process (Listen and Immerse) stays close to the lived experiences of individual participants. It focuses on feelings, memories, and real-life encounters. The second half of the process (View it Wider and Enact/Explore) turns directly toward stories and images. As adults entering conversations with young people, we are not silent partners. We have something to offer, something our collaborators need, but for which they may not know how to ask. We have warehouses of images and stories that give us reason to rejoice that we are who we are, in these unique bodies, holding these sometimes hard-won identities. Our usable past is an essential resource to those whom we accompany as they create identities that resist gender oppression.

WHOSE USABLE PAST?: ACKNOWLEDGING MANY VOICES

My usable past has been constructed from many sources. Primary among them are autobiographies, emancipatory theologies, and feminist biblical studies. Some of that body of evidence and imagery appears in this chapter, particularly as it arises from autobiography—a generous source for glimpses into the ways young people experience spiritual practices that support healing, rather than internalizing the culture's oppressive messages. A deliberate variety of sources becomes especially important as we acknowledge differences of race, ethnicity, gender identity, sexuality, ability, and class.

Three glimpses of adults meeting young people at the crossroads of identity emerge in the stories that follow. These are not neutral stories.[3] They are stories that combat a male-centric worldview shaped by long traditions of white, Eurocentric values. Two of the stories come to us from Black women; one is from a white woman.

These three stories depict girls learning notions of healthy resistance. In them, we see girls soaking up "mother wit," learning "unctuousness as a virtue," and finding ways to love themselves [Cannon 1995, 78–91; Walker 1983, xi–xii]. We also see the presence of "mothering ones"—or more inclusively, "parenting ones." These are people who create environments that nurture young souls engaged in the task of sort-

---

3   In drawing attention to the non-neutrality of these stories, I contend that all education carries with it a particular perspective. See Paulo Freire, *Pedagogy of the Oppressed* (New York: Herder & Herder, 1970).

ing through what it means to be who they are in their body, with their life experiences, as a survivor, and a force to be reckoned with. They are examples, slices of the lives of young people who found ways to hold onto the memory of being created in the image of the Holy. These stories bear testimony to the power of knowing that the Divine Spark resides within us, despite the dominant culture's frequent devaluing and denigration of our lives and experiences.

Autobiographies reveal stories such as these—stories in which we see adult women educating young people in everyday settings. These are lives reflecting difference: difference in race, in class, and in privilege. These differences are lived out in various levels of oppression, from subtle to enormous. For just as we live in a deeply misogynist culture, we also live in a deeply racist culture. Any discussion of the resistance women and nonbinary people must muster to counter cultural oppression must take into account those differences in identity and experience.

I remain most aware of the oppressive forces I experience as a white female. I am also mindful that oppressions are multiplied many times over for women of color. By choosing two stories of Black women, and by using Womanist themes as a lens through which to view these stories, I widen the conversation to include issues of race. Later chapters will widen the conversation further by engaging the voices of Asian-American and Latina/x women as a way of modelling an ever-expanding canon of feminist and liberatory theologies that can enter the girl/friend theology process.

By incorporating stories of women of color into my usable past, I am borrowing from a community that is not my own. I value the written record of women of color alongside personal relationships of mutual support and accountability as I educate myself about structural racism. This record—in both autobiographical and analytical forms—helps me better understand the triple oppression of gender, class, and race facing many women of color. It enables me to acknowledge my own privilege, and it provides a starting point for me to begin the dismantling of racism in my own spheres. Paying attention to the writings of women of color is absolutely necessary if we are to create an inclusive methodology to help build more inclusive realities.

NOT BLOSSOMS, BUT BLOOMING": THREE GLIMPSES OF GIRLS SHAPING IDENTITY

STORY ONE: SAVED FROM SILENCE

Maya Angelou, educator, activist, and poet, tells the story of her young life in *I Know Why the Caged Bird Sings*. Angelou recounts the story of herself as a girl who survived sexual assault and the trauma of testifying against her perpetrator. As a result of these traumas, she stopped talking to everyone but her brother Bailey. For a year, she lived in a blanket of silence, feeling "like an old biscuit, dirty and inedible," until she met a woman who threw her a lifeline. I share a lengthy quote here, as an example of a story that can contribute to our collective usable past in the creation of feminist consciousness.

Mrs. Bertha Flowers, a wealthy black aristocrat, singles out the young Angelou, whose name as a child was Marguerite, for special attention. As they are walking, Mrs. Flowers initiates the following conversation:

> She said, without turning her head, to me, "I hear you're doing very good schoolwork, Marguerite, but that it's all written. The teachers report that they have trouble getting you to speak in class." We passed the triangular farm on our left and the path widened to allow

us to walk together. I hung back in the separate unasked and unanswerable questions.

"Come and walk along with me, Marguerite." I couldn't have refused even if I wanted to. She pronounced my name so nicely. Or more correctly, she spoke each word with such clarity that I was certain a foreigner who didn't understand English could have understood her.

"Now, no one is going to make you talk—possibly no one can. But bear in mind, language is man's way of communicating with his fellow man and it is language alone which separates him from the lower animals." That was a totally new idea to me, and I would need time to think about it.

"Your grandmother says you read a lot. Every chance you get. That's good, but not good enough. Words mean more than what is set down on paper. It takes the human voice to infuse them with the shades of deeper meaning."

I memorized the part about the human voice infusing words.

It seemed so valid and poetic.

She said she was going to give me some books and that I not only must read them, I must read them aloud. She suggested that I try to make a sentence sound in as many different ways as possible.

"I'll accept no excuse if you return a book to me that has been badly handled." My imagination boggled at the punishment I would deserve if in fact I did abuse a book of Mrs. Flowers'. Death would be too kind and brief.

The odors in the house surprised me. Somehow, I had never connected Mrs. Flowers with food or eating or any other common experience of common people. There must have been an outhouse, too, but my mind never recorded it.

The sweet scent of vanilla had met us as she opened the door. "I made tea cookies this morning. You see, I had planned to invite you for cookies and lemonade so we could have this little chat. The lemonade is in the icebox."

It followed that Mrs. Flowers would have ice on an ordinary day, when most families in our town bought ice late on Saturdays only a few times during the summer to be used in the wooden ice-cream freezers.

She took the bags from me and disappeared through the kitchen door. I looked around the room that I had never in my wildest fantasies imagined I would see. Browned photographs leered or threatened from the walls and the white, freshly done curtains pushed against themselves and against the wind. I wanted to gobble up the room entire and take it to Bailey, who would help me analyze and enjoy it.

"Have a seat, Marguerite. Over there by the table." She carried a platter covered with a tea towel. Although she warned that she hadn't tried her hand at baking sweets for some time, I was certain that like everything else about her the cookies would be perfect . . .

As I ate, she began the first of what we later called "my lessons in living." She said that I must always be intolerant of ignorance, but understanding of illiteracy. That some people, unable to go to school, were more educated and even more intelligent than college professors.

She encouraged me to listen carefully to what country people called mother wit. That in those homely sayings was couched the collective wisdom of generations.

When I finished the cookies, she brushed off the table and brought a thick, small book from the bookcase. I had read *A Tale of Two Cities* and found it up to my standards as a romantic novel. She opened the first page and I heard poetry for the first time in my life.

"It was the best of times and the worst of times . . ." Her voice slid in and curved down through and over the words. She was nearly singing. I wanted to look at the pages. Were they the same that I had read? Or were there notes, music, lined on the pages, as in a hymn book? Her sounds began cascading gently. I knew from listening to a thousand preachers that she was nearing the end of her reading, and I hadn't really heard, heard to understand, a single word.

"How do you like that?"

It occurred to me that she expected a response. The sweet vanilla flavor was still on my tongue and her reading was a wonder in my ears. I had to speak.

I said, "Yes, ma'am." It was the least I could do, but it was the most also.

"There's one more thing. Take this book of poems and memorize one for me. Next time you pay me a visit, I want you to recite. "

On that first day, I ran down the hill and into the road (few cars ever came along it) and had the good sense to stop running before I reached the Store.

I was liked, and what a difference it made. I was respected not as Mrs. Henderson's grandchild or Bailey's sister, but for just being Marguerite Johnson [(Angelou, 1969 80–85)].

HOMEPLACE IN A USABLE PAST

bell hooks argues that Black women have always honored spaces such as those in Mrs. Flowers's house: a kitchen out of which flows the sweet smell of vanilla, a living room lined with books, a table at which a girl sits for her lessons in life. In the essay "Homeplace: A Site of Resistance," hooks introduces "homeplace" as one theme that helps bring this story into conversation with the larger historical realities facing Black women involved in identity formation.

In the story we glimpse one woman integrating a pivotal event into the overall picture of her life. Mrs. Flowers's intervention forms a bridge between disparate parts of the girl's life—silence and speech, sparseness, and beauty. It paints, like Van Gogh, "not blossoms, but blooming" [(Berryman 1991, 103)]. We do not see the complete evolution, but rather a glimpse of a person on the way to inventing her adult identity. We see the young Angelou in a moment of transformation. In telling this story, a woman makes meaning out of the events of life that shaped her emerging, multidimensional identity.

We can see this story as part of one woman's "organic formation" toward liberation. It's a snapshot in which the young Angelou learns healthy resistance to the forms of oppression she experienced. Mrs. Flowers provides a holding environment that keeps buoyant the young woman's life project and which provides support through the difficult process of growth and change.

These are spaces in which resistance means opposition to being invaded, assaulted, and destroyed by the system. These are spaces where the injured turn for help in healing themselves. In hooks's treatment, sites of homeplace take on different forms, depending on realities of economics and class. Clearly, Mrs. Flowers's residence represents a relatively privileged version of homeplace. Other depictions of homeplace hooks points to include the dirt-floor residences of enslaved persons, where parents engage their children in life lessons around rituals of hair-combing, meal preparation, and quilt making.

In these kinds of spaces, hooks argues, "all that truly mattered in life took place—the warmth and comfort of shelter, the feeding of our bodies, the nurturing of our souls. There we learned dignity, integrity of being; there we learned to have faith"(hooks 1990, 44). The domestic sphere was a site of both oppression and one of resistance for Black women. Historically, racism, sexism, and colonialism dictated that Black women labored, unpaid, in the homes of white people; and yet, Black women employed the domestic sphere as a site to cultivate power and resistance. In the homeplace, they undertook subversive acts of education. In honoring this history, Womanists name the systems of oppression their foremothers survived, while at the same time celebrating the ways their foremothers resisted. Black women took these conventional roles and expanded them, "to include caring for one another, for children, for Black men, in ways that elevated our spirits, that kept us from despair, that taught us to be revolutionaries able to struggle for freedom"(44).

Angelou became a revolutionary in the struggle for freedom. Having been traumatized by her assault as a young girl and the further traumatizing judiciary proceeding, Angelou hungered for a means to resist. Self-chosen silence was one such means of resistance. By throwing her a lifeline, Mrs. Flowers provided an alternative and more active means of resistance. By the time Angelou graduated from eighth grade, she was the head of her class (Thompson 1994, 36–38). Mrs. Flowers's voice, her attention, the sweet smell of tea cakes, and her mannerisms all combine to create a homeplace; it becomes a platform of resistance. In this story, Mrs.

Flowers responds to Marguerite out of some deep calling of her own, claiming her responsibility to the community by offering herself as a resource in the healing of one young person.

Implications for the Spiritual Formation and Religious Education

In this moment, I seek to learn from a Black woman's story and other Black women's scholarly voices. In doing so, I acknowledge that interpreting voices and experiences not my own comes with the potential of misunderstanding and misappropriating their meanings. However, excluding these voices and stories might constitute a further gap and lack of access for younger generations to the necessary tools for meaning making they face in a more culturally diverse world. I err here on the side of including stories that inform my work but are not from my own culture, hoping to model an inclusive approach to creating a collective usable past. I do so with appreciation of the multiple ways my interpretation is limited and partial.

If some young people lose a sense of their voice in part through the internalization of advice from adults in their life, as Gilligan and Brown maintain, this story provides an alternative. Angelou was, quite literally, "heard to speech." We can understand the hearing provided by Mrs. Flowers as the kind of hearing that Nelle Morton describes, a hearing which "evokes speech—new speech that has never been spoken before" (Morton 1985, 202). This story serves as one piece of evidence supporting the potential of adults to respond to the plight of some young people by listening and providing lifelines.

The story emerges from a community of mentors who claim responsibility for the pervasive difficulties that persist in oppressive cultures. Mrs. Flowers is an example of the community of "other-mothers" who reach out from domestic circles to ever-wid-

121

ening spheres of influence, offering alternatives to the society that inflicts racist and sexist wounds [Collins 1991; James and Busia 1993]. This story provides encouragement for adults to take an ethical stance in support of young people in the midst of identity formation.

Black faith communities in the United States have long created a community of caregivers who interact intentionally with young people, empowering them to integrate healthy forms of resistance into their emerging identities. A contemporary example is the work of Kristi Lauren Adams. Her books *The Parable of The Brown Girl: The Sacred Lives of Girls of Color* and *Unbossed: How Black Girls are Leading the Way* (2020, 2022) tell the stories of emerging identities of Black girls within and at the edges of Black church experience. One particular vignette describes the journey of Hannah Lucas, who at age seventeen co-created the NotOK app with the help of her brother Charlie. The app provides a panic button for teens to contact trusted contacts in the midst of a mental health emergency. In the stories Adams recounts of young Black females, she, like Angelou, shows the construction of identity and meaning from the stuff of everyday life.[4]

The stories told in girl/friend theology need not be mountain-top experiences or high holy moments. More often than not, the most satisfying stories have been those that reflect small simple moments of life—both tragic moments that open us to sitting with deep pain and evil, and also life-affirming moments when grace slips in with a whisper of hope, even amid suffering.

Not all young people are gifted with the instinct toward self-reflection that Angelou honed into a skill for storytelling and used to aid in the narrative construction of identity. But many

---

4   For an interview with Adams on her work, see the podcast *Dear Soft Black Woman*, episode 11, "When Black Girls Lead, We All Win."

might respond to an invitation to tell their stories. Girl/friend theology is a method of spiritual formation that invites adults to model themselves after Mrs. Flowers, empowering young people to name their own realities and engage in healthy resistance. In other words, Mrs. Flowers provides a model for the role of the community in spiritual formation of young people, who do not have to be left to their individual resources in the developmental journey of growing up.

Reclaiming the role of community in human development and flourishing critiques Western, white, male-dominant systems that shape cultural norms around identity, meaning, and purpose. A radically communal worldview—based in African spirituality and the Black church experience—provides a corrective to white normativity. White normativity and its emphasis on the solo journey often goes unquestioned in faith communities and larger realms of US culture (Lewis, Williams, Baker, 2020).

What outcomes might emerge from models of spiritual formation and religious education that center the role of community? If the experiences of diverse communities of women become the starting point for thinking about theology and ethics, new images of God will appear. Might not young people—through their own theological instincts, or through the nudging of a conversation partner—find meaning in the image of God reflected in a Mrs. Flowers or Hannah Lucas? Does that image not have points of connection to scripture and faith tradition? In this way, those images—which have been historically submerged but more recently retrieved from invisibility—might enter into the identity-forming and meaning-making space of adolescence and emerging adulthood. Here is a powerful opportunity to enable people to re-name their reality, to participate in a form of embodied theology that holds the potential to liberate their bodies, souls, and minds from the oppressive constructs that shape their thinking about God, self, and community.

STORY TWO: THE MOTHER OF GOD REVISITED

The second story also comes from the life of a Black girl. Here, poet and essayist Audre Lorde reflects upon the women who "mothered" her into identity, seeking to answer the question:

> To whom do I owe the power behind my voice, what strength I have become, yeasting up like sudden blood from under the bruised skin's blister? My father leaves his psychic print upon me, silent, intense, and unforgiving. But his is a distant lightning. Images of women flaming like torches adorn and define the borders of my journey, stand like dykes between me and the chaos. It is the images of women, kind and cruel, that lead me home [(Lorde 1982, 3)].

She continues to answer her rhetorical question with a series of stories, one of which follows:

> DeLois lived up the block on 142nd Street and never had her hair done, and all the neighborhood women sucked their teeth as she walked by. Her crispy hair twinkled in the summer sun as her big proud stomach moved her on down the block while I watched, not caring whether or not she was a poem. Even though I tied my shoes and tried to peep under her blouse as she passed by, I never spoke to DeLois, because my mother didn't. But I loved her, because she moved like she felt she was somebody special, like she was somebody I'd like to know someday. She moved like how I thought god's mother must have moved, and my mother, once upon a time, and someday maybe me.

124

Hot noon threw a ring of sunlight like a halo on top of Delois' stomach, like a spotlight, making me sorry that I was so flat and could only feel the sun on my head and shoulders. I'd have to lie down on my back before the sun could shine down like that on my belly.

I loved DeLois because she was big and Black and special and seemed to laugh all over. I was scared of DeLois for those very same reasons. One day I watched DeLois step off the curb of 142nd Street against the light, slow and deliberate. A high yaller dude in a white Cadillac passed by and leaned out and yelled at her, "hurry up, you flat-footed, nappy headed, funny-looking bitch!" The car almost knocking her down. DeLois kept right on about her leisurely business and never so much as looked around [Lorde 1982, 4].

UNCTUOUSNESS IN THE USABLE PAST

In this story we glimpse one woman's integration of an alternative figure of authority and power into a preexisting narrative telling her how women should be. As I read this story, the person of DeLois lifts up a form of beauty that resists the white standard, glorifying thin figures and light skin. It also resists some Black female beauty norms influenced by internalized racism, considering straightened hair somehow better than natural hair [Peiss 1994, 103]. As in the Angelou story above, we see a glimpse of "not blossoms, but blooming" in the depiction of the young Lorde trying to peep at the woman's large bosom and, by comparison, reflecting on her own body as lacking enough space for the sun's warmth to shine upon. As Lorde reflects upon the process of a girl inventing her adult identity, we see her choosing to admire and emulate a woman who "loves herself, regardless" [(Walker 1983, xii)]. In telling the story, Lorde makes meaning out of the everyday events of life that shaped her emerging, multidimensional identity. As such, this story provides a glimpse of part of what I want to illuminate as one woman's organic formation toward healthy resistance.

The Womanist theme of "unctuousness as a virtue," explored by Katie Cannon through the life and writings of Zora Neale Hurston, provides a link between Lorde's story and the larger canon of stories surrounding the historical, social, and cultural experiences of Black women. Cannon lifts up the term "unctuousness," as it is used by Alice Walker, to refer to a Black woman's ability to consistently "act sincere in the most insincere situations" [(Cannon 1995, 178)]. According to Cannon, unctuousness emerges in the lives of Black women who "maintain a feistiness about life that nobody can wipe out, no matter how hard they try." Forged out of the historical realities of sexism and racism, unctuousness is a survival strategy often adopted to resist evil and respond to suffering "which is the normal state of affairs" [(90)].

In the life of Hurston, unctuousness included embodying the "mama says" phrases that told her to "jump at de sun" so that she would not have a squinched spirit by the time she was grown. "We might not land on the sun, but at least we would get off the ground," Hurston quotes her mother as saying [(79)]. In such a way, Cannon depicts Hurston l i v i n g into healthy resistance inherited from her mother, rather than internalizing the voice of her father who repeatedly admonished her to adopt a "spirit of docile complacency" [(79)].

Lorde's story provides a possible image of unctuousness as an embodied virtue. This unctuousness is witnessed by and incorporated into her emerging identity, one in which DeLois's prideful walk echoes the woman her mother once was and a gender identity to which she aspires. In her refusal to seek the approval of the neighborhood women, in her comfortable acceptance of dark skin and in her refusal to acknowledge the demeaning taunts of a passerby, DeLois keeps right on moving in an image of "how I thought god's mother must have moved" (Lorde 1982, 4).

Black feminist scholar Regina Austin critiques the use of role models that do not adequately respond to the material conditions that limit young Black women's choices. She used the term "sapphire" to point to the need for a broader repertoire of models of Black womanhood. She would include the "host of non-elite Black women who everyday mount local, small-scale resistance grounded in Indigenous cultural values, values whose real political potential is often hidden even from those whose lives they govern" (Austin 1987, 15). The work of Chanequa Walker-Barnes further broadens the repertoire of models for Black womanhood by examining the burdens of the ideology of the strong Black woman places on women (Walker-Barnes 2014).

Implications for the Spiritual Formation and Religious Education

Like Angelou's story, this portion of Lorde's autobiography adds to the evidence supporting the need for models of spiritual formation that engage young people in theological reflection on their own life stories. To paraphrase Alice Walker, women must scrape the white man off our eyeballs before even trying to get a glimpse of God (Walker 1982, 176).

Glimpses of God that might emerge from Lorde's story break the images of God so embedded in our minds that they seem "glued to our eyeballs." A story like this, incorporated into the storehouse of narratives available to an adult facilitator, could prove useful in leading young people through theological reflection of their own life stories. It could provide a link, allowing girls to realize that they too may someday move with the self-assurance of a DeLois and may incorporate virtues such as unctuousness into their identities while providing the language necessary to recognize such possibilities. Might we encourage young people to tell the stories of role models in their own lives who, like Mrs. Flowers or DeLois, throw lifelines and provide aspirational identities? By telling their stories and making connections to stories from the larger culture that can affirm their worth, young people could begin to learn what it means to resist the internalized voices that operate to belittle, demean, and negate self-worth.

STORY THREE: SHE BELIEVED I COULD FLY

The final story I share comes from the experience of a white woman. In *An American Childhood*, author Annie Dillard remembers a moment in which she learned to resist conventional norms of behavior, while finding the source of sublime joy within her body. This story differs from the earlier two. This story does not arise out of the complex web of oppressions facing women of color. It springs out of the experience of a girl born into privilege by virtue of her skin color, class, and economic status.

Stories of resistance take on a different character in the lives of white girls, who, although oppressed by sexism, do not bear the additional burdens suffered by Black and Brown girls in a racist society. When stories of white women's organic formation toward resistance come into conversation with theology informed by Womanist, *Mujerista*, Asian-Feminist, or Native American perspectives, these stories can provide a resource for the liberatory education of all young people.

Dillard's story reflects an overlapping issue confronting all women. Across many cultures, secular and religious traditions continue to perpetuate dichotomies between the body and the spirit, between rationality and sensuality. This story invites the interplay between these two connected ways of knowing.

In the following story, Dillard is running down the sidewalk, "revving up for an act of faith." She recounts:

> I was conscious and self-conscious. I knew well that people could not fly—as well as anyone knows it—but I also knew the kicker: that, as the books put it, with faith all things are possible.
>
> Just once I wanted a task that required all the joy I had. Day after day, I had noticed that if I waited long enough, my strong unexpressed joy would dwindle and dissipate inside me, over many hours, like a fire subsiding, and I would at last calm down. Just this once I wanted to let it rip. Flying rather famously required the extra energy of belief, and this, too, I had in superabundance . . .
>
> I ran the sidewalk full tilt. I waved my arms ever higher and faster; blood balled in my fingertips. I knew I was foolish. I knew I was too old really to believe in this as a child would, out of ignorance; instead, I was experimenting as a scientist would, testing both the thing itself and the limits of my own courage in trying it, miserably self-conscious in full view of the whole world. You can't test courage cautiously, so I ran hard and waved my arms hard, happy . . .
>
> Up ahead I saw a business-suited pedestrian. He was coming stiffly toward me down the walk. Who could ever forget this first test, this stranger, this thin

young man appalled? I banished the temptation to straighten up and walk right. He flattened himself against a brick wall as I passed flailing—although I had left him plenty of room. He had refused to meet my exultant eye. He looked away, evidently embarrassed. How surprisingly easy it was to ignore him! What I was letting rip, in fact, was my willingness to look foolish, in his eyes and in my own. Having chosen this foolishness, I was a free being. How could the world ever stop me, how could I betray myself, if I was not afraid?

I was flying. My shoulders loosened, my stride opened, my heart banged the base of my throat. I crossed Carnegie and ran up the block waving my arms. I crossed Lexington and ran up the block waving my arms.

A linen-suited woman in her fifties did meet my exultant eye. She looked exultant herself, seeing me from far up the block. Her face was thin and tanned. We converged. Her warm, intelligent glance said she knew what I was doing—not because she herself had been a child, but because she herself took a few loose aerial turns around her apartment every night for the hell of it, and by day played along with the rest of the world and took the streetcar. So, Teresa of Avila checked her unseemly joy and hung on to the altar rail to hold herself down. The woman's smiling, deep glance seemed to read my own awareness from my face, so we passed on the sidewalk—a beautifully upright woman walking in her tan linen suit, a kid running and flapping her arms. We passed on the sidewalk with the look of accomplices who share a humor just beyond irony. What's a heart for?

I crossed Homewood and ran up the block. The joy multiplied as I ran—I ran never actually quite leaving the ground—and multiplied still as I felt my stride begin to fumble and my knees begin to quiver and stall. The joy multiplied even as I slowed bumping to a walk. I was all but splitting, all but shooting sparks. Blood coursed free inside my lungs and bones, a light-shot stream like air. I couldn't feel the pavement at all.

I was too aware to do this, and had done it anyway. What could touch me now? For what were the people on Penn Avenue to me, or what was I to myself, really, but a witness to any boldness I could muster, or any cowardice, if it came to that, any giving up on heaven for the sake of dignity on earth? I had not seen a great deal accomplished in the name of dignity, ever. (Dillard 1987, 88–90)

"LOVING HERSELF, REGARDLESS" IN A USABLE PAST

In this story, we see one woman's attempt to incorporate a moment of embodied ecstasy into her emerging identity as a person who relies on her own internal compass to determine appropriate behavior. Reading this story, we hear echoes of the dramatist's line, "I found God within myself and loved her. I loved her fiercely" (Shange 1977, 63). Once again, Alice Walker's words ring true: this girl is learning to love herself, regardless. Once again, we see a glimpse of "not blossoms, but blooming" as the young Dillard recounts a moment, a slice of life, later remembered as part of what we might call her organic education toward healthy resistance. The girl chooses which voices to internalize, deciding that the embarrassed reaction of the businessman need not, at least in this moment, shape the contours of her inner life.

The young Dillard is experiencing a moment akin to the one my adolescent collaborator Cathy related in her story, "Tomorrow, Then," discussed in chapter 3. Dillard, like Cathy afloat in the reservoir and jogging on campus, was learning to trust her senses, to feel the blood coursing through her veins, and to know that her body is one reliable source of knowing God. Dillard does not trivialize or deny her body, running full tilt and finding joy in this particular form of self-expression. Senses and intuition are the source of her intelligence, as she intuits from the linen-suited woman all she needs to know to confirm the reliability of her internal compass. She senses a moment of connection; real or imagined, it propels her. She finds authority in the trueness of her sensory experiences of feet on pavement, breath pounding, arms flapping. This authority gives her the strength to look foolish in the eyes of the world in order to remain true to the voice within her telling her she can fly.

Implications for the Spiritual Formation and Religious Education

Like the two stories that precede it, Dillard's story supports the call for models of religious education and spiritual formation that encourage young people to reflect theologically about their own life stories. In reflecting on a story with themes similar to Dillard's we can imagine what might happen. A young person might bring to voice the intuitive knowledge that God is both within and outside of us, as near as the next breath, and also affirmed in the deep glance of an understanding other. If this story is part of a body of evidence and imagery possessed by an adult facilitator, it could help counteract notions within the dominant culture that say concerns about our bodies are trivial. We can celebrate bodies as central to a way of knowing God, self, and others that resists dominant norms of culture and religion. Discussion of sensuality can open a conversation about sexuality—a topic that we need to talk about more. Young people, bombarded at an early age with sexual images and decisions about sexual choices, deserve an opportunity to tell stories about their bodies and their relationships in a zone of concern and safety.

Asking such questions as: "How might this story unearth a new interpretation or invert a familiar passage of scripture for you?", "Whose voice is missing from the story or from our conversation around it?", or "Where does power, inequity, or systemic evil show up in the story?" in the midst of a reflection about bodies and relationships might help young people come to articulate an awareness that God is a part of our sexuality, not standing in judgment of it, as patriarchal and conservative portrayals of Christianity would lead us to believe. As in the previous examples—which showed promise for surfacing feminine images of God—a story echoing the themes of Dillard's story might bring forward new ways of thinking about relational images for God. Those images could become a resource in the identity-forming and meaning-making of young adults at a critical time in their lives, before the damaging effects of narrow, wounding views of bodies, sensuality, and sexuality become permanently glued to young eyeballs.

AUTOBIOGRAPHY'S PLACE IN THE USABLE PAST

In these three examples, autobiographical writings afford windows through which to view powerful moments of organic formation. These moments, in turn, inform girl/friend theology.

Elements of a collective usable past in our feminist warehouse include much more than autobiography. The history of women and other under-represented or oppressed people also belong in our collection. Autobiography and memoir, however, make a unique contribution because of their status as "the most democratic form of American letters" [(McKay 1994, 55–59)]. Whereas other literary genres have historically thrown up barriers of exclusion across lines of race, class, and education, autobiography and memoir have been accessible to any literate person and, through oral tradition, to pre- or non-literate persons as well. As early as 1836, Jarena Lee began a long tradition of Black women's autobiographical writing with her text *The Life and Religious Experiences of Jarena Lee, A Coloured Lady, Giving Account of Her Call to Preach the Gospel. Revised and Corrected from the Original Manuscript, Written by Herself.* This was followed by the narratives of enslaved people and spiritual autobiographies, in which Black women used their religious faith to gain selfhood in the face of a society depriving them of all rights [(McKay 1994)].

The writing of autobiography and memoir constitutes a literary construction of self. For women and LGBTQ+ people who endure gender oppression, the act of writing and the creation of self may often occur simultaneously [(Heilbrun 1989, 117)]. In the act of writing an autobiography, people make meaning out of events that shaped their perceptions of the world. Voices that are elsewhere marginalized appear front and center in autobiographies, thus making them "frontier sites where private issues enter public discourse" [(Hine 1997)]. Although they have widely different backgrounds and speak with a multiplicity of voices, Black women's autobiographers "are joined together by their awareness of the impact that race and gender have had on their lives." This common ground accounts for "a strain of radical resistance that runs through even the least overtly political" of Black women's autobiographies [(McKay 1994, 59)]. For these reasons, autobiography and memoir are invaluable pieces in the construction of a usable past that is inclusive of difference and are key resources in the practice of girl/friend theology.[5]

SEA GLASS

During the long hot summer of 1997, I spent a lot of time along the shores of Lake Michigan with my daughter Erin, then two and a half, and our friends. I was hugely pregnant, so I received that clear, cold water and the company of other moms as a welcome tonic each afternoon.

Between building sandcastles, munching on goldfish, and splashing in the waves, Erin and I collected tiny pieces of sea glass. Although the smooth pebble-like fragments also wash up in white and brown, our favorites were Mountain Dew green. Oddly shaped and shockingly green, the fragments kept surfacing all summer long as I unpacked sandy pockets, picnic baskets, and beach towels. Our collection grew to fill a small bowl.

When that summer ended, so did my pregnancy. Our baby Sophia was stillborn from an unknown cause on her due date in late August. During my intense grieving, I found many ways to name the life-giving presence of Sophia, despite the overwhelming sadness of our loss. Somehow, I knew those pieces of sea glass would become important.

Two years later, Erin and her new sister, Olivia, were my daily companions. Landlocked in southwestern Virginia, far from those refreshing Lake Michigan shores and our equally refreshing Evanston companions, I found vast comfort in those pieces of sea glass. They escaped the bowl that sought to contain them. Three sat on my desk, hastily taped up in a moment when I needed inspiration. Arranged

---

5   For a robust list of such resources that center LGBTQ+ lives, go to https://lgbtqreads.com/non-fiction/memoirs-personal-essays/.

in a circle, a dozen of them adorned a scrapbook holding memories of Sophia. Two hung in a window, encased in a beaded purse created for that purpose by a dear friend. Those pieces of sea glass were constant reminders of a physical and personal community that upheld and supported me. They reminded me that the time we spent creating Sophia was not wasted time.

Like the sea glass in my collection, the stories that make up our usable past represent hard but necessary pieces of our life. Strategically placed, they can provide comfort and sustenance in the midst of our daily struggles with depression and anxiety amid the ever-present remnants of patriarchal, white-normative, and heteronormative culture. Audre Lorde reminds us that "for women, then, Poetry is not a luxury." She goes on to write, "The farthest horizons of our hopes and fears are cobbled by our poems, carved from the rock experiences of our daily lives"(Lorde 1984, 36–39).

Constructing a usable past is part of the difficult and necessary work of resisting dominant culture. Our dangerous memories of hope and resistance energize us. We transform angry moments, when we feel the slap of misogyny, racism, homophobia, into artistic expression, carved from our daily lives.

We find glittering fragments of stories scattered among the refuse of the literary and artistic paths we walk. Together, that collection sustains the very personal, yet highly political act of finding and maintaining voice, power, and agency. It reminds us of our potential for self-love that can birth a "belief in the self far greater than anyone's disbelief"(Robinson and Ward 1991, 102). This belief lets us know ourselves as moral agents who can voice our truest convictions, out loud, in public, toward the shaping of a better world.

Girl/friend theology encourages the vulnerable act of sharing our dangerous memories and our usable pasts. These artifacts—mosaics reconstructed from fragments—can be resources in the intergenerational meaning making we must take on if we are to build a world in which all beings can flourish.

CHAPTER FIVE

GOD-TALK IN THE MIDST OF VIOLENCE AND DEATH

To work magic, we begin by making new metaphors.
— Starhawk, *Dreaming the Dark*

Starhawk is a Jewish feminist activist who brought awareness to pagan communities in the 1970s and 1980s as she protested nuclear proliferation. She was a lifesaver to me when, in the midst of my early motherhood, I became troubled by George W. Bush's declaration of war against Iraq. During a war protest in Washington, DC, I woke up a sleeping toddler so she could be present for a moment with Alice Walker and joined hundreds of others in a spiral dance led by Starhawk herself. Under a blue sky adorned with a daytime moon, Starhawk wove a web of community, embodying her vision of feminists reconstructing a world without war.

Where is God when your nation goes to war to gain power and exert control over material resources and foreign governments? Where is God when a gun goes off repeatedly in your neighborhood, and you must reorient your child's bed to be out of the bullet's path? Where is an all-loving God when a parent is abusive? Or when a child becomes hospitalized because their body wastes away from an eating disorder? Traditional beliefs that God is all powerful, all knowing, and all good bump up against reality, especially amid tragedy. When these images of God fall apart and alternative images don't arise, people tend to walk away from belief in God altogether.

Alternative, lifegiving images of a God who is not omnipotent, who is vulnerable, who feels our pain, and who defies our attempts at certainty also exist, even though they often remain hidden from view. These images require excavation and integration if they are to be of any help to real people today.

Adolescents experience violence, both directly and indirectly, on a daily basis. Girls, trans, and gender non-conforming youth experience disproportionate levels of sexual assault, partnered violence, eating disorders, anxiety, and depression. [1] Suicide and homicide are the second- and third-leading causes of death for persons between the ages of fifteen and twenty-four in the United States. For every death, there are at least another hundred nonfatal injuries caused by violence (Center for Disease Control 2018). Adolescents who experience this violence carry heavy trauma in their bodies (Van Der Kolk 2014). Spiritual practices can help them recover from such trauma, even years later (Baker and Reyes 2021).

When given the opportunity to share a story of importance in their lives, six out of fifteen collaborators used the occasion to speak out loud their stories of violence. In chapter 3, Emma shared the story of her close friend's suicide. The two stories I have chosen for this chapter return to a place of tragic pain. The first one, "No Way Out," is a seventeen-year-old's story about the death of her cousin. The second, "Then, One Day, I Saw," is about a friendship between a girl who suffers from an eating disorder and a boy who bears the physical scars of his father's abuse.

---

1   I include eating disorders as part of a long list of violent behaviors, including self-mutilation (known as "cutting"), that girls inflict upon themselves as a way of coping with sex-role expectations. Eating disorders claim the lives of up to a thousand girls a year in the United States. See Jennifer Egan, "The Thin Red Line," *New York Times Magazine* (July 27, 1997): 21– 46, and Carol Lakey Hess, *Caretakers of Our Common House: Women's Development in Communities of Faith* (Nashville: Abingdon Press, 1997), 132–35.

Awareness Alert: References to violence, homicide, eating disorders and physical abuse are intense and may be triggering to some readers. Please take the necessary care for yourself and others as you engage this material or lead a group using it.[2]

STORY #3: NO WAY OUT

Hannah, a seventeen-year-old girl from Chicago, told the following story to a group including me, another adult collaborator, and two other girls, Katie and Elaine. Meeting for a weekend at the home of Elaine, this group spanned diverse religious, racial, ethnic, and economic backgrounds: Hannah is a white Roman Catholic; Elaine is a white Conservative Jew engaged in critiquing her tradition; Peg and I are both white ordained United Methodist ministers; and Katie identifies as African American and describes herself as religiously unaffiliated but a frequent visitor to Roman Catholic and Pentecostal churches. Elaine, Peg, and I are all middle-class and lived, at the time, near Chicago. Hannah comes from a middle-class family and lived in Chicago. Katie, born into a low-income family, left her home of origin at the age of thirteen to live in a group home for girls. When we met, she was working several jobs to help pay her mother's rent. At the time, we all presented as cis-gender heterosexual women.

Hannah told this story on our second day together. We had already shared in several deeply moving sessions. At this point in the weekend, despite the fact that one girl had left and another had taken

---

2   For guidelines on best practices with using trigger warnings, see https://sites.lsa.umich.edu/
     inclusive-teaching-sandbox/wp-content/uploads/sites/853/2021/02/An-Introduction-
     to-Content-Warnings-and-Trigger-Warnings-Draft.pdf. For specific guidelines about
     how to address the topic of suicide when it arises, see https://www.samaritans.org/about-
     samaritans/research-policy/internet-suicide/online-safety-resources/how-talk-about-
     suicide-safely-online/.

her place, common themes were beginning to surface among the stories. Hannah, who had converted to Roman Catholicism in the third grade, was quite active in the life of her parish, having trained and served as a eucharistic minister. Her parents dropped her off on Friday night and whisked her away to figure-skating practice shortly after our weekend retreat of ended. Here is Hannah's story:

NO WAY OUT

This story happened when I was in sixth grade. So, it happened about five years ago. I left out names because it was in the news, and it's just easier for me to talk that way. So I refer to him only as my cousin.

My cousin messed up in his life. He dropped out of school and had kids too young. The worst part, especially having kids, was his involvement with a gang. He was never home. When he was, his girlfriend would often throw him out because he was drunk or high. A couple of years went by. His son was four years old, and his daughter was two years old. I don't believe I'll ever know why, but one night he came home and stayed home. Of course, it was not as simple as that. He flipped back and forth for a while between being a gang member and being a dad. I guess it was his son who provided him with the strength to reach for something better. He got into a drug rehab program. He also attempted to dispel the bonds between him and gang members. I've always heard that you can get out of the gang for finding religion, but I guess finding yourself is not a permissible excuse.

His girlfriend had kicked him out and was not ready to live with him again. For the past year, he had spent his nights crashing at friends' homes or on the street. His parents knew that he was still being harassed by the gangs, so they let him move into the basement. On July 4, his girlfriend decided to bring the kids over. Things went so well. My cousin proved to his girlfriend and his parents that he was finally clean. By this time, his parents had helped him pay off the debts he owed to gang members. You could see this story as a true miracle. A life was turned around and a family was reunited. He had been given a new lease on life. I'd like to end this story here, with this inspirational conclusion and the knowledge that you can always change. But I can't. Although the offenders were never apprehended, we know who they were. On July 6, the gang got my cousin out. They threw a Molotov cocktail through his parents' first-floor window. His parents had both left the house, but as they must have known, my cousin was in the basement. The only exit out was now engulfed in flames. What the gang did not know was that his girlfriend and two kids were still there from the long weekend.

One of the hardest things I've ever had to do in my life is walk into that funeral home and see those two pure white coffins and a pint-sized one in the middle. You may wonder why there were only three coffins. That's the miracle in this story. In his last moments, my cousin saved his daughter. Firemen found her lying unconscious under her dead father. He had shielded her from the poisonous gas and melting flames.

I don't know where exactly they got that priest from at the funeral. I know my aunt was ready to get up and sit him down. He preached to a church that was full of teens. He preached to us about the travesty of gangs and drugs and not to get involved with them. Well, we didn't need him to lecture us on that. The two-year-old girl who stood by the three holes in the ground was all the lecture we needed.

DOING LIVE WITH "NO WAY OUT"

L: LISTEN DEEPLY[3]

The first step of LIVE is L: Listen deeply to the storyteller. I light a candle and signal that it is time for the storyteller to begin. If copies of the story have been circulated, I ask them to be put aside so we can focus on the voice and presence of the storyteller. I invite people to "Listen deeply as the story is read aloud. Listen with the ears of God / Spirit / Creator / Source. Listen with your whole body, without an agenda, paying attention to the feelings the story stirs in you. Listen, as if you are listening to scripture, as if you expect the Holy to show up."

I: IMMERSE IN FEELINGS

The second step is to: Immerse yourself in the feelings. I invite people to "Share the full range of emotions you felt as you listened. Surface feelings that showed up in your body: tense shoulders, change of breathing, tears, etc. Share briefly any stories from your own life that this story called to mind."

As Hannah concluded her story, raw emotions blazed on the faces around the circle. I felt my heart pounding and noticed other

---

3   In the original version, this step was called Experience Near: Feelings, Emotions, and Associations; the third step was called Experience Distance: Images, Symbols and God; the final step was called Going Forth.

visceral reactions, such as heavy sighs and tears. It took several moments before anyone broke the silence.

> *Elaine:* It made me so mad. It *makes* me so mad. The senselessness of the murders, and then, on top of that, the pain inflicted by the priest at the funeral.

Other participants named feelings of anger and sadness. Then Katie, who had previously told us of her childhood in a notoriously violent Chicago housing project, shared close associations with Hannah's story.

> *Katie:* The whole situation is upsetting. It probably was a bottle with alcohol in it. I can honestly imagine someone throwing that bottle in that window. I can understand how you feel because that has happened in my family, so much. That's why we don't have any males in my family. Because they have all been killed senselessly. A lot of those deaths have been gang-related. This was a tragedy. Even if there had just been one death, it would have been a tragedy.

> *Elaine:* The two-year-old is going to grow up knowing that her father died shielding her. She's going to live with that forever.

From pain, the conversation returned to anger, focusing on the religious service that failed to console the congregation, made up mostly of teenagers. Hannah added further details:

> *Hannah:* It was unbelievable. It was all teenagers. You saw rival gang members. A lot of people respected him because he was trying to get out. That's how it got labeled, that he finally got out. They were saying, "He was ours. We took him back. We let him out."

V: VIEW IT WIDER

After allowing for a free flow of emotions in which we acknowledged feelings of anger and sadness, I eventually facilitated a turn in the conversation to the third step in the method, V: View it Wider, asking, "Do you see any symbols or images in this story? Whose voice is missing from this story?" The conversation focused on the lingering smoke after a fire and the image of a father protecting his daughter.

> *Elaine:* I can't get the smoke out of my mind. And how he was trying to protect his daughter. The smoke still lingers, like the lingering effects of a smoky fire five years ago. And it's not going to go away. It's almost like, after the smoke clears, it's still here.

> *Katie:* I also have this other image that stands out, of him protecting her, you know, covering her up. It's like he's not even just protecting her from the smoke and from immediate danger, but almost from the world.

The longer we held these images, the more they came into focus, carrying the discussion from personal loss to critical social analysis. The lingering smoke was the grief that Hannah still works through. The lingering smoke also includes the little girl, whose life was forever maimed by the loss of her family. It was the ongoing reality of violent gangs, who entice young boys to join, yet will not let young men out. And it includes a society in which gangs flourish because they provide young people with protection, a source of income, and a sense of community in the midst of widespread poverty and institutionalized racism. The church, represented by a white priest addressing a hall crowded with mostly Black and Latinx young people, seemed to have nothing to bring to this lingering tragedy.

> *Elaine:* Do you think the lingering effect, that it hurt a lot of people, is going to stop them from doing it again?

> *Peg:* Certainly the priest didn't help. He was at a loss to help them see the lingering effects.

> *Katie:* If you're a member of a gang, you don't want to hear him at this point.

> *Elaine:* I'm visualizing an old guy who has no concept of what's going on. They're not going to listen.

After we had named many connections between the lingering smoke and the evil present in the story, I stepped into my facilitator role and said, "I keep wishing there was an image of water. It just feels overwhelmingly smoky, and water would be an image of God for me here."

God-Talk: A Bent-Over Father Crying Tears of Life

When I asked where God was in this story, two related stories from scripture surfaced. Peg was reminded of the parable of the prodigal son. The parents welcomed back the son who had gone astray—like the ex–gang member—in a demonstration of unconditional love and forgiveness. For Elaine, the little girl's survival against all odds reminded her of Moses' birth narrative. "She must have survived for a special purpose," Elaine said.

Katie identified with Elaine's interpretation. She offered this striking contrast to the image of the out-of-touch priest: God is like the bent-over father who saves his daughter with his tears.

Katie: You might say God really wasn't there. But I think he came late. He was present, because this little girl was saved. It's amazing that he was able to save her. I think that your cousin was playing the God role by protecting her and saving her.

Peg: And with that, with your cousin trying to be the shield for his daughter, it was like his parents were trying to be a shield for him. They provided a sanctuary for him in the basement. It's conflictual for me that one dad can be the God-like shield, and the other dad couldn't shield his children.

In this exchange, Katie became very animated. My adult collaborators and I would later come to recognize this kind of moment as a recurring gift in sessions of girl/friend theology. The energy would shift. One person's voice would become momentarily central, speaking from a grounded place of authority, reminiscent of the prophetic voice in scripture and tradition. Others would fall silent, respecting a deep truth emerging. My collaborators and I would later reflect on having experienced a moment of standing on holy ground.

Katie completed her portrait of God as an ex-gang-member father, crying life-giving tears:

Katie: You have to think that he's sheltering this girl. He's got to be crying. There are tears. That's the water that counteracts all this lingering smoke. If you think of it, that's probably what saved her. There's got to be a lot of smoke in there, but she's getting wet. The tears are evaporating and turning into air for her to breathe. I'm quite sure he was holding her and crying—

Dori: Her father, the tears—

Katie: He had to be thinking, "my child, my child." The water is the tears.

Touched by Katie's depiction of God, Peg affirmed Katie's interpretation.

Peg: My belief about God is that God is crying, too. God is watching this thing happen. God is *at* this funeral…

Katie: God is crying over the priest who is screwing it up. Crying for all these lives that are gathered, but just don't get it.

Peg: Crying and crying and crying. It's those tears that hopefully serve some purpose. We don't think of tears as productive. People think they're a waste of time. But here, the tears are God's tears

The dynamic between Peg and Katie illustrates the adult facilitator's role as supportive and non-authoritarian. Peg, the adult, can introduce an idea, which may connect with the girls' experiences and may not. Here, Peg realized the need to let Katie's speech flow after an early interruption. Later, she supported Katie's interpretation, sharing points of authentic connection between it and her own beliefs.

E: EXPLORE AHA! MOMENTS AND ENACT NEXT STEPS

The final step of the method, E: Explore and Enact, is to underline any "Aha! moments" and name any actions that the story and conversation might cause. Here, I invite questions such as: What surfaced for you that you might keep pondering? What idea had heat or energy for you? What do you want to say out loud so we can help each other hold onto it? What action or next step is emerging for you here? I also might ask what title they would give the story or if they agree with a title I have given it.

As our time grew short, I initiated the final stage of the method by asking if anything in this story moved us toward a new way of being or acting in the world. Hannah responded, sharing her reasons for bringing this particular story to the group: recently, she had begun dating someone with a history of gang involvement. They had broken up after he accused her of "being a white girl in khakis" who couldn't understand his experience as a Latinx person. "I had tried to put the death of my cousin behind me, but when I went out with Juan it all came back," Hannah said. "That's what I have to deal with, and that's why I have to get this out." Although we had come to the end of our formal discussion, the group lingered in support of Hannah and around the complexities of intercultural and interracial relationships. That conversation continued as we ate vegan sandwiches on the back deck.

ECHOES OF FEMINIST THEOLOGY AND ASSERTIONS OF GIRL/FRIEND THEOLOGY

To speak of God as a loving father bent over his daughter crying tears of life is a powerful metaphor. In this instance, girl/friend theology exemplifies the best of hermeneutic tradition by bringing a fresh, new interpretation to the ancient metaphor of God as a father. This offers potential vitality to a metaphor in danger of slipping into irrelevance, at best, or repudiation, at worst.

Feminists have closely dissected the image of God as father with many fruitful results. When women look "beyond God the father," a multitude of lifegiving images flourish. Often retrieving imagery found in scripture and in the writings of medieval mystics, feminist scholars of the Bible and theology depict God as a nursing mother, as a mother eagle, as a midwife, and as a woman giving birth, to name only a few [(Mollenkott 1991)].

Encountering such liberatory images of God was lifechanging for me when I was in my early twenties. It helped rescue a faith tradition that I had come to see as so laden with patriarchy that it could not survive. These submerged strains of Christian tradition created an entirely new pathway for me. I was able to see my calling as one who would lift them up, shout them out, and help others create new pathways of liberating spirituality.

Although non-masculine images of God still remain hidden within many Christian traditions today, I am thankful for the written record of feminists who surfaced them. They would never have reached the light of day without sustained reflection on the nature of metaphor, spurred in part by naming the oppression women experience when God is depicted only as male. In Mary Daly's words:

> The biblical and popular image of God as a great patriarch in heaven, rewarding and punishing according to his mysterious and seemingly arbitrary will, has dominated the imagination of millions for thousands of years. The symbol of the Father God, spawned in the human imagination and sustained as plausible by patriarchy, has, in turn, rendered service to this type of society by making its mechanisms for the oppression of women appear right and fitting. If God in "his" heaven is a father ruling "his" people, then it is in the nature of things and according

to divine plan and the order of the universe that
society be male-dominated [Daly 1973, 13].

To briefly summarize the lengthy critique around the image of
God as father, I turn to the work of liturgical theologian Ruth Duck,
biblical scholar Elisabeth Schüssler Fiorenza, and theologian Sallie
McFague, along with newer research in queer theology.

Duck, in her book *Gender and the Name of God*, argues that the
use of exclusively masculine names for God need to be understood
in light of social context. In contemporary US culture, that means
taking into account the fact that some fathers abuse their children
physically, sexually, and emotionally [Duck 1990, 43–51]. Turning exclusively
to images of God as mother does not suffice. There, too, we see evidence of troubling and abusive relationships. Duck's body of work
loosens the tight hold on patriarchal imagery of God, introducing
hymns and prayers into liturgy that reflect a more expansive and
inclusive understanding of gender identity.

Schüssler Fiorenza's feminist hermeneutic of suspicion aids in this
task by supporting a critical reading of the Bible, which foregrounds
the feminist quest for women's power, freedom, and independence.
Schüssler Fiorenza, although sympathetic to the feminist precau-
tion against using exclusively male imagery for God, nonetheless
makes a distinction between patriarchal and nonpatriarchal male
imagery for God. In her vision, masculine imagery freed from patriarchy can bear life-giving connections with biblical sources. As
an example, she cites the fatherhood of God elaborated in the Jesus
traditions as reflecting "the gracious goodness usually associated with a
mother" [Schüssler Fiorenza 1987, 151]. Rosemary Radford Ruether offers a
similar position, arguing that Jesus's references to God as father are
nonhierarchical and function to overthrow patriarchal imagery that
equates fathers with rulers [Ruether 1975, 67–69].

Breaking down the binary of male and female subjectivity is an ongoing task of feminist scholarship. Naming essentialism as a problem, and flipping characteristics historically attributed to mothers and fathers, for example, assists in this task.[4] By imagining a provider-mother or a nurturer-father, feminists challenge gender roles and expectations and undermine biological and essentialists explanations for gendered behavior [(McFague 1982, 159)]. However, these analyses do not go far enough in critiquing the gender binary, as these feminists still rely on gendered language and stereotypes in order to make their point.

Critique of father-God imagery centers around the nature of metaphor, a topic explored in depth by Sallie McFague. McFague argues that literal interpretations of metaphorical language constitute idolatry. When the Bible is interpreted literally, it becomes an idol and stands in danger of losing its relevance. She writes:

> When a model becomes an idol, the hypothetical character of the model is forgotten and what ought to be seen as *one* way to understand our relationship with God becomes identified as *the* way . . . the distance between the image and the reality collapses: "father" becomes God's primary name, and patriarchy becomes the reigning description of governing relationships on many levels [(McFague 1982, 9)].

In contrast to biblical idolatry, McFague argues for thinking about God metaphorically. Thinking metaphorically involves "spotting a thread of similarity between two dissimilar objects . . . one of which is better known than the other, and using the better-known one as

---

4   See Ellen T. Armour, "Essentialism," in *Dictionary of Feminist Theologies*, ed., Letty M. Russell and J. Shannon Clarkson (Louisville: Westminster John Knox Press, 1996), 88. And also Diana Fuss, *Essentially Speaking: Feminism, Nature, and Difference* (New York: Routledge, 1990).

a way of speaking about the lesser known." Metaphorical theology thus emphasizes personal and relational language about God, but not necessarily as the Christian tradition has interpreted these categories [McFague 1982, 21]. She cites as an example a suppressed strain of feminine imagery within the paradigm of Jewish and Christian history: "Masculine imagery in this suppressed tradition gives credence not to a patriarchal, but to a parental model, with shared characteristics of motherhood and fatherhood" [McFague 1982, 177].

Scholarship emerging from LGBTQ+ authors and allies continues to problematize essentialist categories for God. Tara Soughers, an Episcopal priest who is also the mother of a trans young adult, encourages the church to think beyond the gender binary to expand our imagination of the Divine. She argues that the binary male/female God imagery limits our theological imagination, especially around concepts of the three-in-one nature of God embraced by trinitarian models [Soughers 2018]. Cheryl B. Evans, also the parent of a trans young adult, similarly argues that the Judeo-Christian canon invites us to imagine God beyond the boundaries of male/female, mother/father, brother/sister. In the mystery between fixed gender ideology, these authors argue, robust invitation to imagine God's arises [Evans 2017]. Queer priest Elizabeth Edman reminds us that this thinking has a long tradition in the Christian faith: "There have always been religious leaders who recognized the impulse to question binaries is embedded in an authentic read of Christian tradition," she writes [Edman 2016, Location 996].

Katie's image of God as a bent-over father crying tears of life exemplifies the kind of metaphorical freedom that allows us to imagine God beyond the fixed boundaries of gender essentialism and binary thinking. Katie's story and our reflection upon it rescues the image of "God as father" from idolatry, allowing it to be reinvested with alternative meanings that give it life in an era when many young people reject binary gender norms.

Katie has known gang members. She told of one in particular, an uncle. In him she saw violence, but she also saw something redemptive, something that bears a thread of similarity to what God must be like. The fatherly God she depicts is not Peg's image of the upstairs father, who graciously welcomes back the prodigal son and offers sanctuary in a distant basement. Rather, it is the prodigal son himself: the ex–gang member, a father-God, who holds his daughter close enough to feel his last breath and be drenched by his tears. This is not an all-powerful, faraway God, but one well acquainted with human limitations, suffering, and pain.[5]

The tears of this God offer life, not death. Contrary to some traditional interpretations of God as a father requiring the sacrificial death of his son, we see a God who provides lifegiving sanctuary. It is a relationship that bears resemblance to the one between God and Jesus depicted in Matthew's gospel, where we find a God who says, "This is my beloved child, in whom I am well pleased," and a God with whom Jesus shares tender, pain-filled conversation in the Garden of Gethsemane hours before his execution.

From this session, two closely related assertions of girlfriend theology surface: (1) God is mysteriously omnipresent, but not magically omnipotent. Although we cannot explain it, God *is* at work within human tragedies to create healing potential. God may not fix things, but neither does God abandon us; and (2) God feels our pain and cries with us.

---

5   A study by Joyce Mercer found feminist theology's stress on God's imminence limiting to adolescent females (Joyce Mercer, "Gender, Violence and Faith: Adolescent Girls and the Theological Anthropology of Difference" [PhD diss., Emory University, 1997]). The girls in my research, by contrast, often embraced images of God's imminence as a welcome counterpoint to the images of a predominately transcendent God they had inherited from popular culture and their religious traditions. This is not to imply that transcendent images of God did not seem important to my collaborators: the girls in my study seemed to affirm *both* characteristics in God and exhibited little difficulty in holding the two in tension.

Although I have drawn connections most directly between these assertions and feminist theologies, these assertions also resonate with depictions of God found in process and liberation theology. As John Cobb writes, "Process theologians do not accept the view that God has at every moment the capacity to set things right, but neither does God stand by idly observing the suffering. God is present and active in every event seeking to bring out of it what good can be obtained"(Cobb 1994, 109). In the language of the liberation theologian Gustavo Gutiérrez: "The biblical God is close to human beings, a God of communion with and commitment to human beings. The active presence of God in the midst of the people is a part of the oldest and most enduring Biblical promises"(Gutiérrez 1988, 106).

In this example, we see girl/friend theology offering nonpatriarchal images for God that feminist, Womanist, liberation, and process theologians might all endorse. In this case, the source of this imagery is historically and culturally situated in the real-life experience of a girl who, unfortunately, was forced to witness unimaginable violence and pain. I imagine sessions of girl/friend theology happening with young people, supported by parents, pastors, and other adults who are free to imagine God in ways made possible by the wealth of autobiographies, sermons, podcasts, and books written in these post-gender-binary times. How might they continue the time-honored tradition of finding metaphors for God that emerge from their lived experience, just as Jesus did that day at the well, when in conversation with a formerly outcast woman, he imagined life with God as a fountain of living water.

The next session also engages father imagery and revolves around violence. It echoes the assertion that God is a constant presence who feels our pain, brings healing potential to the suffering, and shares our tears. However, it carries this a step further by introducing the claim that humans participate with God's action in the world. This brings to the foreground an additional assertion of girl/friend theology:

(6) God is most fully alive (incarnated) in us when our eyes are open to the pain of others.

STORY #4: THEN, ONE DAY, I SAW

Sarah, twenty-six, told this story. I recruited Sarah to be a second adult participant in this group, which met every day for a week as part of the Youth Theology Institute (YTI), a summer institute for high schoolers who are interested in the study of theology. Taking place at Candler School of Theology in Atlanta, YTI is one of a network of such programs the Lilly Endowment has funded on seminary campuses over the past decades. This group included five sixteen- and seventeen-year-old girls: Cathy, Kim, Mary, Holly, and Tina. They were from Roman Catholic, Eastern Orthodox, and Protestant faith communities. They were all exceptionally bright, ambitious, and theologically articulate young women from middle- to upper-middle-class white families.

I knew little about Sarah before this first session. She had come highly recommended by a colleague who knew I was looking for a seminary graduate with a feminist commitment to help with my research project. We spoke on the phone a few times to clarify her role and briefly share our views of feminist theology. A graduate of a United Methodist seminary, Sarah described herself as being between religious affiliations. In introducing herself to the group, Sarah said she struggled with the patriarchy she witnessed in the fundamentalist Christian home where she was raised. Going to seminary was a way to answer her questions about God and faith that had been stifled during her formative years.

Following the pattern established in each of my research contexts, I asked my adult collaborator to be the first storyteller. In this way, an adult was able to model self-disclosure, while taking on the vulnerable position of being the first to share. Making sure my younger collaborators are fully aware of the process before bringing their own autobiographies is an attempt to adjust the adult/adolescent power dynamic.

Sarah told this story at the group's first session together:

THEN, ONE DAY, I SAW

Chris was the bane of my existence in ninth grade. I was the stereotypical perfect principal's daughter at a small Christian school, and Chris was the stereotypical bad boy of the class—of the entire school, actually. He was smart, had a quick wit, and was, politically, very astute. And he was critical of—well, of everything and everyone (except for Lydia, who was the prettiest girl in the class). Since Chris was constantly getting into trouble for everything from drinking to talking too much in class, he and my dad, who was the principal, got to know each other really well. I think my dad spent more time with Chris than he did with me, in fact.

The problem was that Chris was every principal's nightmare. He was smart enough to attract a following of admiring peers. He was wild enough to take risks he probably shouldn't take. And he was savvy enough to succeed or get away with most of them. I think my dad probably secretly hated Chris, or hated the anxiety and stress that Chris caused him. But, of course, he never said as much, because hate was a sin. But Dad sure would be glum and very rigidly calm after those days when he'd had to deal with Chris.

Now obviously, Chris didn't like my dad much either. But he knew that if he took his rage out directly on my dad he'd be expelled. So, after being punished by my father—who would often paddle Chris and ask him to repent of his sins and think about what Jesus would have done—Chris would come back into English class or science class and take things out on me. One day he would make fun of my red hair. The next day he would call me fat. The next day he would call me ugly. The next day he would laugh at my father in front of my face. And the next day he would call me a nerd who was going to be a nun her whole life.

Looking back on Chris's words now, I want to laugh, to shrug him off like the annoying little pest he was. But during ninth grade, when I was all awkward angles and insecurities and hopes and fears, Chris was more than a pest: he was a nightmare. And the way he saw or treated me would determine how I felt about myself for the remainder of the day—even the week.

And then one day, I saw the marks on his arm where it looked like somebody had beaten him with a belt buckle. And I overheard him telling one of his friends that his dad had gotten pissed at him the night before. And I started to wonder if Chris was really as tough and uncaring as he wanted me to think. I wondered if he was as lonely inside as I was, just in a different way. I wondered what it felt like to have your dad, not ignore you—like mine was doing—but rather, pay too much attention to you, and not a good attention either, but kind of a painful attention.

And then other things started to happen. I grew a little bit older, I went into the tenth grade. I went to a different school and started feeling depressed. Started feeling anxious and lonely. And I started to lose weight. By the time I turned sixteen and was getting ready to be in the eleventh grade, I had gone from 115 pounds, which was already pretty thin, to ninety pounds. I was anorexic. Everything in my life began to revolve around food or avoiding food, around exercise, and around the scale in the bathroom. I stopped talking to my friends. I stopped going out. I stopped all social activity, and people started to draw away from me. They were afraid. They didn't know what to say or do. Everybody, that is, except for Chris.

I don't know why he didn't run away like the other ones did. But he somehow stayed around. He talked to me. He no longer made fun of me. He treated me like a friend. He was a friend. Why? Perhaps something in his rebellious angry side sensed that I, too, was a little bit angry—that I was pretty miserable, like him, even though I was outwardly the perfect principal's daughter: never sinning, being unkind, or making anything less than an "A." Maybe, like me, parts of him were starving inside, and he knew what it felt like to have no control over your life except what you do with or to your body.

So after all the tension and anxiety over Chris in the ninth grade, I found myself becoming friends with him in the eleventh grade. It's strange, isn't it, thinking about it now—was it me who changed or him? Maybe we both did. Maybe he had grown up enough to recognize that the world was not going to change simply if he got angry and hurt people. And maybe I had grown up enough to realize that life was not going to be good simply if I was always good.

But instead of attacking the world or other people, like Chris had done, I did what lots of women tend to do, I attacked myself. I punished myself for the sins of the world, or of myself. I starved myself down until I almost disappeared, almost as if I were saying I don't deserve or want to be here.

One other thought: maybe Chris and I became friends because at the core of things we were both just hurting kids. We were both sort of disenchanted with life the way we had been taught. I was no longer eager to be perfect. And Chris was no longer eager to be bad. And somewhere between that middle way, between rebellious guy and starving perfect girl, we saw some commonality and we became friends.

It's been a number of years since I heard from Chris. I heard a while back that his parents had sent him into the Marine Corps to shape him up and put some of the "fear of God" into him. I don't know if it would have worked. And as for me, well, I slowly recovered from my anorexia. It took me a good two years to get my weight back up to a healthy level and then another two years to start addressing my own rage and depression and the reasons why I starved myself. But I still kind of carry the weight of it around with me. And I imagine Chris might carry the weight of his own years of being a rebel and being beaten by his father. I wonder if he is as confused about God's love, about grace, and about redemption today as I still am. Maybe not. I miss him. And sometimes I think, I miss God, too.

DOING LIVE WITH "THEN, ONE DAY, I SAW"

L: LISTEN DEEPLY[6]

The first step of LIVE is L; Listen deeply to the storyteller. Because this group had met for girl/friend theology several times, I did not need to set up the agreements for how we would hold the space or describe the steps of the method.

When Sarah finished her story, all participants joined readily into the conversation, and moved quickly into wanting to share their feelings.

I: IMMERSE IN FEELINGS

The group connected at a deep emotional level with the fact that Sarah had suffered from an eating disorder. They shared feelings of self-consciousness, especially regarding their body images and a tendency they notice in themselves to direct pain inward, rather than outward.

> *Cathy:* This made me feel sad, because with girls, I guess it's a generalization, but we seem to push things inside. Chris, when he was angry, he acted out. But girls tend to say, "Something's wrong with me, because this is hurting." And so, Chris acted out and did things to other people with his anger. He didn't go inside himself. Doesn't it seem like that, you all?

---

6   In the original version, this step was called Experience Near: Feelings, Emotions, and Associations; the third step was called Experience Distance: Images, Symbols and God; the final step was called Going Forth.

I mean, the girls I know do that. I know *I* do that. I don't automatically think, "What's wrong here?"

Sarah: Yeah, I think you're right that it implodes instead of exploding.

Kim: Yeah, when someone says something, even if you know the guy's a jerk, it just shatters. It shakes you to your core, and you just feel like sludge.

Holly: And sometimes you tend to believe the bad stuff about yourself instead of believing the good stuff. Like, if someone pays me a compliment, it's hard for me to believe it. But if someone tells me something bad, it sticks. It's easy to find a lot of fault in myself.

All of the participants shared similar experiences, connecting them to aspirations of perfection. Then the talk centered on what it feels like to be singled out or ostracized. The girls acknowledged this happening for both negative and positive reasons, such as appearing to "have it all together."

Kim: Every girl I talk to seems to feel incredibly isolated. Like they don't necessarily fit in. They float from group to group.

Cathy: I was talking to a friend who said, "That just means you have more things figured out than a lot of people around you. "

Kim: I've been told that.

Cathy: But that doesn't do any good. I still feel isolated.

Kim: So, I'm still a social outcast who has a lot of things figured out—

Mary: I feel that way sometimes, like I have so many different aspects of my life that I can't really be categorized. That's isolating.

Tina: It sounds like we're all floaters.

Cathy: Yeah... I'm like that. It has to do with transcending social boundaries. I understand the boundaries, but I don't necessarily see them.

Kim: You never feel like you really fit into the group.

Kathy: Kind of like on the outside, looking in, a social outcast.

V: VIEW IT WIDER

I sensed the talk moving toward images, so in my role as facilitator, I summarized what I had been hearing and moved toward the third step of the method, V: View it Wider, inviting connections to scripture, faith tradition, new interpretations, images of God, evil, or missing voices. But as I often do, especially during initial sessions with a group, I reminded them that any lingering feelings could still be brought into the conversation.

Dori: I want to isolate a few words that seem to encapsulate some of what we're talking about. Let's remember and go back to this idea of transcending social boundaries. I think it's very connected to our feelings about this story. But before we get too far away from the experience of hearing the story, is there anything else that you felt in your body or memories or associations before we move out of the feeling realm? Once we've moved out of the feeling realm and you identify a feeling you can always jump back. This is a very fluid method, so feel free to do that.

When Cathy subsequently started talking, I was glad I had put out one more call for feelings. We stayed in an in-between place, still connected to feelings, yet beginning to move toward images.

Cathy: When you were talking about having to be perfect, I was feeling sick to my stomach. I've never had an eating disorder, but I do worry about my weight, like any American girl. But I've always had this compulsion for perfection. No matter what I've accomplished, it's never good enough. For me, there's always that next achievement that I have to get to…

Other participants shared this compulsion for perfection, saying that it didn't come from their parents, at least not on the surface.

Mary: I know what you mean. The pressure doesn't come from my parents. It's something inside.

Cathy: I don't know how it got planted or embodied in us. You all say it's not your parents. *I* think it's *my* parents. (Laughter) Who makes us think that we need to do this and this and this?

Kim then took us to the second step of the method, answering Cathy's rhetorical question by alluding to the Bible.

Kim: Because it's certainly not there biblically, remember? It's like you're perfect in who you are, a child of God.

Dori: Just be.

Kim: Exist.

Dori: When I was hearing you, Cathy, I remembered the feeling of almost being like an arm of my father, an extension. Whatever the arm did that was good made him look good. Sometimes I just wanted to sever it. I think that's what I did when I moved a thousand miles away from home. It was my way of saying, "I am not your arm." As much as it was his love that made him want me to excel, I needed to have my achievements be my own, not his.

Cathy: That's a lot of how I feel. I can remember being younger and really, I think, believing to some certain extent that what I didn't do right was going to be reflected in how much my dad loved me. You know what I mean? That felt horrible. That's a bad feeling. That's not a healthy way to envision how you should be, or your perfection.

V: VIEW IT WIDER

Kim had already initiated the third step in LIVE, V: View it Wider. After this very animated discussion of feelings and emotions, we moved deeper into to a discussion of images.

> *Dori:* Is there a guiding metaphor or an image that comes to you? We've talked about this idea of transcending social boundaries and the link to the story is the bad boy and the good girl meeting someplace in the middle. What images, as you think back to the story, seem significant?

> *Mary:* For me, it's like the understanding that everyone has problems in their own life. I remember when I realized that we all carry things with us. That was a big thing for me: other people have struggles.

> *Kim:* I think there's something like a revelation that comes at some point in high school that not everyone's family is the way yours is. There is no normal. And I hear about these people who have been abused, and it's all they've known. And they think it's normal, and I think my life is normal. But there isn't a set normality.

> *Cathy:* And also I think that you start to develop a different kind of relationship with your friends in high school at a deeper level. You begin to see the mechanics of their family functions. And it's true there is no perfect thing. It is weird to see all the different perspectives. In terms of an image or a related

story, I thought immediately of *The Breakfast Club*. I thought of you as that girl and him as that guy.

We talked for several moments about the movie *The Breakfast Club*, a cult classic that celebrates an unlikely coalition of high school friends.

Sarah: I actually just watched it a month ago. It made me cry again because of the feelings of all these kids. They're all estranged and alienated from each other. Once they finally sit down and start opening up, they finally start to realize how each person is just human. The hard part is then going back to school and figuring out how you're going to deal with it now. I always wanted them to make a sequel to the movie to see if they actually continued talking or if they just drifted.

Holly: You cried when you saw that?

Sarah: Uh-huh. I cry at movies. Did you cry?

Holly: I don't cry at movies. What was it that made you cry?

Sarah: The last little speech. It was the ending scene when I realized Judd Nelson's character was getting in touch with the fact that he was human and could be taken care of by somebody—and that he was lonely, and that it was okay to admit that. That sort of broke it open. It made me cry, both because I thought it was really cool and because I wondered what in his life is going to help him sustain that. You know, he has an abusive father and all that sort of stuff. Is he going to be able to stay alive and stay passionate about things?

From this tender and vulnerable discussion of the movie, Kim brought us back to scripture, where a few distinct images of God began to emerge from the story.

God-Talk: Seeing the Scars

Two stories from Jesus's life, one of which had been discussed in a YTI class earlier in the day, surfaced.

> *Kim:* I thought of the woman who touches the hem of Jesus's garment. I have the idea that with anorexia and eating disorders, I would want to be healed. If there was just one thing that would make me all whole and better again—

> *Sarah:* Yeah, a healing touch. That's a great image.

> *Mary:* I'm thinking about Jesus being at the well. We were talking about that story this morning— how Jesus talked to this woman who he was never supposed to talk to, because she was in this subjugated category. He was not even supposed to talk to women, and especially not to *her*. It wasn't right for the perfect kid to be friends with the rebel. The social boundaries got crossed.

At this point, I affirmed the connections the girls were making. "With these stories in mind," I asked, "how do you see God in this story?"

Cathy became very animated.

Cathy: Well, the spirit of God was definitely inside of you when you saw the scars on Chris's arm and you thought, "What is this?" You could've overlooked them. Many people would have just dismissed them or thought he deserved them. But that perception— God was in that perception.

Dori: I like that idea. God is present in the compassion, in being able to see the scars.

Sarah: Just like in *The Breakfast Club*. That's what allowed them to transcend social boundaries.

Cathy: Their common element, their wound, brings them together.

When this engaging banter came to a pause, Sarah rolled her eyes, leaned back in her seat, exhaled deeply and said:

Sarah: This is fascinating to me. When I wrote this, I was thinking about who God was for me, and because of my issues with God, I would have said God was the distant or unreachable father here. Either my father or Chris's father. I'm used to seeing things in a more negative or pessimistic way. To hear you all immediately point to God as being in me, the spirit that was able to see the scars—I hadn't thought of it like that before. It's just a completely different way of seeing it, and it's helpful.

Cathy: Well, I think God is in the scars.

Dori: God is in the scars?

Kim: And your eyes, that you see them.

E: EXPLORE AHA! MOMENTS AND ENACT NEXT STEPS

When I noted the time and asked to move into the final part of the session, they were a little resistant. A strong feeling of celebration buzzed in the air: Sarah, an adult, expressed genuine appreciation for new insight the girls had given her. The session provided an emotional catharsis for her. Although these girls had been together in a group of sixty young people for two weeks, discussing topics of faith, this was the first time they had met together in an exclusively female space. In the previous ninety minutes, they had shared deeply on emotional and spiritual levels.

When we approached our closing moments, Kim had this to offer:

> *Kim:* I think what sticks with me most is that your friendship, later on, was based on this thing that had hurt you both and made you so uncomfortable. Your pain becomes the basis of an important friendship.

> *Cathy:* So many times we don't see the scars—

> *Dori:* The scars become the source of healing, the hem of the garment. When we find a way to see the scars, Chris no longer is the bane. He turns out to be the balm?

As this session ended, everyone wanted to linger. We spent the rest of their free time reflecting on what had just occurred and simply hanging out. Cathy mentioned how good it felt to be in the company of other girls. "Some talks you can only have with your girlfriends, like at a sleepover," someone said. That comment led me to name this process girlfriend theology!

I am grateful for moments like these, when a zone of safety provided a shift in the status quo of power dynamics. In this instance, young people led meaning making for themselves, grounded in their own life experiences. Adult participants welcomed this agency, affirming the new understandings that arose. The adults intentionally encouraged this shift, purposefully stepping back from the usual norms of adult power and privilege to allow younger voices to dominate the conversation.

I came to understand these moments of intentional power shift—along with dedicated time and space for people who experience similar kinds of oppression to make meaning "outside the gaze" of their oppressors—as a signature characteristic of girl/friend theology. This is what, across the decades of doing this work, keeps me committed to it. Yes, these moments can happen anywhere at anytime when attentive peers or adult allies walk alongside an organically arising moment in which someone finds liberatory, feminist consciousness. And it also happens in circles like these that are intentionally set aside to create the conditions for liberatory spiritual formation to take place

Girl/friend theology and other forms of democratizing spiritual practices contribute to the deconstruction of patriarchal, colonial, white supremacist, and hegemonic values that harm people and the planet. In addition to girls, what other oppressed groups of people might benefit from the creation of zones of safety, outside the gaze of their oppressors? What might be the lasting value of such temporary zones of safety? As we uproot negative images of God—such as that of a ruler or all-powerful father—we replace them with images that free us to imagine our agency, power, and resourcefulness. These new mental models support us in our personal healing and well-being, as well as in our collective efforts to shift culture in ways that affirm the agency, power, and resourcefulness of all people.

ECHOES OF FEMINIST THEOLOGY AND ASSERTIONS OF GIRLFRIEND THEOLOGY: SOLIDARITY, SACRAMENT, METAPHOR

In the last step of LIVE: E: Explore Aha! Moments and Enact Next Steps, this group touched on three theological themes: solidarity, sacrament, and metaphor.

In identifying God in the moment of perceiving another's oppression, they were echoing a major theme of liberation and *mujerista* theology as defined by the work of Ada María Isasi-Díaz (1996). She calls for North American churches to move from an ethic of charity to an ethic of solidarity and mutuality in their treatment of Latin Americans. The first step toward such a move, Isasi-Díaz writes, is crossing borders and making friendships. As Cathy mentioned in our discussion of Sarah's story, it is common to assume a person deserves the scars they hold, but Sarah instead found a way to be in solidarity with Chris's suffering. Modeling Jesus's compassion, Sarah chose not to blame the victim, but to see the scars as a sign of common suffering and an invitation to relationship. The participants affirmed God's presence in the compassion felt toward another person's wounds. In doing so, they uncovered the dynamics of solidarity as part of their impulse to navigate across social boundaries for the sake of deeper, more mutual understanding.

A second theological theme arising in our conversation is that of sacrament. In this story, our conversation danced around the fringe of an affirmation: that is, God is present not only in our compassion, but in the scars themselves. To see God's presence in the everyday is to experience an inbreaking of the holy into the profane. This is a sacramental moment in which "we have eyes to see and ears to hear" [Vogel and Vogel 1994, 20]. Significantly, in this case, it is a wound—an image deeply ingrained in Christian symbolism—that inspires this sacramental moment.

A third theological theme that surfaced in this story points back to McFague's work on metaphorical theology and father-God imagery. The fathers in this story—one distant and aloof, the other physically abusive—illustrate the argument of many feminist scholars that father language for God should be altogether abandoned. The metaphor of the father, for many people, can trigger painful memories of hierarchy, subordination, and patriarchal authoritarianism. As Roberta Bondi poignantly summarizes:

> The primary and earliest place we do learn about fatherhood, human and divine, is from our own fathers, but the fatherhood we learn about is not unfallen fatherhood. In the world of experience, because our own fathers were wounded, even when they long to, they never do perfectly image God's fatherhood. Without even meaning to, and sometimes even trying very hard not to, they have wounded us, their children, by the way they were fathers, just as we wound our own children, and so, without intending to, our fathers pass on a wounded image of God's fatherhood as well (Bondi 1995, 28).

Although we have seen how the image of God as father can be salvaged and invested with nonpatriarchal meaning, painful memories of earthly fathers point to the need—recognized by so many feminist and queer theologians—for alternative ways of naming and imagining God. While fully developing an alternative metaphor of God as friend, McFague points to numerous other generative images and their relational nature. The potential metaphors for God, she writes, are too various to enumerate: liberator, comrade, creator, mother, friend, rock, thunder, lover, brother, teacher, sister, light, fire, defender, sustainer, nurturer, advocate, and so on. The images which tumble from the mouths of those experiencing the liberating love of God are not meant *to describe God* so much as *to suggest the new quality of relationship* being offered. Hence, religious metaphors and the models that emerge are not pictures of God, but images of a relationship; as such, they are nonrestrictive, highly particular, and subject to ongoing revision and reimagination [McFague 1982, 165].

As Jesus identifies with the suffering of others through his life and death, Sarah identified with the suffering of another. In seeing Chris's scars, Sarah was, like Jesus, transcending social boundaries and entering into solidarity with another. Thus, eyes that see the scars—a primary image for God that surfaced from our conversation around Sarah's story—enter McFague's litany of "nonrestrictive and highly particular" metaphors for God that we invite into ongoing revision and reimagination [186]. In her model of God as friend, McFague draws attention to the imminent nature of God, echoing both Hannah's and Sarah's story sessions. She writes, "Rather than stressing the protection, comfort, and redemption of individuals *apart from* others and the world, the friendship model emphasizes sacrifice, support, and solidarity *with* others and the world. God is our friend who suffers with us as we work to bring about a better existence for suffering humanity" [186].

These two story sessions pull a thread of connection between four assertions of girl/friend theology: (2) God feels our pain and cries with us; (6) God is most fully alive (incarnated) in us when our eyes are open to the pain of others; (1) God is mysteriously omnipresent, but not magically omnipotent. Although we cannot explain it, God *is* at work within human tragedies to create healing potential. God may not fix things, but neither does God abandon us; and (7) church, at its best, is a community of compassion, a resource in our healing, and a potential agent of change in the world. Each of these assertions surfaced as we held Hannah's and Sarah's stories.

GOD-TALK IN THE MIDST OF VIOLENCE AND DEATH

In this chapter, through thick descriptions of two additional girl-friend theology sessions, the voices of young people spoke. They spoke through the stories themselves, through their group conversations, and through connecting their images to existing voices in written theology. The result is a meeting place—a site where adult theological meaning-making both informs and is informed by the voices of young people as they come of age.

In both of these sessions, adults made available their usable past as a potential resource in the lives of young women who deal with violence. This usable past slips out of tidy categories, such as literary or biblical. It lapses momentarily into the very personal. Taken together, perhaps it is best termed a "spiritual" usable past, because our spiritual selves integrate diverse resources—literary, personal, emotional, and biblical—to aid in our "whole-making"(Thurman 1986, 76)

Sarah entered the storytelling space vulnerably, bringing part of her intimate struggle with an eating disorder. As is often the case as we deal with the effects of grief, violence, or addictive behavior, we recover in bits and pieces, not all at once. Sarah, in sharing part of her process of recovery, met girls at the crossroads where adolescence and adulthood overlap. She did so without allowing the focus to center solely on her, but allowing the conversation to be about all of us, engaged together in God-talk among girlfriends.

Sometimes it seems as if only a miracle can counteract the centuries of male-centric bias and white-normativity within Christianity. Many people who enter into serious reflection on this tradition decide to leave it: the hurtful history seems too much to overcome. I do not blame them. However, my young colleagues in these two story circles encourage me that we can reclaim our tradition. We work small *miracles* by making new metaphors, salvaging fragments submerged by patriarchy. Transforming a tradition laden with a patriarchal bias requires these new metaphors. Girl/friend theology offers us these: God as a bent-over father crying tears of life and God as imminently present in the moment when our eyes are opened to another's scars.

In the process of voicing these metaphors, the young people did much more than create two new metaphors: they learned *how* to create them communally, from life experience, in a safe-enough place where doubt and critique of tradition can be steps toward transforming and embracing evolving tradition.

Frequently as I engage others in this playful, creative process, a discomfort arises: Is *any* metaphor for God okay? Are there limits on the ways we are free to name God through this method? Occasionally, an idea arises with which others disagree. In those moments, I welcome the nuances of the different interpretations, reminding that we do not all have to leave with the same conclusions. I remind participants that this is not a neutral exercise; it is biased toward a particular wisdom tradition that prioritizes liberation for those who've experienced oppression.

Was the image of God that surfaced freeing to people who've experienced oppression? Did our interpretations of scripture bend toward the ones Jesus would call the least of these? Did the metaphor for God emerge from scripture or uncover a new perspective on a sacred text? Did it bring forth a quiet, hidden, or submerged element of religious tradition? Did the image meaningfully intersect the stories and analyses of history's losers, rather than its winners?

Within these questions are four sources—scripture, tradition, experience, and reason. Known as John Wesley's quadrilateral, these four sources provide a way of measuring the ideas that surface, without creating new boundaries of what is "okay," but rather, trusting participants to the ongoing, collective work of finding the stories and images that call them to life.

In girl/friend theology circles, I found that erring on the side of inclusion works best. So much of mainstream Christianity in America continues to be censored through the lens of white, male interpretation. Loosening those interpretations and inviting ourselves into theological meaning making takes courage. History tells us we may be disregarded, or worse, excluded from community as heretical or unorthodox.

Taking heart from Starhawk, who weaves healing community in the midst of structural violence, I draw a wide net, welcoming the critical, unorthodox, or surprising images of God, even if they make me pause, turn to wonder, or feel uncomfortable.

CHAPTER SIX

DRAWING FROM OUR OWN DEEP WELLS

BORROWING WITH CARE ACROSS CULTURES AND TRADITIONS

Rilke was right when he said that God is to be found in our
roots. And there is no end to our sending them deeper.
—Gustavo Gutierrez, *We Drink from Our Own Wells:*
The Spiritual Journey of a People

I come from a land of strawberries, oranges, and adolescent awakenings.

I am thirteen years old, lying on a single bed a few inches away from a screened window that opens onto a dark spring night. As I lie awake, strains of music float across the yard, the garden, the pasture, and the pond, tracing a path I know well in daylight. I sit up and look out the window, peering in the darkness toward the source of this guitar music, accentuated every few minutes with a loud shout and an outbreak of applause. I see only faintly the lights of the party, dimly piercing the darkness. I lie back down and listen to the music, slipping through the window in my mind, bare feet first collecting dew from the yard, then deep rich soil from the garden. In this imaginary journey, I slip between two pieces of barbed wire and jump over the drainage ditch, following the light and the music across the wide pastures and around the edge of the pond to the other world that lies about a quarter mile from my bed. This world of farmworkers—immigrants from Mexico—who come to my rural neighborhood each winter to pick strawberries arouses my curiosity. I study Spanish in my spare time and befriend the sons and daughters who ride the school bus with me.

I am seventeen, eighteen and nineteen, and on the edges of my maturing thought process, I hold an awareness of injustice, an awareness of arbitrary borders separating "us" and "them." During these years, through fits and starts of overheard conversations and a subversive teacher or two, I came into a space between two meanings: the meanings of childhood, cloaked in family and sheltered by views I did not know I can question, and the inchoate meanings of adulthood, moments of awakening to political and spiritual realities and an awareness of the choice to question, to criticize, to think for myself.

When I look back on my own adolescence, I see a white girl, growing up in a modest ranch house in the middle of an orange grove in Central Florida with some awareness of race and class, but very little sense of my own ethnicity. My parents—dad, a social worker and, mom, a registered nurse—were both first generation college-educated. This was significant because my dad—a first generation Ukrainian immigrant—saw education as the only way out of the difficulties that plagued his childhood. Despite knowing I was half Ukrainian, I had only a little curiosity about that lineage until 2018, when I began exploring an ancestral framework for healing cultural wounds.[1]

---

1   I wrote about this process in the essay "Learning to Walk with My Ancestors" in the journal *Religious Education* 117, no. 2 (2022): 99–101, which can be accessed here: https://www.tandfonline.com/doi/abs/10.1080/00344087.2022.2060467.

From this perspective, I embrace my thirteen-year-old self with compassion. Curious, drawn to a culture not her own, she grew into a feisty eighteen-year-old journalist, who argued with editors about the importance of writing about the plight of the immigrant farm-workers—not just the wealthy white landowners—when an early frost devastated the strawberry crops.

But the way I exoticized my adolescent attraction to the world of the farmworkers looks like racism to me now. When I was a young feminist practical theologian envisioning better models of spiritual formation and religious education, "slipping through the barbed wire fence" sufficed as a metaphor for borrowing from my Womanist, *Mujerista*, and Asian-feminist sisters in the construction of new models of spiritual formation and religious education. I used the image of border crossing to write about borrowing images, artifacts, and stories from cultures not my own. Now, I see that metaphor as trivializing the actual danger of people who cross borders at great risk every day. This awareness reveals the white privilege I repeat-edly learn to acknowledge, sit with, and resolve to continue facing with honesty.

Across the decades, many women and men of color risked invest-ing in me. They accompanied me on my journey of unlearning the racism inherent in my upbringing. I am grateful for their gifts of time and energy, just as I am grateful for the work of Black, Indigenous, and other authors of color. All have been worthy mentors in the on-going work of dismantling whiteness in the larger world and with-in myself. Because of the gifts of their perspectives, I am able to critique my former scholarship as limited and falling short of goals to which I aspire today. To excise this book of that moment, however, seems intellectually dishonest, and so I retain it, choos-ing to let it remind me of my limited perspective and to commit to ongoing learning.

Today, I look to a new metaphor: I draw from the wells of my Ukrainian ancestors to find stories, images, and artifacts to help me live into a better future. In doing girl/friend theology, I also borrow with care from the deep wells of others, particularly Womanists, *Mujerista*, and Asian-Feminists. Drawing from our own deep wells—a metaphor Peruvian liberation theologian Gustavo Gutierrez borrows from Bernard of Clairvaux—offers an apt description of what I hope to practice here as I borrow with care across cultures [Gutierrez 1984].

Welcoming an expansive palette of images, voices, and stories from multiple contexts around the globe is necessary if we are to invite the creation of new theologies with deep roots for the sake of healing the world's pervasive wounds. Liberatory or emancipatory theologies—those that prioritize the most vulnerable people and critique dominant mental models—can help young people find agency and resilience in the face of personal and collective struggle. Spiritual practices that connect us to a bigger story can serve as an antidote to despair, presenting a deep reservoir of resources for creating a future where there is room enough for all to flourish.

In chapter 4, I showed how autobiographical stories tracing resistance to gender oppression can become part of a robust usable past. I wove reflections on these autobiographies with Womanist theology, modeling how these sources can aid the feminist education and spiritual practice of young people. If we can glimpse ourselves reflected in such stories, we can tease out images of God, self and others that help us create more life-sustaining theologies in our own blood and bones. In this chapter, themes from *Mujerista* and Asian-feminist theologies speak to gender oppression across and beyond their specific cultures of origin. Because I integrate Womanist theology more thoroughly throughout the whole of this project, I do not look at it as closely here. In touching on these three perspectives and highlighting the particular gifts they bring to my practice of girl/friend theology, I hope to spark readers' creativity toward multiple theological perspectives not named here, even and especially newer emancipatory theologies that are ever emerging.

MUJERISTA THEOLOGY: CONTEXT, METHODS, THEMES

Politician and activist Maria Antonietta Berriozábal tells a story about her adolescence: She grew up in a Mexican-American neighborhood and household in the southwestern United States. Here, she experienced connection to her family, God, and her wider community as resembling a shawl, woven of many threads and wrapped around her. This shawl gave her life meaning and orientation. It helped define her vocation as being in service to the community. As she left junior high school and entered a high school outside her neighborhood, she found many of the treasures valued by her culture and community now largely ignored in normative, white, American culture. The resulting identity crisis caused her to doubt the dearly held beliefs that had given her life meaning[Berriozábal 2012].

Ethnographic research conducted by the American Association of University Women (AAUW) in the 1990s documents similar journeys. In a 1996 study, the AAUW identified girls, usually of Latin American descent, whom they called "border crossers" because of the involuntary cultural border crossing required of them. The success of these girls, as they wade through the difficult adolescent waters of junior high and high school, depends largely upon the similarities or differences between the school's culture and the girls' culture of origin. If the school culture values the treasures of her community, the girl will usually find a wide arena in which she can carve out a successful niche. If, however, the school culture values the dominant culture's norms to the exclusion of cultural diversity, the girl might be labeled a troublemaker and will find successful avenues of achievement severely limited [AAUW 1996, 31].

In the following section, I explore the context, theological method, and key themes of *Mujerista* theology as it emerges in the writings of theologian Ada María Isasi-Díaz, a significant leader in its development. I do so mindful that she is one of many voices adding to the plurality that is *Mujerista* theology. I also do so mindful of young people who, in the process of growing up, must necessarily cross borders into racist and violent territory.

HISTORICAL CONTEXT OF MUJERISTA THEOLOGY

Mujerista theology emerged during the 1970s and 1980s, along with many other theologies undertaking the task of unmasking the white, Western, androcentric bias of dominant US theology and white feminist theologies. Acknowledging their roots in liberation theology, Hispanic feminists in the United States expressed long-held feelings of marginalization within the largely white, middle-class circles of feminist theology. They voiced their own theological method, visions of God and the church, and biblical interpretation as they centered race, ethnicity, gender, social class, and, sometimes, sexual orientation. This movement included women primarily of Mexican, Puerto Rican, and Cuban descent and sought to claim a common identity among these groups, while not erasing the differences each brought based on their nation of origin and other socioeconomic factors.

Isasi-Díaz, who migrated to the United States from Cuba as a teenager, became a primary leader of this grassroots development. She led retreats of Hispanic women and articulated a vision of theology as a liberatory praxis of Hispanic women oppressed by ethnic prejudice, sexism, and poverty in the United States [Ruether 1998]. This vision grew out of Isasi-Díaz's formative experiences as a Catholic nun serving for three years among a community of the poor in Lima, Peru.

Her liberatory praxis includes: (1) enabling Latinas to understand the struggles of their daily lives within the context of the many structures that oppress them and stand in need of change; (2) helping Latinas to imagine and define their preferred future; and (3) challenging Latinas to understand how the prevailing oppressive systems in society—including organized religion—have internalized within them attitudes of self-effacement that contribute to their sense of powerlessness and lack of voice. This three-part analysis encourages Latinas to engage communally in the fight or *la lucha*, the empowering struggle for the liberation of all people. For Isasi-Diaz, *la lucha* becomes a source of hope as Latina women begin to challenge that which would otherwise require their servitude or self-abnegation. The result is a strong sense of moral agency accompanied by communal and individual self-worth [Isasi-Diaz 1995].

In addition to this primary goal of empowering and enabling Latinas, *Mujerista* theology has a secondary goal: to effect change, contributing to a refashioning of the mainline theologies that currently support the status quo in North American church and society.

THEOLOGICAL METHOD OF MUJERISTA THEOLOGY

In *Mujerista* theology, biblical exegesis is a communal task in which the word of God, *la palabra de Dios*, refers not to what is written in the text, but to how the stories and their applications aid in struggles for survival. Through continued resistance to traditional or fundamentalist interpretations of scripture, Ada Maria Isasi-Diaz encourages *mujeristas* to discover the Bible as a wealth of new information providing stories that serve as interpretive keys in the struggle for liberation [Isasi-Diaz 1995, 161]. Literary and historical analysis of the text serves to uncover details of the biblical story that resonate with the contemporary lives of Latinas. For example, Shiphrah and Puah, the midwives who foreshadow the Exodus event, serve as models: They are risk-taking women whose defiance and resistance parallel the strength of Latina women using their moral agency to shape the future of their people.

Mujerista theology uses techniques of qualitative research to place the lived experiences of Latinx women at the center of the theological task. The qualitative research tools Isasi-Díaz draws upon are ethnography and meta-ethnography.

Ethnography refers to the gathering of stories, primarily through intensive retreats and interviews. The retreats involve interconnected movements of storytelling, analysis, liturgy, and strategizing. The goal for Isasi-Dias was to hear women articulate the events of and the meanings arising from their everyday lives—that which constitutes their common and shared reality. This process hears women into speech as it provides a forum for women to reflect upon their lives and discover meanings communally, thus developing their individual and collective voices [(Isasi-Diaz 1995)]. In addition to retreats and interviews, *Mujerista* theology uses other ethnographic techniques, such as participant observation in popular religious rituals and practices occurring in the everyday lives of women.

Meta-ethnography refers to the interpretation of these ethnographic accounts. As the theologian reviews the accounts of retreats and interviews, key metaphors and themes emerge. She notes commonalities and differences arising from the women's stories and process of meaning-making. These key themes become generative words that resonate with and express the life situations of Latinx women. These words are then "translated" by the writer/theologian. As a central part of this task, the theologian returns these translations to the community to check their authenticity. In this way, the method stays rooted in the community, remaining in a dialogic tension between the professional theologian and the lay theologians—women to whom she is accountable. Isasi-Díaz calls this a joint search for understanding and meaning.

This method provides a critique to dominant theological norms by beginning with the lived experience of women, rather than beginning with the understandings and practices considered to have important religious significance. Thus, *Mujerista* theology becomes a subversive act that allows new theological questions to arise. Isasi-Díaz provides a compelling example of this by contrasting views of Jesus within Latin American male theology. While some would ask how Jesus can be presented to make him more central and accessible to common folk, *Mujerista* theologians would ask why the majority of Latinx women do not relate to Jesus in the first place. This move results in a focusing of attention on the centrality of Mary within the popular religious lives of women. By asking a different question, new understandings about the presence of the divine in everyday life emerge.

Isasi-Díaz approaches the Bible by asking how it can enhance the moral agency of Latinx women, centering the struggle for liberation as the lens through which to view the Bible. The Bible becomes a strategic tool for women to define their preferred future. Thus, in their interpretation and appropriation of the Bible, *Mujerista* theologians seek stories that can serve as sources of hope. Biblical depictions of persons, including Jesus, who struggled for survival become the canon within the canon, helping Latinas define a heritage of resistance to domination and oppression.

Patrick Reyes, a practical theologian of Mexican-American roots, pays homage to his *Mujerista* colleagues and ancestors in his book *Nobody Cries When We Die*. Reyes significantly expands on the theme of *la lucha*, using his own life experience growing up in Salinas, California to focus on the community, his vocation to survive, and the ways his grandmother called him to life [Reyes 2018]. He applies this theme to address toxic masculinity and cultural domination within his context, which is helpful to me as I imagine girl/friend theology widening its focus to multiple forms of gender oppression alive in our midst.

THEMES OF MUJERISTA THEOLOGY

Three key themes of *Mujerista* theology emerge as necessary correctives to theology in North American churches and as helpful in the context of girl/friend theology. They are *lo cotidiano*, mutuality and solidarity, and a high anthropology.

Lo Cotidiano. *Lo cotidiano* refers to the starting point of *Mujerista* theology—the lived experience of Latinx women. As well as being a descriptive term, it refers to an interpretive, or hermeneutical, task and sets up the foundational stance of *Mujerista* theology.

Descriptively, *lo cotidiano* refers not only to the daily chores associated with caring for families and maintaining households, but also to an analysis of the various systems of class, race, and gender oppression that affect the daily lives of women. Relationships of family and community, systems of authority, and expressions of faith are part of this daily lived experience.

As part of the hermeneutical task, *lo cotidiano* refers to processes that shape Latina thought, interpretation, and action. These are necessarily subjective, as Latina women's perceptions of the world are not all the same. It is important to acknowledge these differences, rather than mask them. Thus, *lo cotidiano* is constantly shifting—a transitory and subjective articulation of events as they occur close to home in the struggle to put food on the table, find jobs, move relatives across the border, and raise children. It is not an objective, removed, or abstract hermeneutical category.

Lastly, *lo cotidiano* is a way of knowing, an epistemology. It has to do with claiming women's daily experience—varied, complex, and infused with difference—as the starting point of shaping reality. This means "rescuing" what has been deemed unimportant in traditional theological systems. Daily lived experience, traditionally seen as a trivial and untrustworthy epistemological source, becomes the primary source of authentic relationship to the divine. This is a subversive act, making possible the reinterpretation of scripture and tradition from an admittedly subjective and provisional point of view [Isasi-Díaz 1996, 65–73].

This theme provides especially important insight for girl/friend theology. Young people's everyday lives are not trivial. Sharing the story of sexual harassment on the bus, a hurtful racial micro-aggression, or a history of familial violence may be the starting place for finding a reliable hope. Acknowledging and addressing such pieces of everyday life in spaces constructed with care for one another is the necessary first step in constructing ongoing, living, relevant religious traditions and life-sustaining spiritual practices. Engaging such a process, young people become organic intellectuals who reflect critically on their everyday lives, finding moral agency and means of resistance to oppression.

Mutuality and Solidarity. Isasi-Díaz proposes a shift in the way mainstream theology approaches ethical behavior. Traditionally, the church has seen charity as the appropriate Christian ethical behavior. She proposes that, in order for mutuality to exist between the oppressed and the oppressors, this must change. The appropriate Christian ethical response must be solidarity—specifically, understanding the interconnections between the rich and the poor, the oppressed and the oppressor. She defines solidarity as both a theory and a strategy.

Solidarity is the understanding that allows us to see all humanity as intrinsically linked, meaning the privileges of some are connected to the oppression of others. As strategy, solidarity implies forming relationships of mutuality between the oppressed and the oppressors. In these relationships, we may develop a critical awareness of the ways in which our own daily lives and actions contribute to the oppression and domination of others. As we listen to oppressed communities, those of us with privilege of any sort may enter the struggle for liberation alongside those most directly affected by structures that oppress.

The shift from charity to solidarity is an example of one way *Mujerista* theology alters theological categories within and beyond a Latinx frame of reference. This shift is essential to dismantling the legacy of imperialism for which Christianity is responsible (Jennings 2020). It is especially important that those engaged in ministry and spiritual formation with young people in North American faith communities find ways to bring this corrective into our practice. Understanding the ways in which *Mujerista* theologians welcome the presence of those who join in a community of solidarity enables white North American Christians to move away from the responses of guilt and sympathy, toward more helpful stances of solidarity and mutuality. It also helps us affirm youth who claim their agency in dismantling the oppressions that negatively affect their lives and the world.

High Anthropology. Isasi-Díaz articulates a high anthropology and a low Christology. She rejects the notion that Jesus's suffering was greater than all other human suffering. For *Mujeristas*, suffering is not the central motif of the Christian story; it is rather *la lucha*, the struggle against such suffering. The party, or *fiesta*, occurring in the midst of life's struggles, celebrates ongoing resistance to the causes of suffering. *La fiesta* celebrates the community of solidarity, that which energizes the ongoing struggle.

Isasi-Díaz uses the powerful phrase *permítanme hablar*, which means "allow me to speak," to articulate her high anthropology. Unless Latinx women's voices are heard and received, dominant structures will continue to undermine their humanity. Unless they come to value their own stories, their own voices, their own realities, and their own theological formulations, they may continue to internalize dominant culture's objectification of their body/selves. Thus, *Mujerista* anthropology is "from within" and "from below," as it centers not on an abstract view of humanity but on a particularized context.

I share with Isasi-Díaz this high anthropology and lift up the importance of *permítanme hablar* in the lives of young people who are struggling to create identity amidst oppressive forces. Girl/friend theology prioritizes the voices of young people claiming identities-in-the-making. Significant ideas and images about God will emerge from these contexts. These ideas and images are crucial to updating the archaic and often harmful theologies inherited from past generations. As opposed to traditional religious education models, which begin with scripture and move toward life experience, girl/friend theology moves in the opposite direction, from the ground up. Thus, it is "from below" and "from within."

BORROWING FROM OUR ONE ANOTHER'S DEEP WELLS

Making connections between *Mujerista* theology and girl/friend theology reveals why careful borrowing from one another's deep wells matters. One goal of girl/friend theology is to create a feminist method of religious education and spiritual practice for young people who come from varying social and cultural contexts. Therefore, it must take into account the theologies arising from people who reflect varying races, ethnicities, classes, and sexual orientations. An appreciative encounter with *mujerista* theology contributes to a wider understanding of what it means to be a feminist in contemporary American culture.

A second goal is to allow those young people who inherit privileges of race, class, ability, or ethnicity to be able to critique the dominant culture in which they find themselves and to begin to critique this privilege as part of their call to live ethically, in right relationship with others. In order to critique dominant culture, they must be aware of cultural forms that provide correctives to Western, white, patriarchal structure. *Mujerista* theology provides examples of cultural norms that value everyday lives, stress the importance of community, lift up the potential of humans, and invite the formation of coalitions.

Adopting themes from *Mujerista* theology entails relating its historical context. It is important not to transplant the concept of *lo cotidiano*, for instance, into a middle-class North American context, without rooting this image within an oppressed community. Borrowing across cultures calls us to a heightened awareness of the histories of cultural looting. Along with that comes a heightened commitment to borrow with permission, mutuality, and care.

ASIAN-FEMINIST THEOLOGY: CONTEXT, METHOD, THEMES

When Asian-feminist theologians turn a critical eye toward Western theology, they name many of the same realities that feminists around the world expose in Eurocentric, neo-orthodox methods of speaking about God and humanity, but they do so from a perspective that is uniquely positioned in their experiences of gender oppression within Asian contexts [Chung 1990]. Two central critiques in-

192

clude Western theology's exclusive reliance on biblical paradigms and its hegemony over the definitions of norms and categories of theology.

An enormous amount of diversity exists within Asian-feminist writings. While most Western feminist theologians share a cultural and religious background rooted in the three Abrahamic traditions, Asian-feminist theologians, "despite certain common cultural biases, have extremely diverse histories, religions, cultures, and traditions" (Chung 1990, 7). I refer specifically to the work of two foremothers of Asian-feminist theology, Korean theologian Hyun Kyng Chung and Hong Kong-born Kwok Pui Lon, in what follows.

HISTORICAL CONTEXT AND THEOLOGICAL METHOD OF ASIAN-FEMINIST THEOLOGY

In the mid-1980s, Asian women began publishing critiques of Western theology and male-dominated Asian liberation theologies. A leader in this movement, Chung identified three major settings that were central to the emergence of a feminist, liberation-oriented theological consciousness among Asian women. Those settings were the Christian Conference of Asia, the Ecumenical Association of Third World Theologians (EATWOT) and the Asian women's theological journal, *In God's Image* [Chung 1990].

Asian-feminist theologies grow out of stories—stories set in common, everyday experiences of life. This method of doing theology, although implicit in many liberation theologies, receives explicit articulation from Asian feminists. The clearest articulation of this methodology comes from the Women's Committee of the EATWOT. Chung describes this method as three circular steps: storytelling, critical social analysis, and theological reflection. [Chung 1990, 104–109].

Step One: Storytelling. Kwok, whose scholarship focuses on feminist and postcolonial theology, writes that Indian, Burmese, Japanese, and Chinese women all have a "treasure chest" of lullabies, songs, myths, and stories that give them a sense of identity and a vision for the future. Opening this treasure chest is the first step to doing theology, she writes. At EATWOT gatherings and writings, the storytelling step begins with women from diverse backgrounds listening carefully to one another as they relate the particularities of their lived experiences. Stories of family resilience, domestic violence, political activism, survival of sexual abuse, and resistance to forms of cultural and religious imperialism, for example, serve as the starting point for asking questions about God's presence and activity in the world.

The power of these stories lies in their tangible nature. They reflect concrete life experience rather than abstract metaphysical concepts. This embodied historiography methodology emerges from an understanding of history as a construct that leaves out the stories of the oppressed. Behind the objective truths of written history lie hidden realities, which are exposed as Asian women tell their stories and move into acts of solidarity. Embodied historiography invites the whole person, immersed in the complex web of political, social, economic, and personal factors that determine her options in life.

Step Two: Critical Social Analysis. Sharing stories leads to the second step in this theological method: critical social analysis, which involves looking intently at the larger picture. What is going on politically, economically, and socially that shapes this story? In a story about sexual abuse, for example, questions concerning patriarchal culture and the harm it inflicts on women's bodies emerge. In the story of a woman whose exposure to Christian missionaries robbed her of her native spirituality, questions of cultural bias and hegemonic religious practices emerge. When the larger contexts of personal stories are examined, they may reveal multiple layers of gender oppression, economic exploitation, and social discrimination. This step exposes the cultural and psychological patterns that perpetuate women's oppression. It is a process of conscientization, of bringing to awareness interlocking systems and enlarging the vision of women engaged in struggle at the grassroots level.

Step Three: Theological Reflection. After taking a critical look at the social influences that set the stage for the story, this method moves to theological reflection. Chung names four sources for Asian women's theological reflection: women's lived experience, engaged subjective reason that takes sides, tradition, and scripture. God is not revealed outside of humanity, but rather within the Asian woman's experience of suffering and hope. The Bible is part of this step, but only as appropriated from the starting point of lived experience.

The goal is to bring Asian women's lives into dialogue with the traditions of Christianity. It is a practical theology, one that does not perpetuate the age-old interpretations of the Bible that are laden with Western assumptions, patriarchy, and colonialism. Rather, it selects the stories that give meaning to women's lives, critically examining inherited interpretations. Chung notes that this last step in the theological method is called *hyun jang* theology, which means it centers around the places where historically meaningful events are transpiring.

In this theological reflection, ethical commitments are necessarily intertwined. The litmus test of this method is whether it contributes to the authentic personhood of women, fosters just communities, and develops caring and respectful attitudes toward all of creation. Chung determines if a theology is "good theology" by discerning whether it untangles the Korean woman's *han* (the sin of internalized self-hatred) and thus liberates her from bondage. If it enables *han* to continue to accumulate, it is bad theology, regardless of what other purposes it might serve to the church or its traditions [Chung 1990, 42–43].

THEMES OF ASIAN-FEMINIST THEOLOGY

Kwok critiques traditional Western theology for its focus on a narrow and mystified view of the Bible. Although acknowledging the power and authority of stories found there, she asserts that religious imagination based on the Bible alone is apt to exclude women's experiences [Kwok 1994]. Among the classic trappings of Christianity that missionaries brought with them to Asian cultures was the stress on studying Hebrew, Greek, Latin, and German, while denying the importance of indigenous linguistic heritages. Further, the theologies of Augustine, Aquinas, Tillich, Barth, and other European men defined the implicit norms of theology, setting the categories in which Asian theologians were trained to function. Scholars of Asian origin who trained in Europe and North America were forced to spend most of their time trying to understand a spiritual reality through concepts and symbols that did not resonate in their own hearts and minds. This forced assimilation of Western theology, Kwok argues, was a disservice to her people and the whole church.

When integration between the indigenous and the transplanted takes place, Kwok maintains, a plurality of voices replaces the unified discourse of traditional theology. New norms of theology emerge as the practices of communities within their particular struggles for liberation. Chung argues that women, especially, must reclaim their right to speak about God and generate new symbols from their own experience, thus participating fully in the process of myth- and symbol-making. To this end, she writes:

> Only when we Asian women start to consid-
> er our everyday concrete life experiences as the
> most important source for building the religious

meaning structures for ourselves shall we be free
from all imposed religious authority (Chung 1990, 5).

Understanding the three-step method of Asian-feminist theology as practiced by EATWOT enriches what we do in girl/friend theology. Just as Chung asks, "Who is Jesus?" and "Who is Mary?" from an Asian woman's perspective, girl/friend theology asks questions such as these from the perspective of culturally situated young people in the midst of shaping their identities. In both cases, the answers contribute to a refashioning of Christian symbols and images. The four-part method of story theology used in girl/friend theology shares many of the assumptions underlying Asian feminists' three-step circular process of storytelling, critical social analysis, and theological reflection. To reveal these connections, we turn to three significant themes of emancipatory theology exemplified in Asian-feminist theology: (1) theology begins with sharing stories of lived experience; (2) theology is communal, rather than individual work; and (3) theology connects sin with structural causes of oppression through critical reflection on history, systems, and power.

Theology begins with sharing stories of lived experience

Just as "the Indians, the Burmese, the Japanese, and the Chinese all have stories that give meaning and orientation" to their lives, North American young people—specifically those who've experienced racial or gender oppression—have stories, particular to their subcultures, that shape their approach to life. These stories, for those who have experienced trauma, violence, or marginalization, will often be tales of surviving struggle, pain, suffering, and oppression. For Asian women, these repositories may be lullabies and folktales; young people in the US might find these themes arising from hip-hop, Tik Tok, graffiti, skateboard performance, street drama, spoken word poetry, and other forms of personal narrative.

Unlocking these deeply textured, culturally imbued treasure chests of stories—shining a flashlight on these gems so they show up more clearly as such—is a step in helping youth understand the realities in which they live and in helping them create ever-more life-giving realities to inhabit. A spiritual practice for young people that draws out the value, beauty, and innovation of their own cultural artifacts could be lifesaving. It is in keeping with the theological tradition of Asian feminists that values meaning-making from the bottom up and seeks to make visible hidden realities.

Theology Is Communal Rather Than Individual Work

The Asian-feminist motif of God as community-in-relationship, allows women to move out of individualism into a stance of honoring their responsibility and connectedness to the community. Spiritual practices that support the individual's ability to rely upon others as sources of meaning-making in their lives embodies this image of God as community-in-relationship.

This relational understanding calls forth images of God that expand the ones we typically inherit within hyper-individualistic Western cultures. It can free young people to imagine how they experience God/Creator/Universe/Spirit arising from their concrete, everyday realities as relational human beings caught up in the web of friendship, family, romantic relationship, and the larger world. As Chung writes, "In this image of God as the community in relationship, there is no place for only one solitary, all-powerful God who sits on the top of the hierarchical power pyramid and dominates all other living beings"(1990, 49). As young people adapt this understanding of relationships and community, we could expect liberating images of God to emerge, adding to the creation of the "many theologies" Kwok celebrates within Asian theological contexts. As theology becomes the product of the whole community, a new understanding of the word "theologian" emerges. Young people creating meaning out of their daily experiences might claim for themselves the role of theologian, coming to understand themselves as stakeholders in the emergence of new, lifegiving forms of Christian tradition.

Theology connects sin with structural causes of oppression

A theology that emphasizes personal sin often places blame for oppression on the victims themselves. Women and girls exiting fundamentalism report being made to feel at fault for their abuse at the hands of male clergy [Klein 2018; Easter 2016]. A young woman's clothing choice, her body language, or the very structure of physiology is sometimes interpreted—in theologies emphasizing personal sin—as being the cause of the sexual misconduct of others.

In contrast, Asian-feminist and other liberatory theologies engage critical reasoning that takes sides with those suffering oppression, looking to find the source of oppression within the larger context of structural systems of patriarchy and other supremacies. These emancipatory theologies locate sin and evil in economic, political, and social realities that women come to identify as having oppressive effects in their lives. As Asian women come to name these systems, they can mobilize to change them, while at the same time freeing themselves from internalized oppression.

At the onset of adolescence, young people begin to be able to think abstractly. The developing brain's ability to do formal operational thinking allows the emergence of critical thinking skills. A young person can now critique the familial and cultural norms they were born into. A young person begins to experience connections between alternative versions of history, diverse perspectives, and larger systems, thus forming the basis for understanding of and active resistance to systems of oppression.

BORROWING FROM ONE ANOTHER'S DEEP WELLS

In girl/friend theology, peers and adult mentors become companions in the process of critical thinking, increasing the individual's and the group's capacity to shift theological understandings, for example, from an emphasis on personal sin to an understanding of corporate sin and structural oppression. This theological shift allows individuals to name their participation in sinful structures and in internalizing oppression, while mobilizing themselves to be agents of change to dismantle those structures. In a move similar to the liberatory process of Asian-feminist theology, spiritual practices emerge as a potential support to sustain a young person's discovery of meaning and purpose.

Spiritual practices such as girl/friend theology can become the site of new mental models about God, self, and community. These new mental models support one's mental well-being, as one glimpses a sense of purpose where there was meaninglessness or a sense of community where once there was social isolation. Even if momentary, these glimpses can provide sustenance for personal resilience, as well as emerging activism, as a young person discerns their own agency as a change maker around social ills such as structural racism, climate devastation, and gun violence. Participants in girl/friend theology frequently remark "we are not alone" and "we are not alone in this work!" They recognize the gift of being part of a community and a sense of "something more" as a force in the world which accompanies them in world-building and world-repair. This connection between the individual and the communal, the personal and the political, comes into sharper focus when we see it happening among diverse women, from varying contexts, around the world. Drawing with care from one another's deep wells makes visible the interconnecting themes that arise from similar yet distinct communities resisting gender oppression as they experience it in their lived realities.

WOMANIST THEOLOGY: ITS CONTEXTS, METHODS, AND THEMES

Of the three women's emancipatory theologies I use as key sources for girl/friend theology, Womanist theology is the one I most thoroughly integrate into my theory and practice. Because I draw from this source elsewhere, my emphasis on it here will be brief.

HISTORICAL CONTEXT OF WOMANIST THEOLOGY

Linda Moody provides a helpful summary of the emergence of Womanist theology, dating its articulation to Audre Lorde's 1979 letter to Mary Daly. In this letter, Lorde critiqued Daly's generalizations of white, middle-class women's experience as being normative for all women [Lorde 1996]. Womanist theology is critical of white feminist thought that does not acknowledge the interconnectedness of race, class, and gender. It also critiques Black male theology for its gender bias. Womanist theology offers distinct methodologies and biblical hermeneutics based on sources previously unacknowledged as authoritative (or made altogether invisible) within Western theology. Those sources include Black women's contemporary experiences, the narratives of enslaved people, biographies of African American women, and African American spirituals.

A defining moment in the historical emergence of Womanist theology was Alice Walker's four-part definition of "womanist" in her 1983 book *In Search of Our Mothers' Gardens*. Based on this definition, to be a Womanist means: (1) To act grown-up, responsible, and in charge; (2) to love other women, sexually and/or non-sexually and to be committed to the survival and wholeness of all people,

201

male and female; (3) to love music, dance, the moon, the Spirit, food, roundness, struggle, the folk, and to love yourself, regardless; and (4) to be Womanist is to feminist, as purple is to lavender. This evocative definition provided a common point of reflection for foremothers of Womanist theology [Walker 1983, xi–xii].

THEOLOGICAL METHOD OF WOMANIST THEOLOGY

Based on Walker's four-part definition, Delores Williams articulates four methodological principles of Womanist theology. First, the methodology is intentionally dialogical, consciously seeking to remain in conversation with diverse communities while continuing to focus on those struggling against multiple layers of oppression, such as that experienced by women of color and their children. Second, it is liturgically informed, using the ritual life of the historically Black church tradition in the US as a source for theological reflection, while critiquing the homophobia, sexism, and classism found there. Third, Womanist theological methodology seeks to be didactic, reshaping the ethical and moral life of the church and society based on its critiques. Last, the methodology is committed to both reason and experience as sources of imagery and metaphor. In addition, Womanists believe that theology should engage ethical practice and reject divisions between the sacred and the sexual.

BIBLICAL HERMENEUTICS OF WOMANIST THEOLOGY

Womanist theologian Jacquelyn Grant approaches the Bible with the question, "Who do Womanists say that Jesus Christ is?" For her, Black women's own experience of oppression and God's witness as a liberator within that context provide the lens through which to read and interpret the Bible. In this way, Womanists hold in tension two sources of revelation—the Bible and Black women's experience. Through this hermeneutic, Jesus emerges as a highly personal manifestation of God, one who feels pain, knows of the struggle, and provides comfort in the midst of oppression [Grant 1989].

For Delores Williams, the liberatory acts of God must be seen alongside the biblical witness of times when God does not act as a liberator. The story of Hagar—a surrogate mother and enslaved woman who is banished to the wilderness—offers a paradigm of survival, not of liberation. Hagar's story provides a point of critique, acknowledging that God does not always liberate. Some people, most often the ones with whom the biblical writers *do not identify*, are left in subordinate positions—as is Hagar [Williams 1995].

In this paradigm of struggle and survival in the wilderness, Williams sees many parallels between Black people's experiences, as reflected in the narratives of enslaved people, and the experiences of Black Americans in contemporary society, where oppression continues despite the promises of the civil rights movement. In light of these parallels, the tendency of Black male theology to focus on the liberating God of the Exodus falls short. Hagar encounters God in the wilderness, a place where one learns to survive and where one is transformed. Born of this critical biblical hermeneutic is the need for Womanists to turn to extra-biblical sources—especially West African sources—to provide what woman-inclusive correctives to non-liberating aspects of scripture and tradition.

KEY THEMES OF WOMANIST THEOLOGY

Among the many generative themes within this body of literature, three arise as particularly crucial in integrating womanist thought into a feminist model of religious education for young people. Having discussed these three themes individually in previous chapters, we summarize them briefly here.

The first is Alice Walker's insistence on acknowledging the presence of adolescent girls. Walker's definition of Womanist, which describes the experience of girls as "acting womanish," serves as a badly needed corrective to white liberal feminist theology and to the theological perspective found in some mainline white churches in North America [Walker 1983, xi–xii]. For the most part, the experience of adolescent girls—as well as young LGBTQ+ people—has been invisible in these realms.

The second is bell hooks's concept of homeplace as a site of resistance. White feminists often portray domestic life as a sphere of menial labor and drudgery. In contrast, hooks reminds us of the importance of homeplace for Black women: it is where survival skills are passed down from parents to their offspring. By reframing domestic life as a position of power rather than subservience, Black women create "a way outta no way" to ensure the survival of their people [hooks, 41–49].

The third is Katie Cannon's concept of "unctuousness as a virtue," drawn from the life and works of Zora Neale Hurston. Cannon builds upon Alice Walker's definition of unctuousness as "the ability to act sincere in the most insincere situations" and a "feistiness about life which no one can knock out" in her analysis of Hurston's life. Working during the Harlem Renaissance, Hurston was often forced to cater to the whims of the white patrons who funded her ethnographic research in her Black-led central Florida hometown. There, Hurston gathered in rich detail the stories, songs, and survival strategies of her people. Using the unctuousness instilled in her by her mother, Hurston was able to maneuver within systems of white oppression, carving out enough room to create a lasting cultural repository. Cannon sees Hurston's life as an example of what it means to live to one's full potential, despite the limiting factors of racism [Cannon 1995, 91–100].

BORROWING FROM OUR ONE ANOTHER'S DEEP WELLS: AN ETHIC FOR APPROPRIATION AND RECIPROCITY

In her book *Mujerista Theology*, Isasi-Díaz tells of her sadness, anger, and frustration in trying to "plant her garden" in the soil of white feminism. Transformed by the womenchurch movement and hopeful when entering into community with white feminists, Isasi-Díaz was disappointed to discover the racism there. When she tried to plant her garden—replete with memories of her Cuban childhood and immigrant experience—she found it unwelcomed [Isasi-Díaz 1996, 16–21]. Unfortunately, this has often been the experience of Black, Indigenous, and other people of color seeking to engage in theological discourse across the boundaries of ethnicity, race, and economic status.

Out of this painful history grew academic discourse among some of the Womanist, feminist, and *Mujerista* theologians and ethicists who take part in the American Academy of Religion. One result of these conversations was naming the joined concept of "appropriation and reciprocity" as an ethical guide in theological border crossings [Eugene 1996]. Appropriation refers to taking the stories, metaphors, concepts, or modes of discourse of one group or culture with the intent of converting them for one's own use. White persons have historically wrongly appropriated the cultural reserves of Black, Indigenous, and persons of color without caring about the specific experiences out of which they grew, about whether interpretations retain integrity of meaning, or about giving something back. This constitutes misappropriation and breeds distrust.

Reciprocity moves toward restitution of this kind of misappropriation. It refers to entering into relationships of mutuality and accountability. It also means giving back to the community from which one borrows and respecting the communities from which the artifacts and discourse arises. An understanding of appropriation and reciprocity serves as an ethical guide for women engaging in shared theological reflection across borders of race, ethnicity, and class.

Making connections between the writings of *Mujeristas*, Asian feminists, and Womanists can enlist these voices in helping young people reshape their spiritual lives and practices. A more fulsome repertoire of theologies representing wider perspectives supports both young people and the adults seeking to update their own theological commitments, to be offered as lifelines to the young people in their care. While acknowledging the critical differences between these culturally specific theological perspectives and various contemporary contexts, I nonetheless see similarities that hold great potential for healing across social locations.

These three specific theological expressions—*Mujerista* theology, Asian feminist theology, and Womanist theology—each emphasize that the daily lived experience of those who have been oppressed because of their gender identity is the most valid starting the starting point for reflection about God. They each share a high anthropology, believing and acting as if real lives and bodies matter and provide avenues toward knowing God. They all confirm Chung's belief that spirituality is found "not in only university desks, but in kitchens, laundries, fields, and factories"[(1990, 89)]. Finally, they all believe theology must take sides with the poor and oppressed, opening possibilities for coalitions across borders of differences.

Adults aware of the writings of *Mujeristas*, Asian feminists, and Womanists possess something of immense value to young people who are constructing their religious and spiritual identities: the knowledge of narratives spoken in first languages that contribute to a wider repertoire of imagery than currently exists within mainstream theology in the United States. This knowledge is especially critical to young Black, Indigenous, and other people of color, as this story from Gloria Anzaldúa illustrates:

> In the 1960s, I read my first Chicano novel. It was *City of Night* by John Rechy, a gay Texan, son of a Scottish father and a Mexican mother. For days I walked around in stunned amazement that a Chicano could write and get published ... When I saw poetry in Tex-Mex for the first time, a feeling of pure joy flashed through me. I felt like we really existed as a people [Anzaldúa, 1987, 59–60].

This flash of pure joy occurs when echoes of one's experience as a person of color enters public discourse. I see the potential for replicating this flash of pure joy if feminist pastors, youth workers, and teachers—armed with a curation of their communal usable pasts—create pathways to share these with young people constructing their religious and spiritual identities. Campus minister Terri McDowell Ott illustrates such a flash of pure joy she experienced in a student's life. After getting to know a young Latina student named Jocelyn on her predominantly white campus, Ott, a white woman, invited Jocelyn to read *Mujerista Theology* with her over the summer. Jocelyn reported that the reading "rocked her world" and described, with a huge smile on her face, that the book seemed to read her mind, putting to words a precise reflection of her own life experience. "I had to stop every few minutes and reread—I just couldn't believe it. Isasi-Díaz dives into ideas or thoughts that we know as Latinas," Jocelyn told Ott. Jocelyn became an intern in Ott's campus ministry and quickly recruited fourteen other Latina students—some Christians and some spiritual-but-not-religious—who were attracted to the study of theology written by a Brown woman like themselves [Ott 2018].

When young people see themselves and their culture reflected more regularly, they know that they come from long lines of culturally creative spiritual innovators, and they may be more likely to find their own place in that ongoing lineage. Seeing such representation might support a young person's inchoate yearnings to craft a life of meaning and purpose that resists and expands conventional expectations.

That was my yearning as an adolescent, lying awake, imagining the worlds beyond my bedroom window, and hungering for a spirituality supported my political awakenings. This yearning—a common characteristic of adolescent identity formation — often wanes, unnoticed and unsupported [Heilbrun 1989]. Worse, spiritual hunger gets pathologized or medicated [Miller 2021].

We need models of spiritual exploration, formation, and religion that support the developmentally appropriate critical thinking of young people. Drawing with care from one another's deep wells an result in new access to tools for addressing our culture's woundedness.

CHAPTER SEVEN

BREASTFEEDING WOMEN AND YOUNG VEGANS

GIRL/FRIEND THEOLOGY AS EMBODIED PEDAGOGY

> I do not see religious practices as separate from everyday experiences. This is what I introduce to my students—to see your whole life as spiritual practices.
> —Kwok Pui Lon, quoted in *Encyclopedia of Women and Religion in North America*

In February 1999, the following letter appeared in the *Evanston Review*, a weekly newspaper in a city just north of Chicago:

Dear Editor:

Is breastfeeding offensive?

As the mother of a two-month-old daughter, I spend much of my time breastfeeding. In between, I take part in everyday activities such as grocery shopping, visiting the library, and working out at the gym. Every once in a while, my infant daughter demands a feeding when I find myself away from my rocking chair, smack in the middle of a public place.

Recently, this happened at Northwestern University's Henry Crown Sports and Aquatics

Center. After discreetly nursing my daughter in the most private of two seating areas, I was asked by a childcare worker to visit the facility director's office. There I was gently told that my action had offended another gym patron. I was informed that, although the facility "does not have a policy against" breastfeeding, I would have to nurse in the women's dressing room or to cover myself with a blanket while nursing. Taken off guard, I nodded a quick assent and, after a few brief words, left the director's office.

Since that moment, I have become increasingly dismayed that I was asked to hide a perfectly natural, healthy act. I have also learned that Illinois law protects my right to breastfeed in public by stating that breastfeeding does not constitute indecent exposure. There is currently federal legislation pending to ensure nationwide standards supporting breastfeeding in the workplace and other public spaces.

Up until now, I have not felt the need to speak out about breastfeeding. I have never attended a La Leche League International meeting, although I support that organization's goal to decrease global health risks by increasing breastfeeding.

Now I see that breastfeeding is an act with very public implications.

If I choose to take the advice of the facility director, hiding while breastfeeding, I implicitly teach a new generation of parents that breastfeeding is somehow indecent, lewd, or offensive. If I enter the dressing room to nurse, I am left to sit on the floor or in a very uncomfortable position on a bench, teaching a new generation of parents that putting extra wear and tear on a mother's body is inconsequential. If I go one step further, expressing breast milk in private to bottle-feed my baby when we are in public, I teach a new generation of parents that increasing a mother's already heavy workload is acceptable. The last step would be to give up on breastfeeding altogether. Had I not been an experienced mother convinced of the benefits of breastfeeding, I might have chosen this step when confronted with the request not to nurse in public.

Breastfeeding is not a lifestyle choice. It is a significant medical choice for my baby. The American Academy of Pediatrics guidelines strongly endorse breastfeeding during the first year of life as the best way to ensure a child's long-term health.

Despite the obvious health benefits of breastfeeding, an anonymous gym patron has found my simple act of mothering offensive. In an era when young women succumb to eating disorders, in part due to society's ideal of feminine beauty, opportunities to be offended abound: a woman's breast serving its biological function should not be one of them. I believe the patron's complaint should not have been passed on to me. It should have stopped at the listening ear of the director, who could have explained my legal right and done a bit of breast-feeding education at the same time.

Despite laws, many obstacles—including embarrassment and lack of cultural affirmation—stand in the way of women breastfeeding. I hope our community will benefit from a positive public discussion of breastfeeding, thereby enabling and encouraging women to do what is best for their infants.

Sincerely, Dori Baker

The day this letter appeared, my phone rang off the hook. I got calls from my midwife, my nurse practitioner, my older child's preschool director, and total strangers. "The same thing happened to me and I never nursed in public again," said the nurse practitioner. "I've always wanted to go back and change that." "You go, girl!" said Roberta, whom I had never met. She told me that for years she regretted shamefully retreating to the stall of a public restroom after being asked not to nurse in a restaurant. "I read the letter to my sons over dinner," said the preschool director. "They think it's no big deal to see a woman nurse in public." All of the women called specifically to thank me for responding in public to a very private affront. As my friend Sue empathetically stated, "I'm sorry this happened to *you*. But I'm glad it happened to someone who knew how to respond."

On the day I nursed Olivia in the gym, I didn't feel particularly able to respond. On hiatus from my writing, research, and teaching because of my new baby, my days were spent in the foggy haze of repetitive tasks central to childrearing. Going to a gym that provided childcare was a way of providing myself a brief respite from the constant needs of an infant and a preschooler. Not engaged in a teaching community of feminists, women, and girls (except that of my own daughters), I was out of the habit of feminist consciousness.

When confronted, I responded directly from my own veneer of nice and kind, politely silencing my initial instinct to say, "This is *not* my problem." For a moment, I felt shame and embarrassment. Maybe I *had* been wrong to nurse in public. Maybe I *had not* been as discreet as I intended to be. As I loaded my children into the car, my body helped me remember a feeling beyond shame and embarrassment—that of anger. As I drove home, my adrenaline began to flow and my heart rate increased as I began to find a voice for the anger. When I got home, I phoned a friend for encouragement, sat down at the computer while my children napped, and figured out how to respond.

Remembering this incident jolts me back to an awareness of the permeable borders between public and private, body and mind.[1] The personal is political, and my mind is "wreathed in flesh and warm" (Wright 1987, 18). Although I may lapse into the habit of compartmentalizing, the realms of public vs. private and body vs. mind are not separate. Nor are politics and theology easily separable. Giving voice to my indignation was a political act birthed by a profoundly theological instinct. The voice in me that needed to speak out grows directly out of my connection with a divinely feminine face of God that I have come to know through Hebrew and Christian scriptures, interpreted through many layers of experience, tradition, and reason. It is partly by naming myself as created in the divine image that I

---

1   My experience here resonates with that of Bonnie Miller-McLemore, who writes, "Daily, I become entangled in the ambiguous oppositions between so-called public and private life. On the one hand, my 'private' vocation as devoted mother collides head-on with my religious and feminist hopes for justice and equality in a 'public' world not structured for, and even hostile to children. On the other hand, my 'public' vocation as professor clashes with my religious and maternal desires for creation, nurturing, and sustenance in the 'private' world of child's play and domestic routine. My life refuses to fall into the traditional dichotomy between private and public arenas that Western society has fostered." Bonnie Miller-McLemore, *Also a Mother: Work and Family as Theological Dilemma* (Nashville: Abingdon Press, 1994), 30–31.

am able to embrace the image of a breastfeeding woman as being nuanced with holiness.

The letter did not address theology, but it did address pedagogy: I made the claim that breastfeeding teaches. Choices about where and how women nurse their babies are *shaped by culture*, but they also hold the potential to *reshape culture* in ways that are more life-affirming than the status quo. Voicing our dangerous memories can unleash change. Dangerous are the memories of shame, embarrassment, and anger I felt that day in the gym. Powerfully, dangerous are the memories of hope and solidarity that emboldened me when friends and strangers called to celebrate my act of resistance.

I look back on this story from my young mothering days with a quiet pride. I am glad I was bold enough to speak my truth in those days before social media, when a letter to the editor was one of only a few platforms for citizen journalism. I am also glad that today we have so many outlets for garnering support for individual and collective acts of resistance.

In this chapter, I draw connections between breastfeeding in public and what was then the very beginnings of the vegan movement. I've left the stories that follow relatively untouched, because the example of veganism, at least as I experienced it, is evidence of young people using their private lives as public outcry. As I look back from the vantage point of 2023, veganism is an example of how culture can and is changing because of young people resisting the status quo, individually and collectively. Gender neutral bathrooms, boycotting racist and misogynist companies, working to end gun violence, and reducing single-use plastics are all issues around which young people are organizing and successfully changing culture.

At the outset of this project, my goal was to fashion a theological response to the psychological literature calling attention to the complex web of difficulties facing girls. I hoped this response would equip young women with a usable past, a connection to their faith story, and a heightened ability to voice the dangerous memories that can both give them life and help them mobilize cultural change. Along the way, I kept broadening the focus on gender oppression of girls to also include concerns of LGBTQ+ people and boys subjected to the effects of toxic masculinity. The biblical faith tradition, when it centers the voices of historically marginalized communities, offers resources for repairing the tragically skewed vision of what it means to be created in the image of God for girls, boys, and gender-queer folk alike.

Critical pedagogy is a field of study that examines teaching practices, acknowledging that no education is politically neutral. Borrowing from Brazilian educator Paulo Freire, critical educators build the case that teaching practices can empower subjects to become agents in the process of social change. The teacher becomes a "transformative intellectual" who critically engages culture with the aim of creating more just public spheres (Hernandez 1997, 10).

In the language and concepts of critical pedagogy, breastfeeding teaches. Even though I was not engaged in a teaching community with the young people working out in the gym or the retirees walking the track, I was potentially informing their politics of parenting.

If breastfeeding teaches, so does veganism. Veganism is a lifestyle that involves abstaining from eating, wearing, purchasing, or supporting the use of animal byproducts. A choice I first learned about from my young adult collaborators in this project, veganism makes a political statement out of the very personal act of eating. Comparable to my choices regarding breastfeeding, choices about veganism can reshape culture. Non-vegan parents who wish to keep a sacred quality in shared family meals find ways to accommodate their vegan young people around the dinner table. Webpages, cookbooks, and cooking shows devoted to vegan recipes testify to this.

When two of our teenage neighbors with whom we regularly shared meals became vegan, we learned to eat eggless chocolate cake and to read carefully the labels on bread and pasta packages. Conversations with vegan friends widen my vision. Although I have not adopted their practice, I have tuned into the debate and read with newfound attention accounts of the conditions in our nation's meat, dairy, and egg industries. As practiced by my friends, veganism teaches: it contributes to the creation of a culture more mindful of the need for the ethical treatment of animals.

Over the past twenty-five years, interpretations and practices surrounding veganism have changed dramatically. Mainstream American culture has become attuned to the devastating ways in which the creation of animal byproducts leads to further climate destruction. Since the years of my original research for *Girlfriend Theology*, plant-based substitutes have come to line the shelves of groceries across the country. Fast-food chains now provide affordable vegan options and large corporations are abandoning products created through cruelty. Veganism, a private lifestyle with a very public statement, actively reshaped culture and led to substantive changes in capitalist consumption following the late 1980s.

As I immersed myself in the world of girls and young adults, I learned to pay attention to veganism, as well as many other significant ways this group speaks through their bodies. As symbols, these markers sometimes speak more than words say. As I neared the conclusion of my research, I realized that "the body" was not *one* theme that frequently surfaces in young people, rather, it is an ever-present awareness at play in the lives of young people. Body image consciousness is amplified, both positively and negatively, by social media culture today.

As Sara Shandler writes in an anthology of girls' voices called *Ophelia Speaks*, "I do not have a cute nose, perfect skin, long legs, a flat stomach, or long eyelashes. My awareness of these facts makes my body a backdrop for my everyday life . . . My stomach, back, skin, knees, hair are always in my peripheral vision. Never my sole focus (I'm too healthy for that!), but always just tickling at my consciousness"[(Shandler 1999, 39)]. Joan Brumberg's historical study of girls' bodies echoes this first-person account, "Girls today make the body into an all-consuming project in ways young women of the past did not" [(Brumberg, 1997, xvii–xx)].[2] Henry Giroux makes a similar point about bodies from the perspective of working- and lower-class youth. He writes that, especially in the absence of hope for economic security, "one forever feels the primacy of the body"[(Giroux 1996, 5)].

This has only heightened in the decades since *Girlfriend Theology* was originally published, due to the influence of social media on body image in teens. In 2021, whistleblowers within Facebook and Instagram shared documents showing that developers of these social media platforms were aware of their negative mental health consequences, particularly for girls.

"Thirty-two percent of teen girls said that when they felt bad about their bodies, Instagram made them feel worse," a March 2020 slide presentation posted to Facebook's internal message board. "Comparisons on Instagram can change how young women view and describe themselves," it went on to state. [3]

Girl/friend theology engages bodies as a significant source of knowing, teaching, and learning. Across the hundreds of sessions

---

2   Brumberg's study compares diaries and journals of contemporary female adolescents with those from nineteenth- century white America. She finds adolescent female angst about bodies to be persistent across time, but that "it is the historical moment that defines *how* [a girl] reacts to her changing flesh." Earlier women's mention of their bodies refers to efforts to avoid vanity and self-indulgence. The "cult of true womanhood" deemed self-control, service to others, and belief in God to be more important than beauty. Contemporary journals of adolescent girls, Brumberg writes, show persistent pre- occupation with bodies — including weight, complexion, clothes, and piercings — as second only to peer relationships.

3   https://www.wsj.com/articles/facebook-knows-instagram-is-toxic-for-teen-girls-company-documents-show-11631620739.

I've hosted through the years, bodies were always central. I remember energized circles in which vegan teens and breastfeeding adults, sprawled on couches and sitting cross-legged on floors, discussed body piercing, dating, and sneaker collections, alongside eating disorders, anxiety, and sexual violence. This body-talk was part of our God-talk.

It became important to me along the way to listen explicitly to what my collaborators say in, through, and about their bodies. How are they reacting to and resisting dominant culture's standards of beauty? How are their spirits being diminished by the implicit expectations regarding thinness, whiteness, and the other culturally approved edicts of attractiveness? When Asian American women remember their adolescent bodies, they sometimes recall deep longings to change the shape of their eyes to look more Western. "I yearned in front of the mirror, wishing for a face that would save me from ridicule and shame. A white face would make others respect me, I wanted them to respect me. I knew that whiteness was part of what was required to have power in the United States," writes Hyo-Jung Kim [1991, 99]. Lanika, a girl writing in an anthology of African American girls' voices, remembers the tyranny of taking ballet lessons in a space clearly designed for white girls:

> Even the tights for ballet are not meant for black people. The tights are pink ... and blend in with white girls' skin. But when I put those pink tights on, you can see my brown skin coming through ... I told my ballet teacher that I wasn't even tryin' to wear pink tights because they are not made for me ... And then there's the hip issue. Ballerinas are also supposed to be real petite, you know, with real small waists that curve in real slightly and then curve back out only a little bit

> more. But your hips are not supposed to stick out,
> and mine do. Sometimes my teacher will tell me
> to put my hip down, and I have to tell her that
> that is where it is, and it's not going anywhere,
> never mind down! (Carroll 1997, 33)

How might voices like these—if taken seriously by those who design spaces, methods, and environments—change the way we teach and form? Might we, the listeners and the speakers, co-design educational environments that truly welcome young people as they are, in a great variety of body shapes, sizes, and colors? Few educational spaces explicitly encourage diverse bodies. Even fewer educational spaces encourage thinking about the connections between body-talk and God-talk like we foster in girl/friend theology. I call this an embodied pedagogy because so many of the characteristics of the spaces we created point to the explicit welcoming and affirming of bodies. I draw links between the embodied pedagogy of girl/friend theology and the postmodern critique of education that grows out of the field of critical pedagogy.

BODIES MATTER: THE POSTMODERN CRITIQUE

Bodies and minds are connected. All teaching is political. All knowing is historically and socially situated, tinged through and through with relationships of power and social dynamics. Taking into account these varied voices of postmodernity, the fields of critical pedagogy and cultural studies have, during the past two decades, chipped away at the ideal of an unbiased education formed from classics of the Western canon. Critical educators call for a restructuring of educational institutions and processes so that they cease to privilege those the Westerner, the male, the straight, and the economically advantaged. In contrast to education as the reinforcement of domination, they posit "education as the practice of freedom" [hooks 1994, 6].

Although this critique aims at creating public educational spaces and methods that will make fully participatory democracy possible, it also provides a guide for how we teach and learn spiritual practices. If religious education and spiritual practice is to contribute to equipping persons to participate more robustly in public discourse, we must integrate a critical postmodern notion of resistance into our theory and practice. The writings of Henry Giroux, Peter McLaren, Mary Belenky and her coauthors, and bell hooks provide guides for religious educators who seek to engage in education as the practice of freedom [Giroux and McLaren 1994; hooks 1994; Belenky et al. 1986]. Akilah Richards, founder of the unschooling movement, furthers these critiques, disrupting the idea of intergenerational relationship to talk instead of "intergenerational partnerships" in which adults support young people's autonomy and recognize their sovereignty [Richards 2020]. After briefly defining critical postmodernism, I will explore the ways in which these writings inform religious education and spiritual formation generally and girl/friend theology particularly.

CRITICAL POSTMODERNISM AND CRITICAL PEDAGOGY

Various and sometimes contradictory discourses fall under the banner of postmodernism. In my use of the term, I refer to four critiques classified as postmodern: a rejection of modernism's meta-narratives; a debunking of the authority of positivistic science; an attack on the belief in a unified goal of history; and deconstruction of the Enlightenment ideal of an autonomous self, acting independently of history [Giroux and McLaren 196]. The effect of such critiques is to turn attention to the local, the specific, and the partial, with the resulting awareness that knowledge is socially constructed.

Tom Beaudoin adds texture to this definition. From his perspective as a member of the first generation to come to maturity during postmodernism, Beaudoin describes some of the cultural events that mark the social and political memory of his generational peers. These include the shifting views of family life as a result of an unprecedented divorce rate; a pervasive fear of nuclear annihilation, epitomized by the 1983 television broadcast of *The Day After*, and the 1986 explosion of the space shuttle *Challenger*, watched by schoolchildren across the country because a teacher was on board. Events such as these, coming as they did after the Vietnam War and the Watergate scandal, contributed to the "cultural crisis" inherited by the postmodern generation, alternatively known as Generation X [Beaudoin 1998, 11]. Subsequent generations experienced similar disruptions and political upheavals, further eroding trust in the grand narratives that once held the promise of cohesive meaning-making structures. The first decades of the twenty-first century, for example, gave rise to the era of "fake news," even as algorithms on YouTube and Facebook created ever-deepening rabbit holes of competing truth claims.

In the midst of competing discourses of truth, postmodernism is often posited as an era in which the quest for meaning is futile. Taking a lead from Giroux and McLaren, I note a distinction between *ludic* postmodernism—which tends toward nihilistic reflections on the heterogeneity of realities in which meaning is inevitably unascertainable—and *critical* postmodernism, which does not give up on finding meaning. Critical postmodernism aims at the creation of diverse public spheres in which different perspectives encounter one another and participate in mutual meaning-making. These kinds of shared, collaborative, non-coercive spaces of meaning-making point to what's possible as we imagine creating spaces for re-envisioning spiritual and religious understandings.

BORDER PEDAGOGY

For Giroux and McLaren, postmodern ideas about contingency and the loss of certainty are not harbingers of the triumph of nihilism. Rather, they represent a state of possibility. Given this stance of openness, Giroux and McLaren construct a "border pedagogy" which offers new possibilities for engaging the memories, histories, and stories of those who have experienced oppression [1994, 39]. The borders refer to the physical and cultural realms of meaning that are historically and socially constructed and that both limit and enable particular identities and social forms. These borders may include areas as simple as a specific neighborhood and as complex as multiracial identity. Critical educators equip students to become border-crossers as learning involves shifting parameters of place, identity, history, and power.

Specific implications of border pedagogy include: The belief that curriculum can best inspire learning when it builds upon the tacit knowledge students already possess; the view of the student and teacher as co-learners in a process of discovery in which students become the subjects, rather than merely the objects, of history; and the acknowledgment that certain experiences and accounts of history have been excluded from the oppressor's discourse, leading to the need for the excavation of and sharing of counter-memories. This excavation attempts to recover communities of memory and their stories of struggle that can provide sources for culturally specific meaning and identity.

ENGAGED PEDAGOGY

Ideas on teaching emanating from the works of bell hooks's find good company among Giroux's work. Influenced by Freire and the

Buddhist monk Thich Nhat Hanh, hooks sought to reform education so that it holistically engages the mind, body, and spirit. She advocated for classrooms where passion has a place, and where students learn to think differently about gender, race, sexuality, class, ability, and privilege. This is knowledge that informs action, allowing students to lead transformed lives. hooks acknowledges that this kind of teaching can be frightening. She tells of the fear she felt when a black student, during the course of a class exploring internalized racism, announced to everyone her decision to stop straightening her hair. "Nothing about the way I was trained as a teacher really prepared me to witness my students transforming themselves," hooks writes [hooks 1994, 196]. In transforming herself, the student became the teacher, challenging hooks to continue to integrate her theory and practice.

Specific implications of hooks's engaged pedagogy include: the assumption that teachers will address the connection between students' overall life experience and the knowledge they are acquiring in the classroom; the view of the classroom as a communal place in which teachers strive to create participatory spaces for sharing knowledge; the belief in teaching as a sacred vocation involving the sharing of not only information, but also the intellectual and spiritual growth of students; the belief that there is no such thing as politically neutral education; and the belief that honoring and respecting the reality and experiences of BIPOC requires new pedagogical processes and styles of teaching [hooks 1994, 13–22]

CONNECTED TEACHING

Giroux's vision of "border pedagogy" and hooks' vision of "engaged pedagogy" echo the concept of "connected teaching" expressed in the 1986 collaborative effort *Women's Ways of Knowing*. Focusing specifically on methods of teaching and learning that empower women's public voice and action, Mary Belenky and her coauthors would agree with Giroux and hooks that education is never politically neutral.

Other specific implications of "connected teaching" include: (1) the image of teacher as midwife, collaborating with students to bring new knowledge to birth [Harris 1988, 83]; (2) the freedom for teachers to claim their own vulnerability, at times finding the courage to think out loud with students, rather than creating the illusion that knowledge is the already complete, private possession of the teacher; and (3) the welcoming of diversity of opinion, which involves looking at the subject of inquiry through the students' multiple viewpoints [Belenky et al. 214–229].

PEDAGOGICAL INNOVATIONS AND RELIGIOUS EDUCATION

These critical educators envision radically transformed spaces of education and formation. Their vision is not utopian, but rather engages the quest for meaning in the midst of life's real struggles over power, wealth, and authority. Reverberations of these critiques echo in the field of religious education and spiritual formation.[4] For just as the hegemonic Enlightenment worldview of rational science and pure, objective ways of knowing held sway in public education, it also seeped into the core of religious faith and became ingrained,

---

4 Harris, *Women and Teaching*; Michael Warren, *Youth, Gospel, Liberation* (San Francisco: Harper & Row, 1987); Mary Elizabeth Mullino Moore, *Teaching From the Heart: Theology and Educational Method* (Minneapolis: Fortress Press, 1991); and Daniel Schipani, *Religious Education Encounters Liberation Theology* (Birmingham, AL: Religious Education Press, 1988). These religious educators fall under the category of "Educating for Social Transformation" in the typography of the field offered in Jack L. Seymour, *Mapping Christian Education: Approaches to Congregational Learning* (Nashville: Abingdon Press, 1997). They draw on Paulo Freire's work, or adaptations of it within the realm of religious education.

handed down from generation to generation [Cobb 1997]. Churches often portray theology as a body of knowledge, doctrines, and creeds to be ingested, rather than a process of meaning-making in which humans engage with each other and with God. Churches often view scripture as a literal source of unchanging truths, instead of as a story of particular people in specific historical settings that embodies particular truths. Religious education has often adopted a banking model, in which teachers act as if students are empty vessels to be filled with correct understanding [Friere 1970, 63]. Introduction to Christian faith in confirmation classes traditionally follows this banking model, focusing on the memorization of scripture or creeds, without prioritizing the formation of spiritual practices, the creation of meaningful community, or the acknowledgment of doubt as part of healthy developmental process.

Many religious educators use the ideas of critical postmodernism to nudge the church into claiming its role as an agent of change in the world. Just as Giroux's goal for public education is the creation of "transformative intellectuals" equipped to participate in pluralistic democracies, the goal of these religious educators is to equip persons of faith to be public theologians engaging in ethical discourse shaped by their religious commitments. This is not the hegemonic discourse of the religious right, which seeks to impose its theological interpretations on issues such as abortion rights, gay marriage, gender neutral bathrooms, and prayer in public schools. Rather, it is discourse akin to liberation theology, in which grassroots organizations learn to see the political realm as a locus of God's activity in the world and seek to bring God's justice to issues such as systemic racism, unfair distribution of the world's resources, and species demise.

Critical postmodernism proves fertile ground for reimagining education. It provides the connections between border pedagogy, engaged pedagogy, and connected teaching, and gives birth to numerous other pedagogical innovations. Megan Boler's pedagogy of discomfort, for instance, stands in the same tradition. In this model, students with diverse identities and experiences of oppression learn to identify their individual privilege, if applicable, and collectively engage in cultural critique that results in reliable ally-ship [1999, 176].

Cutting across all these pedagogical innovations is an awareness that bodies matter, for it is in our bodies that we experience the specifics of history and culture, as I did when breastfeeding Olivia in the sports center.

EMBODIED PEDAGOGY: THE GIRL/FRIEND THEOLOGY CLASSROOM

In chapter 2, I set the stage for girl/friend theology to take place within a haven of hospitality, referring to the process as openended and flexible. The aim of this process is not grand conclusions, but rather to have each participant leave with their own awareness or set of conclusions, some of which may be mutually agreed upon, and some of which may be individually held. This type of open-ended process is evocatively described by Anne Game as a "disturbing pleasure" in which "the risks of infinity, with hints of madness . . . are far preferable to the safety (and possibly bad faith) of closure" [1991, 191].

The process includes the disciplines of keeping confidentiality and honoring the silence, as described in the Covenants of Presence introduced in chapter 1.

Over time, these initial guidelines evolved and new ones emerged. Often the participants suggested changes, informally structuring the space where transformative learning about God, self, and others could take place. Many times, I recognized these changes only in retrospect, naming and incorporating them into later instructions to a different group of girls. As I thought about these guidelines, I often heard echoes of women's writings, and so point to those writings in the footnotes, when they provide further illumination. The guidelines for embodied pedagogy that emerged are:

1. Bodies, whenever possible, should be comfortable. We seek rooms with couches, armchairs, and carpet. Water bottles, Starbucks cups, and Diet Coke cans sprinkle the scene. We welcome bathroom breaks, crossed legs, and bare feet.[5]

2. We pay attention to our physical surroundings as having potential effects on our moods and the content of our thoughts. For example, we might move outside on a warm day when the sun is shining. What we see and feel there might influence what we think and say.

3. If we meet over meals, we honor individuals' food choices without stigmatizing dietary restrictions.

4. Different bodies have different stories to tell. We lovingly embrace and respect differences of skin color, body shape, and dialect that influence an individual's experience navigating our society. We accept and celebrate the differences that mainstream culture consistently attempts to "other."

5. Emotions are explicitly welcomed. One part of the story session deals specifically with the articulation of emotions, but emotions also emerge unbidden at other moments. We pay attention to the

---

5   This attention to bodily comfort is in stark contrast to what I remember of my own religious and secular education as an adolescent and young adult. It brings to mind bell hooks's comment: "When I first became a teacher and needed to use the restroom in the middle of class, I had no clue as to what my elders did in such situations." *Teaching to Transgress*, 191.

emotions released through our bodies in the form of tears, adrenaline surges, increased heart rates, the impulse to reach out to touch someone, or the feeling of being "sick to my stomach." All of these are clues to emotional terrain that we may be able to speak about, but also may be either too difficult or impossible to articulate.

6. Disagreement and conflicting interpretations are welcome. Although a common understanding often emerges, we do not ignore differences of opinion to maintain a facile consensus. When disagreement occurs, we notice raised voices or defensive body language. We remain present with both sides of the exchange, modeling the ability to disagree without harming one another.[6]

7. We acknowledge the fluidity of our emotional/cognitive selves. Although we are often able to structure our participation, talking about feelings at one point and saving ideas for another, we recognize the connectedness of our emotional and intellectual ways of knowing. We remind ourselves that "the method is flexible" and we can return to any step at any time. We always err on the side of compromising the method, rather than silencing a person.

8. We honor the occasional need to maintain confidentiality and trust one another to hold

---

6   Emilie Townes provides a helpful metaphor for this kind of exchange. The "ring shout" of traditional black religious practice allows for diverse voices within a space of equality. Unlike a monologue or a chorus, the ring shout is not pperformative and does not require harmony. "Voices of the Spirit: Womanist Methodologies in Theological Disciplines," *Womanist* 1 (Summer 1994): 1–2.

our stories with sensitivity and care. Because action is a desired outcome, we do not offer blanket confidentiality. Often, the action that emerges is a new behavior resulting from a new way of thinking about God, self, and others. These new ways of thinking may be helpful to others and may warrant sharing. Blanket confidentiality would confine the learning to the story session. Requested confidentiality protects participants' sensitive information, while affirming the ongoing process of communal meaning-making outside of the story session.

9. Silence is holy. When chosen, silence is a way of honoring one another's deep sharing. However, *being silenced* degrades us. We do not hush, gloss over, or ignore one another.[7]

10. Interruptions, usually considered rude in group settings, happen all the time. They are the hallmark of a community making meaning together. In the flow of thinking, we usually do not stop to say, "excuse me." However, we encourage participants who contribute frequently to step back when those more hesitant to speak take the floor.

11. Often, a participant claims their authority and begins to speak boldly, even prophetically, seemingly unaware of those around them. We honor that moment as one in which they have been "heard

---

7   On the experience of literally being hushed, journalist Ann Taylor Fleming writes, "Down the corridors of my preteen years, the word I remember hearing the most was 'hush' or some variation on it, a quashing chorus of 'shhs' that inevitably greeted one of my characteristically high-decibel riffs on the world and served to intensify my feeling of choking" (1994, 170).

to speech." We entertain the possibility that God may be choosing to be present among us in the form of their prophetic utterance.[8]

12. As adults and young adults, we journey together. For adults, girl/friend theology can provide a privileged glimpse into adolescent lives and as experienced travelers, adults with a feminist conscience have much to offer. Along with that experience and age comes a power differential. Adults practice the discipline of not saying too much, especially avoiding the instinct to judge or provide remedies for perceived adolescent problems.

These twelve guidelines form part of the introduction I provide before beginning girl/friend theology with a new group. By sharing these guidelines, I affirm at the outset that bodies will be treated with honor and respect. In keeping with the pedagogical innovations cited earlier in this chapter, "embodied pedagogy" acknowledges political commitments. A primary political commitment of girl/friend theology is the feminist principle that bodies and minds are integrated, not split. This underlies the accompanying conviction that theology is not a disembodied process, but rather a way of knowing that can and should engage the body, mind, and spirit. This contributes to a revision of patriarchal and oppressive streams of Christian thought and practice that did not honor bodies of women, people of color, and youth [(Paulsell 2002)].

In intentionally curated spaces such as this, body-talk can inform God-talk, and vice versa. The clearest example of this occurred during Emma's story, related in chapter 3. Emma, somewhat surprised, real-

---

8   Kathleen Norris defines prophets as "the carriers of hope through disastrous times." This is a fitting image for adolescent prophets, who can describe a landscape adults are often unable to see. *The Cloister Walk* (New York: Riverhead Books, 1996), 45.

ized she was wearing Rachel's shoes, just as we finished talking about Rachel's death. Wearing the shoes of a deceased friend came to be seen as a way of honoring the dead and keeping her memory alive. Emma's shoes and the instinct to wear them helped to make sense of the church's age-old tradition of preserving relics, such as the remains of a saint's fingertip. The image of the saint's fingertip, in turn, helped us understand the sacred quality of the shoes on Emma's feet. We named connections between our bodies and ancient traditions, celebrating a new/ancient meaning emerging in our midst.

Another example of body-talk informing God-talk occurred during Hannah's story, as related in chapter 5, when Katie talked about the father bending over his daughter in the midst of smoke and flames. As Katie vividly imagined the posture of the father and the daughter, she named his tears as the source of her survival. In his crying, the father revealed an aspect of God for us. We named connections between an ancient image and a contemporary body, replacing an image of God as toxically masculine with the ability to cry.

In these moments, the intentionally body-welcoming space we created contributed to the flow of our conversation, resulting in the ability for surprisingly new meanings to arise as we excavated ancient sources through the lenses of embodied feminist critique.

WHY GIRLS AND WOMEN NEED EMBODIED PEDAGOGY

In describing embodied pedagogy, I envision a trauma-informed space in which learning takes place on many levels. In such learning environments, the content of women's emancipatory theologies, women's communal usable past, and various faith traditions travel through processes that engage bodies, minds, and spirits. Thus, the teaching becomes intentional practice, actively seeking emancipation, healing, and transformation [(Chopp 1996, 222)]. Creating such learning contexts is critically important at this juncture of history and culture, because many educational experiences—both formal and informal—operate to damage the integrity of body, mind, and soul. When my friend, Lisa, was a teenager, her parents took her to a psychiatrist because she exhibited "lesbian tendencies." The doctor said she was going through a stage that would pass. Lisa tried to abide by this "diagnosis." But her body would not let her. Whenever Lisa was in the presence of a girl she liked, she had to leave the room to vomit. Lisa experienced confusion of body, mind, and spirit during adolescence and well into her early adult years. A deeply religious person, she tried her best to adopt the behavior her church, parents, psychiatrist, and culture deemed appropriate. Her body stores many memories of those years of repression [(VanDerKolk 2014)].[9]

Many bodies store memories of old wounds.[10] They bear testimony to the fact that cultural norms, which can become embedded in family systems, often have pernicious effects on bodies across the spectrum of race, class, gender identity, sexuality, and ethnicity. Some teens engage in self-harming behavior, or struggle with body dysmorphia. Some young people rely on substances as a coping mechanism. Their bodies are their voices, and they are shouting loudly.

---

9   For a thorough discussion of some of the specific developmental issues facing adolescent girls coming out as lesbians, see Beth Zemsky, "Coming Out against All Odds: Resistance in the Life of a Young Lesbian," in *Women, Girls and Psychotherapy: Reframing Resistance*, ed. Carol Gilligan, Annie G. Rogers, and Deborah L. Tolman (Binghamton, NY: Haworth Press, 1991), 185–99. See also Gerald Unks, *The Gay Teen: Educational Practice and Theory for Lesbian, Gay, and Bisexual Adolescents* (New York: Routledge Press, 1995) and Leanne McCall Tigert and Timothy Brown, *Coming Out Young and Faithful* (Cleveland: Pilgrim Press, 2001).

10   Ruth Behar, in telling about a year of her girlhood spent in a body cast, writes eloquently of this, stating that "the body is a homeland—a place where knowledge, memory, and pain is stored by the child." *The Vulnerable Observer: Anthropology That Breaks Your Heart* (Boston: Beacon Press, 1996), 30.

Theorists believe one factor causing the life-threatening disorders of anorexia nervosa and bulimia is white culture's standard of thinness as epitomizing beauty. Becky Wangsgaard Thompson suggests that girls' bodies suffer cultural wounds. In her study of Black, Latina, and white girls struggling with eating disorders, she discovered a wide range of traumas out of which their disordered eating grew. Racism, sexism, classism, ableism, homophobia, transphobia, sexual and emotional abuse, and cultural erasure all inflict deep wounds on young people in the process of meaning-making [1992, 50].

Clinicians note a significant increase in the rate of life-threatening obesity among low-income adolescents. Young people living in historically impoverished communities lack access to healthy, affordable food options, and to information focused on living a healthy lifestyle both through diet and exercise. Families struggling to pay their bills, or living in a food desert, may be forced to purchase food at the local fast-food chain or gas station. The lack of adequate public health care further complicates the long-term health risks of obesity

Self-harm, understood as intentionally harming oneself without necessarily experiencing suicidal ideations, is an increasingly prevalent teenage phenomenon that has gained attention only in the past few decades [Walsh and Rosin 1988]. Jennifer Egan, in an investigative report for the *New York Times Magazine*, followed one adolescent girl during several months of treatment for self-harm. Egan describes the life of sixteen-year-old Jill McArdle (a pseudonym) as full of self-scrutiny. When she was fourteen, a boy spread harmful lies about her sexual behavior. Depressed and anxious, Jill turned to self-injurious behavior as a coping mechanism. She felt that engaging in self-harm would distract her from her anxiety and anguish. Soon, self-harm became an unhealthy habit. Researchers who study self-harm conclude that it begins as a coping mechanism. As Egan writes: "People harm themselves because it makes them feel better;

they use physical pain to obfuscate a deeper, more intolerable psychic pain associated with feelings of anger, sadness, or abandonment . . . It can also jolt people out of states of numbness and emptiness—it can make them feel alive"[(Egan 1997, 21–40)]. The behavior, similar to eating disorders and substance abuse, can become a compulsion, eclipsing all other thoughts and actions.

Adolescents use their bodies in ways both healthy and unhealthy to cope with trauma and exert control over whole selves. These examples of physical harm point to the untold internal pain young people sometimes undergo in their journey to adulthood. Contemporary youth hold varied identities along the lines of race, class, gender, sexuality, ability, and ethnicity; common to them all are the conflicting, and at times toxic, messages about the value of their body/selves. Sometimes people find healthy paths of resistance and grow into adulthood spiritually, physically, and emotionally unscathed. But sometimes they rely on unhealthy forms of resistance, behaviors that often continue into adulthood.

Gilligan's hope to see girls and women dancing at the crossroads of female development stems from a feminist vision that "one day, the underground knowledge women have stored inside themselves since girlhood will cease to be merely psychologically corrosive and become, instead, a public resistance that will remake the world"[(Behar 1996, 131)]. Such a vision may seem utopian. But linked to transformative social action, utopian visions can become seeds of change. Any remaking of the world will require multiple paths of resistance. One such path involves the creation of alternative spaces in which the bodies, minds, and spirits of all young people—female, male, and nonbinary—can emerge free from the limiting constraints of gender oppression. An embodied pedagogy provides clues toward the creation of such spaces.

CHAPTER EIGHT

GOD-TALK AT THE CROSSROADS OF SOULS

Some women will just "happen" to Race through these
fields and pick up Messages of an Other and better world . . .
Such . . . women will hear ripples of merriment, echoes of
distant yet familiar raindrops, sunbeams. We will experience
"coincidences," syn-Crone-icities, meetings at crossroads of
species, of souls. We'll Race and Race and leap with deer and
hop with rabbits. With ladybugs we'll climb tall stalks of grass.
With barnacles we'll hug the rocks of seashores. With snakes
we'll glide through gardens. Like butterflies we'll skit from
flower to flower. Our Hour will come. It has already.
— Mary Daly, *Pure Lust: Elemental Feminist Philosophy*

Between birth and death, we navigate multiple uncharted transitions. One of the most treacherous is adolescence and emerging adulthood. Young people at this transition need companions, midwives who are willing to deal with the messiness of life and to celebrate the clear, shining moments as they come. Throughout this project, I have attempted to outline a path developing such relationships within the context of faith communities. As we conclude, we turn finally to the relationships that my participants formed in girl/friend theology. Out of such relationships grew a particular vision of God, which I describe as a meeting at the crossroads *of souls*. The Christian tradition possesses a strong, albeit hidden, custom of creating such crossroads in the lives of women. These women's spaces *within the church* have been crucial for the development of feminist consciousness *outside the church*. In this way they have transformed society [Lerner 1993, 220–246]. Might inclusive meaning-making spaces such as those envisioned in this book play a role in this ongoing tradition, transforming society in such a way that people of all genders more fully reflect the image of God?

A RESOUNDING CRY FOR MENTORS

Young people need adults who are willing to enter into relationships with them. This resounding cry for mentors echoes across cultures, traditions, and disciplines.

Two sociological studies published in the early twenty-first century examining male and female adolescence point to the importance of adult role models. In looking at resilient youth—those young people who are "invulnerable, successful-despite-the-odds"—Joy G. Dryfoos cites the importance of youth having an attachment to a caring adult. She writes, "The best documented fact in the extensive US literature on youth is the importance of social bonding between a young person and an adult." She points to the development of "safe havens" within communities as providing "safe passage" in a landscape otherwise devoid of traditional rites of passage from childhood to adulthood [Dryfoos 1998, 39; 262].

Patricia Hersch titled her ethnographic study of high school students *A Tribe Apart*, referring to the sheer amount of time contemporary adolescents spend outside the presence of adults. "The teenager has been classified as a remote being," wrote one of her adolescent collaborators. "There is an unspeakable distance between youth and the grown-up world" [Hersch 1998, 30]. Hersch concludes her study with this plea:

> What kids need most from adults is not just
> rides, pizza, chaperones, and discipline. They need
> the telling of stories, the close ongoing contact so
> that they can learn and be accepted. If nobody
> is there to talk to, it is difficult to get the les-
> sons of your own life so that you are adequate-
> ly prepared to do the next thing. Without a link
> across generations, kids will only hear from their
> peers [Hersch 1998, 364].

Joan Jacobs Brumberg's research on the adolescent female body
reaches a similar conclusion, but from a historical perspective. Today,
girls' bodies are maturing sexually at a younger age. This is happening at a time when cultural mores regarding sexual behavior are in
flux. The result of this convergence, Brumberg writes, is that girls
need help making "sense of their own emotions, as well as the social pressures that are part of the postvirginal world" [Brumberg 1997, 209].
Calling for women to enter relationships with girls, she writes:

> I think that most girls desire and profit from
> connection with their mothers, their aunts, their
> women teachers, and even their friends, and that
> individual autonomy has been oversold as a mod-
> el for female development and for social life in
> general . . . As we prepare girls for the 21st cen-
> tury, we need to initiate a larger multigeneration-
> al dialogue that speaks to the reality of earlier
> maturation [209].

Writing at the overlap of adolescent development and feminist
theology, Joyce Mercer agrees. In looking for ways to promote
"wholeness and thriving" among adolescent girls, Mercer lifts up
five categories of social practice that seem to benefit girls in educational, religious, and clinical settings. One such category is practic-

es that invite deep, sustained conversations between girls and adult mentors. She writes that these relationships support the vitality and well-being of adolescent girls. In her study, girls communicated that they do not often get the chance to talk about their lives in substantive ways with adults. Girls affirmed the need for in-depth conversations about God, ethics, romance, the future—and the value of simply having someone listen to them for an extended period of time [Mercer 2008].

This echoes the findings of Carol Lee Flinders, who writes, "One of the subtler aspects of the debate over 'voice' and 'silence' is that there is an immense difference between having permission to speak and enjoying the hope that *someone might actually listen to you.*"

Mentoring relationships are reciprocal. Throughout her work, Hersch comments on the mutuality of the friendships she formed with adolescents. Glimpsing their worlds changed her world in positive, life-affirming ways. Gilligan and Brown also note this phenomenon, taking it from the personal to the political realm; not only do adult-adolescent relationships have the power to help girls, they have the power to transform society:

> When women and girls meet at the crossroads of adolescence, the intergenerational seam of a patriarchal culture opens. If women and girls together resist giving up relationship for the sake of "relationships," then this meeting holds the potential for societal and cultural change [Gilligan and Brown 1998, 232].

The tradition of "other-mothers" in the lives of Black women exemplifies this dynamic in a mentoring relationship. "Other-mothers," a role whose origins can be traced to West African cultures, are those women in the community who share child-rearing responsibilities with blood mothers [Collins 1991]. Through other-mothering, the lives of women and girls intersect to transcend private realms and to have public impact. Beverly Jean Smith describes the effect of a community of other-mothers who looked after her, her sisters, and female cousins while growing up. Smith writes, "Surrounded by a large group of women: family, friends, and neighbors, I have always felt connected while acting alone . . . I entered the world with a voice, and all of these women have helped me sing"[(1991, 98)].

A woman's sustained involvement with a girl other than her own daughter is unusual today, unless the relationship is the result of a professional role as teacher, professor, nurse, doctor, nutritionist, psychologist, social worker, or pastor [(Brumberg 1997, 198)]. These professionals sometimes step beyond their job descriptions, throwing the lifelines girls use to pull themselves through difficult times. These women are the Mrs. Bertha Flowers, the DeLois, and the "linen-suited business woman in her fifties" of girls' *organic* educations as discussed in chapter 4. Girls need intentional, explicit education that leads toward wholeness. The cry for mentors resounds and girl/friend theology provides one way of answering the call.

FROM SOLO TO COMMUNITY: MENTORING CIRCLES

Sondra Higgins Matthaei modifies the term "mentor" to characterize a specific relationship within the faith community. She defines a "faith mentor" as a "co-creator with God who, as a living representative of God's grace, participates in the relational, vocational, and spiritual growth of others" [(1996, 20)]. I widen Matthaei's definition to the image of a faith-mentoring circle and add the element of feminist consciousness to describe the relationships that girl/friend theology seeks to create. Throughout the literature on mentoring, one-on-one relationships are usually in focus. Yet several barriers make such relationships risky to both adults and adolescents. First, women may feel intimidated by the prospect of getting to know young people, who often present themselves as indifferent. Second, often burdened with responsibilities of professional and family life, women fear creating close relationships that hold the potential for long-term responsibility. Third, without some common bond through which to initiate the mentoring relationship, women wonder, "What are we going to talk about?" and young people might wonder, "What about me does she want to fix?" Lastly, no matter what safeguards are in place, one-on-one relationships run the risk of leading to the abuse of power. Sadly, many people report being emotionally and sexually abused by their pastors, counselors, and therapists. This potential exists no matter the gender identity of the mentor or adolescent. The threat of abuse and the fear of false accusations of abuse both contribute to an air of risk surrounding one-on-one mentoring relationships. With these risks under consideration, the image of a "mentoring circle" creates a path through some of these barriers.

In the research for the first edition of this book, I created mentoring circles: groups composed of two adult women and between two and four adolescent girls. For the purposes of my research, the groups were necessarily short in duration. Although significant mentoring occurred in these short periods of time, I envision girl/friend theology happening at a slower pace that allows for long-term relationships to develop and grow. In such mentoring circles, one adult mentor alone is not fully responsible. Adults share responsibility with each other and with the young people for the relationships that form and the content of the sessions. Mentoring circles are mutual and reciprocal, acknowledging that adults need the companionship and insight of young people as much as young people need the companionship and insight of adults. The life story that each participant brings determines the content of the conversations. As participants take turns bringing the story, they take turns setting the agenda. In mentoring circles, adults are not trying to fix adolescent problems. Instead, they are opening the texts of their lives as potential resources to adolescents.

When the element of feminist consciousness is added to such mentoring circles, the vision of girl/friend theology is complete. Gerda Lerner defines "feminist consciousness" as:

> (1) the awareness of women that they belong to a subordinate group and that, as members of such a group, they have suffered wrongs; (2) the recognition that their condition of subordination is not natural, but societally determined; (3) the development of a sense of sisterhood; (4) the autonomous definition by women of their goals and strategies for changing their conditions; and (5) the development of an alternative vision of the future (Lerner 1993, 274).

As adult women and adolescents bring and find commitment to feminist ideals within mentoring circles, they join in an ancient chorus of voices that has worked throughout history *within the church* to create the very elements of feminist consciousness Lerner describes.

The emphasis here is on girls and women, but I can easily imagine it widening to welcome anyone who has experienced oppression because of their gender identification or sexual orientation. A young friend, Theo, who identifies as nonbinary, recently moved to San Francisco to launch a career and live in a place free from the constraints of their conservative Evangelical family and surrounding culture. Theo told me how surprised and delighted they were when, upon being recruited to sing in an Episcopal choir in the Bay Area, they found a welcoming circle of gay men and nonbinary people deeply engaged in Christian community. This circle mentors Theo in forms of Christianity that came to life during this church's response to the HIV/AIDS crisis of the late 1980s. It provides unimaginable solace and comfort to Theo as they navigate the spiritual, financial, and emotional challenges of young adult development.

My mentor, feminist historian and theologian Rosemary Radford Ruether, described this kind of liberatory environment as "women/church." While I haven't discovered the nonbinary name for this movement, I celebrate the many pockets of spiritual care, spiritual practice, and deeply mutual community sprouting up across the United States, as churches fade in usefulness and relevance to young adults. An example is The Dinner Party, founded by Lennon Flowers, which started in the Bay Area as a safe place for people experiencing grief to gather regularly around a meal for companionship. Liberated from belief or dogma, this gathering provides spiritual sustenance which also forms people in new practices. Humans, innately spiritual beings that we are, will find ways to meet our spiritual needs, even when those needs are best described as simply human ones. It is with this same spirit of inclusivity in mind that I trace the historical value of "female clusters" as providing safe space that might be adapted for use by similarly gender oppressed communities today.

FEMALE CLUSTERS: REVIVING AN ANCIENT TRADITION

Lerner uses the phrase "female clusters, female networks, and social spaces" to refer to the pockets of history where women's intellectual activity flourished, despite patriarchy. In the absence of such groups, "individual women had to think their way out of patriarchal gender definitions and their constraining impact as though each of them were a lonely Robinson Crusoe on a desert island, reinventing civilization" (Lerner 1993, 220). Biographies that focus on such exemplary female lives "explain only themselves." They serve the political purpose of affirming notions of the heroic, but they do not challenge official histories (Smith 1993). However, when the female subject is located in her political and social context, alternative histories sometimes emerge.

Lerner provides this kind of structural analyses of the societies in which women's thought gained momentum. She examines clusters of learned women, seeking to determine what supported their existence. Throughout history, groups of religious women often provided the "cultural prodding" necessary for women to advance intellectually and educationally. For women to think, to write, and to enter the marketplace of ideas, a specifically female audience was required. In Lerner's analysis, women mystics and cloistered nuns were the first to achieve such audiences. She traces the first documentation of an individual woman's life to the seventh-century writing of *The Life of St. Radegund,* by the nun Baudovinia [1993, 249]. Lerner points to this writing as the beginning of a long tradition of "sister books" in which younger nuns paid homage to their predecessors through written biographies. Although the primary impetus for these writings may have been the spreading of religious views or providing heroic images for sister nuns to emulate, they function significantly as the earliest written record of women's history. It is no accident that female clusters supporting women of note were often religious: during a variety of historical moments, the argument for women's equality often rested on theological and biblical grounds [Ruether 1998, 5].

In addition to being in the church, such female networks also emerged within courts and families of nobility, where women of wealth had access to education. Lerner writes of one such group of matriarchs, "we see in this clustering an inter-generational laying-on of hands by which the transmittal of knowledge to women becomes a family tradition" [1993, 220]. Female clusters, female networks, and social spaces are the shoulders on which future generations of women *could have* stood, had they been aware of their inheritance.

However, as Lerner points out, most of their writings were lost without a trace to the women who followed.

For over a thousand years, women reinterpreted the biblical texts in a massive feminist critique, yet their marginalization in the formation of religious and philosophical thought prevented this critique from ever engaging the minds of men who had appointed themselves as the definers of divine truth and revelation [(1993, 275)].

She concludes that individual efforts could not lead to collective advancement, because "women did not know that other women before them had already engaged in this enterprise of re-thinking and re-vision" [(275)].

Similarly, Rosemary Radford Ruether notes that alternative visions of community structured around egalitarian practices existed within early Christian traditions. These were never completely submerged within orthodoxy, but neither were they made fully visible. She summarizes the situation, which borders on the tragic:

> Nevertheless, fragments of the alternative vision were continually rediscovered in Christian history by women mystics, female religious communities, and popular Christian movements, some of which came to be defined as "heretical." A host of such popular movements in the late Middle Ages constantly *came close to rediscovering* a countercultural egalitarian Christianity opposed to the patriarchal and hierarchical church [(Ruether, 1986, 35 emphasis added)].

Evidence of women (and genderqueer folk) thinking, writing, and publishing throughout history—work done against formidable odds in order to claim their worth and autonomy—is available to us now as a result of the academic and informal research of modern women's and LGBTQ+ movements. A primary goal of the women's movements in theology has been to retrieve and interpret these hidden strains of women's thought and activity—to make of it a usable past. Armed with that usable past, women of today have what women of past generations lacked: the ability to move from private realms to transform public spheres.

Female clusters on the fringes of the church became centers for the flourishing of women's intellectual and theological capacities. From that fringe, they contributed significantly to the slow but inevitable building of voices that could finally be heard at the centers of power and authority. We might also suppose that those female clusters were not all adults, nor were they all gender-conforming. Girls entered convents, cloisters, and monasteries at young ages. Although they may be difficult to hear, young peoples' voices entered that chorus as well. I imagine such female clusters revived in contemporary communities of faith, where, finally standing on the shoulders of giants, women, girls, and nonbinary people might hear their voices carry farther than they ever have before.

GOD-TALK AT THE CROSSROADS OF SOULS

In the ongoing adaptation of girlfriend theology to girl/friend theology, adults and young people talk about their lives, their feelings, their faith, and their ongoing action, meeting at the crossroads *of souls*. In doing so, they paint a picture of God using their worlds, bodies, and images. What emerges, however, is not so much a finished product as it is an ongoing process—not the blossom but the blooming. Revisit with me the four stories we analyzed, pointing to those moments of blooming, that crossroads of souls.

In Emma's story, we accompanied a journey of grief. We remembered the innocent bliss of playground friendships and we experienced deep sadness when her friend died from suicide. We found hope in the image of "church" as a group of friends gathering spontaneously to acknowledge their loss and offer mutual support, in spite of the failure of the designated church to do so. We gasped with Emma when she realized she was wearing the shoes of her deceased friend. When she named the sacred significance of the shoes on her feet, we all stood with Emma on holy ground for one still moment of recognition.

In the second story, Cathy took us with her to a remote swimming hole where she and her friend caught a glimpse of what heaven might be like. As we entered Cathy's world, we imagined ourselves floating on that red raft, staring into the clouds and locking eyes with the Holy One. At the same time, we felt the threat of Bigfoot lurking in the woods and the pervasive knowledge that, as women, we cannot float freely and adventurously wherever we wish. In a brief moment of forgetting that pernicious reality, we glimpsed "a foretaste of glory divine." Our bodies were the source of that glimpse, revealing to us that our lives are like fifth gospels, sites where God continues to reveal God's self to us.

In the third story, our eyes burned from the smoke of a lingering fire that killed Hannah's relatives. We stood with Hannah as three caskets were lowered into the ground and one young girl faced a lonely recovery. We saw God in the image of the girl's father, a young man who had tried to right an earlier bad decision but found the path towards improvement impossible to realize. Amid fire, he rescued his daughter by shielding her with his body. We honored the moment when Katie stepped forward, remembered the members of her family who had died from gang violence, and prophetically gifted us with the image of God as a weeping father.

In the final story, we revisited times when we hated our bodies and worried about our weight. We felt compulsion for perfection as a driving force, causing us to forget our capacity to question standards of achievement or beauty. Then, with Sarah, one day, we saw. We saw the scars on another human body, and we felt compassion—the kind of compassion that enables the transcending of social boundaries into a space where solidarity can happen. We celebrated Sarah's sacramental moment, the moment in which God's presence was made real through another person's wound. We smiled when Sarah shared her fascination that God was not the distant father but more like her, a compassionate one who feels pain. And when it was all over, none of us were quite ready to leave the comforting presence of a newfound female cluster.

The seven theological assertions I made at the beginning of this project changed as I proceeded. I struggled to let them reflect the specific notions about God to which the girls testified. As I carefully listened to what the girls and women said, I revised the assertions. Many of them are embedded in the brief summaries above, but the list bears repeating:

1. God is mysteriously omnipresent, but not magically omnipotent. Although we cannot explain it, God *is* at work within human tragedies to create healing potential. God may not fix things, but neither does God abandon us (story #3 and story #4).

2. God feels our pain and cries with us (story #3 and story #4).

3. We have direct access to God through our bodies (story #1 and story #2).

4. Our lives are like "fifth gospels." Our life stories are sacred texts where God continues to reveal God's self (story #1 and story #2).

5. We go to church to "*share* God, but not find God." Religious institutions can affirm our hunches

about God but do not usually introduce us to God for the first time (story #1 and story #2).

6. God is most fully alive (incarnated) in us when our eyes are open to the pain of others (story #4).

7. Church, at its best, is a community of compassion, a resource in our healing, and a potential agent of change in the world (story #1 and story #4).

This list provides only the briefest sketch of a richly textured portrait of the God who emerged at the crossroads *of souls* where girls and women met. In many ways, this God is different from the God most of the girls inherited from their faith traditions. Some of my young collaborators had already altered their images of God before they agreed to take part in girl/friend theology. The work of transforming traditions was not altogether new to them, but the girls seemed to breathe a collective sigh of relief at being able to speak out loud these potentially "unorthodox" images of God and find them embraced, affirmed, and urged onward. The adult collaborators, likewise, enjoyed moments when one of their hard-won theological transformations was greeted with a resounding "aha."

The God at the crossroads *of souls* is not the fortress, the rock, the king, or the writer of an unalterable plan for human history. This God moves and breathes within us and beyond us. This God reflects our passions and inspires new action in the world. When God takes on new shapes and forms, we change as well. Human bodies—*all* human bodies—take on new significance. They are not trivial or base but are avenues to the holy, means by which a living, moving, breathing God continues to express God's self in an ever-evolving creation. The image of the church alters as well. It, too, becomes alive and flexible, moving to adapt to evolving patterns of human behavior. It is not a place to go only for answers but a gathering of companions who bring their questions, their needs, and their passions for transforming the world.

This picture of God and God's relationship to humans is woefully incomplete. Numerous categories of theology do not surface here. The rest of the list—as long as infinity itself—is left to be written. What other characteristics of the God-human relationship might emerge if adults and young people continue to meet—not only at the crossroads of young adult development, where the border separating us from them becomes very thin—but also at the crossroads *of souls?* At this crossroads, the border between self and other becomes less marked. In this space, their lives cross, and there is no name for it. This space is best described with a story.

IN MY GRANDMOTHER'S GARDEN [1]

On the afternoon of the day my grandmother died, the trees in my family's orange grove burst into fragrant bloom, the surest sign of a Florida spring. That night, I fell asleep in the bed of my adolescence. Strawberry season was in full swing, and my Latinx neighbors celebrated in the light of an almost-full moon. I could hear their lively, thumping guitar music on the other side of the barbed wire fence.

A day later, I led my grandmother's memorial service, just as she and I had planned. We were a small circle of family and friends gathered by the lake in her backyard, where for years she had rescued stray cats and fed hot dogs to a wild blue heron. As we told each other about her life, a hawk watched from a nearby tree, then took flight. A butterfly drifted lightly above. My elder daughter handed out tissues when she noticed tears, and my youngest daughter tested unfamiliar laps. I fingered a piece of sea glass, and read aloud these

---

1   The imagery here recalls several sources, including Alice Walker, *In Search of Our Mothers' Gardens* (San Diego: Harcourt Brace Jovanovich, 1983), and Ada María Isasi-Díaz, *Mujerista Theology: A Theology for the Twenty-first Century* (Maryknoll, NY: Orbis Books, 1996).

words, which I had found scribbled in the margins of my grandmother's journal dated 1964, a year after I was born: "God is so large he requires all life to express himself." My soul whispered an amen: God *is* that large. He is and She is.

There, in my grandmother's garden, I gave thanks for my inheritance: for the women in my life who had helped me find voice; for those friends and teachers who taught me to cross borders in search of good soil; for the midwives who had helped me birth babies and ideas; for the ancient ones, women upon whose shoulders I stand when I don my priestly robe to witness to the Holy One in our midst; and for the chorus of women's voices that have brought us this far.

I also gave thanks for the young people with whom I had recently journeyed. They gave me new eyes to see "church" as a quiet circle gathered in their grief. They gave me a renewed image of God as father to stand beside my hard-won image of God as mother. They gave me a sacramental way of viewing another person's pain. And they gave me a resounding reminder that God *still* waits for human bodies through which to express God's self, writing fifth gospels again and again.

They have more to give. Young people's visions of God will transform the world. Their day will come. It has already.

BIBLIOGRAPHY

Adams, Khristi Lauren. 2022. *Unbossed: How Black Girls are Leading the Way*. Minneapolis: Broadleaf Books.

—. 2020. *The Parable of the Brown Girl: Sacred Lives of Girls of Color*. Minneapolis: Fortress Press.

Allen, Samantha. 2020. *M to (WT)F: Twenty-Six of the Funniest Moments from My Transgender Journey*. Audible Audiobook.

American Association of University Women. 1996. *Girls in the Middle: Working to Succeed in School*. Washington, DC: AAUW.

———. 1992. *How Schools Shortchange Girls*. Washington, DC: AAUW.

Angelou, Maya. 1969. *I Know Why the Caged Bird Sings*. New York: Bantam Books.

Anzaldúa, Gloria. 1987. *Borderlands/La Frontera: The New Mestiza*. San Francisco: Aunt Lute Books.

Armour, Ellen T. 1996. "Essentialism." In *The Dictionary of Feminist Theologies*, ed. Letty M. Russell and J. Shannon Clarkson, 88. Louisville: Westminster John Knox Press.

Arnett, Jeffrey Jenson. 2004. *Emerging Adulthood: The Winding Road from the Late Teens through the Twenties*. New York: Oxford University Press.

Austin, Regina. 1987. "Sapphire Bound." Paper presented at the American Association of Law Schools Workshop for Women in Legal Education, Washington DC.

Baker, Dori Grinenko. 2005. "Evoking Testimony Through Holy Listening: The Art of Interview as a Practice in Youth Ministry." *Journal of Youth and Theology* 4, no. 2 (2005): 53–68. https://doi.org/10.1163/24055093-90000137.

———. 2006. *Love Letters in a Second-Hand Hope Chest, in Parker, Evelyn. The Sacred Selves of Adolescent Girls.* Cleveland: The Pilgrim Press.

———, ed. 2010. *Greenhouses of Hope: Congregations Growing Young Leaders Who Will Change the World.* Rowman and Littlefield.

———. 2012. *The Barefoot Way: A Faith Guide for Youth, Young Adults, and the People Who Walk with Them.* Louisville: Westminster John Knox Press.

———, and Darlene Hutto. 2019. *The Guide to Discernment Retreats.* The Forum for Theological Exploration, https://issuu.com/fteleader/docs/guide_to_discernment_retreats_final_digital.

———, and Patrick B. Reyes. 2021. "Recovering Joy for Young People in the Afterburn of Violence." *Journal of Youth and Theology* 20, no. 1 (2021): 22–45. https://doi.org/10.1163/24055093-02001001.

———, and L. Callid Keefe-Perry. 2016. "Clearness Committees Revisited: Gathering Young Adults for Contemplative Discernment," in *The Prophetic Voice and Peace Making.* General Board of Higher Education in the United Methodist Church.

Baker-Fletcher, Karen. 1996. "Womanist Voice." In *Dictionary of Feminist Theologies*, edited by Letty M. Russell and J. Shannon Clarkson, 316–317. Louisville: Westminster John Knox Press.

Bass, Dorothy, ed. 1997. *Practicing Our Faith: A Way of Life for a Searching People.* San Francisco: Jossey-Bass.

Bass, Dorothy, and Don C. Richter. 2002. *Way to Live: Christian Practices for Teens.* Nashville: Upper Room Books.

Bateson, Mary Catherine. 1990. *Composing a Life.* New York: Plume.

Beaudoin, Tom. 1998. *Virtual Faith: The Irreverent Spiritual Quest of Generation X*. San Francisco: Jossey-Bass.

Behar, Ruth. 1993. *Translated Woman: Crossing the Border with Esperanza's Story*. Boston: Beacon Press.

———. *The Vulnerable Observer: Anthropology That Breaks Your Heart*. Boston: Beacon Press, 1996.

Belenky, Mary Field, Blythe McVicker Clinchy, Nancy Rule Goldberger, and Jill Mattuck Tarule. 1986. *Women's Ways of Knowing: The Development of Self, Voice, and Mind*. New York: Basic Books.

Berriozabal, Maria Antonieta. 2012. *Maria, Daughter of Immigrants*. San Antonio, TX: Wings Press.

Berryman, Jerome. 1991. *Godly Play: A Way of Religious Education*. San Francisco: HarperSanFrancisco.

Bolen, Megan. 1999. *Feeling Power: Emotions and Education*. New York: Routledge.

Bondi, Ruth. 1995. *Memories of God: Theological Reflections on a Life*. Nashville: Abingdon.

Bowler, Kate. 2018. *Everything Happens for a Reason and Other Lies I've Loved*. New York: Random House.

Bronfenbrenner, Urie. 1979. *The Ecology of Human Development*. Cambridge, MA: Harvard University Press.

Brown, Ann L. 1992. "Design Experiments: Theoretical and Methodological Challenges in Creating Complex Interventions in Classroom Settings." *Journal of the Learning Sciences* 2, no. 2 (1992): 141–78.

Brown, Lyn Mikel. 1991. "Telling a Girl's Life." In *Women, Girls, and Psychotherapy: Reframing Resistance*, edited by Carol Gilligan, Annie G. Rogers, and Deborah L. Tolman, 71–86. Binghamton, NY: Haworth Press.

Brown, Juanita. 2005. *The World Café: Shaping Our Futures through Conversations that Matter*. Berrett-Koehler.

Brumberg, Joan Jacobs. 1997. *The Body Project: An Intimate History of American Girls*. New York: Random House.

Bruner, Jerome. 1969. *On Knowing: Essays for the Left Hand*. Cambridge, MA: Harvard University Press.

Burbank, Beth. 1987. "Reflecting upon Stories as a Way of Doing Theology in CPE." *Journal of Supervision and Training in Ministry* 9 (1987): 147–57.

Cannon, Katie Geneva. 1995. *Katie's Canon: Womanism and the Soul of the Black Community*. New York: Continuum.

Carroll, Rebecca. 1997. *Sugar in the Raw: Voices of Young Black Girls in America*. New York: Crown.

Centers for Disease Control and Prevention, National Center for Injury Prevention. "Violence in the United States," https://www.cdc.gov/injury/wisqars/pdf/leading_causes_of_death_by_age_group_2018-508.pdf.

Chopp, Rebecca. 1996. "Praxis as the Shape of Theology." In *Dictionary of Feminist Theologies*, edited by Letty M. Russell and J. Shannon Clarkson, 222. Louisville: Westminster John Knox Press.

———. 1995. *Saving Work: Feminist Practices of Theological Education*. Louisville: Westminster John Knox Press.

Chung, Hyun Kyung. 1990. *Struggle to Be the Sun Again: Introducing Asian Women's Theology*. Maryknoll, NY: Orbis Books.

Cobb, John B., Jr. 1994. *Lay Theology*. St. Louis: Chalice Press.

———. 1997. *Reclaiming the Church: Where the Mainline Church Went Wrong and What to Do about It*. Louisville: Westminster John Knox Press.

Cole, Thomas B. 1999. "Ebbing Epidemic: Youth Homicide Rate at a 14-Year Low." *Journal of the American Medical Association* 281, no. 1 (January 1999).

Collins, Patricia Hill. 1991. "The Meaning of Motherhood in Black Culture and Black Mother-Daughter Relationships." In

Double Stitch: Black Women Write about Mothers & Daughters, edited by Patricia Bell Scott, Beverly Guy-Sheftall, Jacqueline Jones Royster, Janet Sims-Wood, Miriam DeCosta-Willis, and Lucie Fulz. Boston: Beacon Press.

Crain, Margaret Ann, and Jack L. Seymour. 1996. "The Ethnographer as Minister: Ethnographic Research in Ministry." *Religious Education* 91 (Summer 1996): 299–315.

———. 2003. *Yearning for God: Reflections of Faithful Lives.* Nashville: Upper Room Books.

Critser, Greg. 2000. "Let Them Eat Fat: The Heavy Truths about American Obesity." *Harper's Magazine* (March 2000): 41–47.

Csikszentmihalyi, Mihaly, and Mark Freeman. 1986. "Adolescence and Its Recollection: Toward an Interpretive Model of Development." *Merrill-Palmer Quarterly* 32, no. 2 (April 1986): 167–85.

Daly, Mary. 1973. *Beyond God the Father: Toward a Philosophy of Women's Liberation.* Boston: Beacon Press.

———. *Pure Lust: Elemental Feminist Philosophy.* San Francisco: Harper, 1992.

Denzin, Norman K., and Yvonna S. Lincoln, eds. 1994. *Handbook of Qualitative Research.* London: SAGE Publications.

DiAngelo Robin. 2018. *White Fragility.* Boston: Beacon.

Dillard, Annie. 1987. *An American Childhood.* New York: Harper and Row.

Donovan, Ursula, and Rosalind Gibson. 1996. "Dietary Intakes of Adolescent Females Consuming Vegetarian, Semi-Vegetarian and Omnivorous Diets." *Journal of Adolescent Health* 18 (1996): 292–300.

Duck, Ruth. 1990. *Gender and the Name of God: The Trinitarian Baptismal Formula.* New York: Pilgrim Press.

Dryfoos, Joy G. 1998. *Safe Passage: Making It through Adolescence in a Risky Society.* New York: Oxford University Press.

Easter, Ashley. 2017. *The Courage Coach: A Practical, Friendly Guide on How to Heal from Abuse.* Self-published.

Edman, Elizabeth, M. 2016. *Queer Virtue: What LGBTQ People Know about Life and Love and How it Can Revitalize Christianity.* Boston: Beacon.

Egan, Jennifer. 1997. "The Thin Red Line." *New York Times Magazine,* July 27, 1997, 21–46.

Eisner, Elliot W. 1996. *The Educational Imagination.* New York: Macmillan, 1979.

Erikson, Erik. 1982. *The Life Cycle Completed: A Review.* New York: W. W. Norton.

Eugene, Toinette M. 1996. "Appropriation/Reciprocity." In *Dictionary of Feminist Theologies,* ed. Letty M. Russell and J. Shannon Clarkson, 15–16. Louisville: Westminster John Knox Press.

———. "Moral Values and Black Womanist Thought." *Journal of Religious Thought* 41, no. 2 (1984 –85): 2–34.

Faludi, Susan. 1991. *Backlash: The Undeclared War on American Women.* New York: Crown.

Fleming, Ann Taylor. 1994. *Motherhood Deferred: A Woman's Journey.* New York: G. P. Putnam's Sons.

Flinders, Carol Lee. *At the Root of This Longing: Reconciling a Spiritual Hunger and a Feminist Thirst.* San Francisco: Harper & Row, 1998.

Fowler, James. 1981. *Stages of Faith: The Psychology of Human Development and the Quest for Meaning.* New York: Harper & Row.

Fox, Matthew. 1983. *Original Blessing.* Santa Fe: Bear & Co.

Freedberg, Louis. 2000. "Borderline Hypocrisy: Do We Want Them Here, or Not?" *Washington Post,* February 6, 2000, B1.

Freire, Paulo. 1970. *Pedagogy of the Oppressed.* New York: Herder & Herder.

Fuss, Diana. 1990. *Essentially Speaking: Feminism, Nature, and Difference*. New York: Routledge.

Game, Anne. 1991. *Undoing the Social: Towards a Deconstructive Sociology*. Toronto: University of Toronto Press.

Geertz, Clifford. 1989. *Works and Lives: The Anthropologist as Author*. Stanford: Stanford University Press.

Giddens, Anthony. 1991. *Modernity and Self-Identity: Self and Society in the Late Modern Age*. Stanford: Stanford University Press.

Gilligan, Carol. 1982. *In a Different Voice: Psychological Theory and Women's Development*. Cambridge, MA: Harvard University Press.

Gilligan, Carol, and Lyn Mikel Brown. 1992. *Meeting at the Crossroads: Women's Psychology and Girls' Development*. New York: Ballantine Books.

Giroux, Henry A. 1996. *Fugitive Cultures: Race, Violence, and Youth*. New York: Routledge.

Giroux, Henry A., Colin Lankshear, Peter McClaren, and Michael Peters, eds. 1996. *Counternarratives: Cultural Studies and Critical Pedagogies in Postmodern Spaces*. New York: Routledge.

Giroux, Henry, and Peter McClaren, eds. 1994. *Between Borders: Pedagogy and the Politics of Cultural Studies*. New York: Routledge.

Grant, Jacquelyn. 1989. *White Woman's Christ and Black Woman's Jesus: Feminist Christology and Womanist Response*. Oxford: Oxford University Press.

Groome, Thomas. 1991. *Sharing Faith*. San Francisco: HarperSanFrancisco.

Gunning-Francis, Leah. 2015. *Ferguson and Faith: Sparking Leadership and Awakening Community*. St. Louis: Chalice.

Gutiérrez, Gustavo. 1988. *A Theology of Liberation*. Maryknoll, NY: Orbis Books.

Gutierrez, Gustavo. 1984. *We Drink from Our Own Deep Wells: The Spiritual Journey of a People*. Maryknoll, NY: Orbis.

Habermas, Jürgen. "A Review of Gadamer's *Truth and Method*." In *The Hermeneutic Tradition: From Ast to Ricoeur*, edited by Gayle L. Ormiston and Alan D. Schrift, 213–244. Albany: State University of New York Press, 1990.

Haegele, Katie. 2000. "Pack a Punch." *Feminista!* 3, no. 8 (February 2000): 1–6.

Hall, G. Stanley. 1904. *Adolescence: Its Psychology, and Its Relations to Physiology, Anthropology, Sociology, Sex, Crime, Religion, and Education*. New York: Appleton.

Hancock, Emily. 1989. *The Girl Within*. New York: Fawcett Books.

Haraway, Donna. 1988. "Situated Knowledges: The Science Question in Feminism and the Privilege of the Partial Perspective." *Feminist Studies* 14, no. 3 (Fall 1988): 58–72.

Harris, Maria. 1988. *Women and Teaching: Themes for a Spirituality of Pedagogy*. New York: Paulist Press.

Heidegger, Martin. 1962. *Being and Time*, translated by John Macquarrie and Edward Robinson. New York: Harper and Row.

Heilbrun, Carolyn. 1989. *Writing a Woman's Life*. New York: Ballantine Books.

Hernández, Adriana. 1997. *Pedagogy, Democracy, and Feminism: Rethinking the Public Sphere*. Albany: State University of New York Press.

Hersch, Patricia. 1998. *A Tribe Apart: A Journey into the Heart of American Adolescence*. New York: Ballantine Publishing Group.

Hess, Carol Lakey. 1997. *Caretakers of Our Common House: Women's Development in Communities of Faith*. Nashville: Abingdon Press.

Heyward, Carter. 1980. *Touching Our Strength: The Erotic as Power and the Love of God*. San Francisco: HarperCollins.

Hine, Carlene Clark. 1997. Class lecture, Northwestern University Avalon Lecture, March 8, 1997.

hooks, bell. 1994. *Teaching to Transgress: Education as the Practice of Freedom*. New York: Routledge.

———. *Yearning: Race, Gender and Cultural Politics*. Boston: South End Press, 1990.

Horn, Stacey S. 2004. "Mean Girls or Cultural Stereotypes?" *Human Development* 47, no. 5: 314–20.

Hurston, Zora Neale. 1996. *Dust Tracks on a Road*. San Francisco: HarperCollins.

Isasi-Díaz, Ada María. 1993. *En La Lucha/In the Struggle: Elaborating a Mujerista Theology*. Minneapolis: Fortress Press.

———. 1996. *Mujerista Theology: A Theology for the Twenty-first Century*. Maryknoll, NY: Orbis Books.

———. 1995. "*Mujerista* Theology's Method: A Liberative Praxis, a Way of Life." In *Mestizo Christianity: Theology from the Latino Perspective*, edited by Arturo J. Bañuelas. Maryknoll, NY: Orbis Books.

James, Stanlie M., and Abena P. A. Busia, eds. 1993. *Theorizing Black Feminisms: The Visionary Pragmatism of Black Women*. London: Routledge.

Jennings, Willie James. 2020. *After Whiteness: An Education in Belonging*. Grand Rapids, MI: Eerdmans.

Johnson, N. G., and Roberts, M. C. 1999. "Passage on the Wild River of Adolescence: Arriving Safely." In *Beyond Appearance: A New Look at Adolescent Girls*, edited by N. G. Johnson, M. C. Roberts, & J. Worell, 3–18. American Psychological Association. https://doi.org/10.1037/10325-016.

Kaner, Sam. 2014. *Facilitator's Guide to Participatory Decision-Making*. San Francisco: Jossey-Bass.

Kang, Nam-Soon. 1998. "Creating 'Dangerous Memory': Challenges for Asian and Korean Feminist Theology." *Ecumenical Review* 49, no. 1 (January 1998): 21–31.

Kegan, Robert. 1982. *The Evolving Self: Problem and Process in Human Development.* Cambridge, MA: Harvard University Press.

———. 1994. *In Over Our Heads: The Mental Demands of Moral Life.* Cambridge, MA: Harvard University Press.

Kim, Hyo-Jung. 1991. "Do You Have Eyelashes?" In *Women, Girls, and Psychotherapy: Reframing Resistance,* edited by Carol Gilligan, Annie G. Rogers, and Deborah L. Tolman, 201–212. Binghamton, NY: Haworth Press.

Kindlon, Dan, and Michael Thompson. 1999. *Raising Cain: Protecting the Emotional Life of Boys.* New York: Ballantine Books.

Kingsolver, Barbara. 2002. *Small Wonders.* New York: HarperCollins.

Klein, Linda Kay. 2018. *Pure: Inside the Evangelical Movement That Shamed a Generation of Young Women and How I Broke Free.* New York: Touchstone.

Kleiner, Art. 2019. *The Wise Advocate: The Inner Voice of Strategic Leadership.* Columbia University Press.

Kwok, Pui Lan. 1994. "Mothers and Daughters, Writers and Fighters." In *Frontiers in Asian Christian Theology: Emerging Trends,* edited by R. S. Sugirtharajah. Maryknoll, NY: Orbis Books.

Lancaster, Roger N. 1994. *Life Is Hard: Machismo, Danger, and the Intimacy of Power in Nicaragua.* Berkeley: University of California Press.

Lee, Jung Young. 1995. *Marginality: The Key to Multicultural Theology.* Minneapolis: Fortress Press.

Lerner, Gerda. 1993. *The Creation of Feminist Consciousness: From the Middle Ages to Eighteen-seventy.* New York: Oxford University Press.

Lewis, Stephen, Matthew Wesley Williams, and Dori Baker. 2020. *Another Way: Living and Leading Change on Purpose.* St. Louis: Chalice Press.

Limón, José. 1991. *Dancing with the Devil: Society and Cultural Poetics in Mexican- American South Texas*. Madison: University of Wisconsin Press.

Lorde, Audre. 1984. *Sister Outsider*. Freedom, CA: Crossing Press.

———. 1982. *Zami: A New Spelling of My Name*. Watertown, MA: Persephone Press.

Lowenhaupt-Tsing, Anna. 1993. *In the Realm of the Diamond Queen*. Princeton, NJ: Princeton University Press.

Matthaei, Sondra Higgins. 1996. *Faith Matters: Faith Mentoring in the Faith Community*. Valley Forge, PA: Trinity Press International.

McAdams, Dan. 1993. *The Stories We Live By: Personal Myths and the Making of the Self*. New York: William Morrow.

McClaren, Peter. 1994. "Multiculturalism and the Post-Modern Critique: Toward a Ped- agogy of Resistance and Transformation." In *Between Borders: Pedagogy and the Politics of Cultural Studies*, ed. Henry Giroux and Peter McLaren. New York: Routledge.

McFague, Sallie. 1982. *Metaphorical Theology: Models of God in Religious Language*. Philadelphia: Fortress Press.

McIntosh, Peggy. 1989. "White Privilege: Unpacking the Invisible Knapsack." *Peace and Freedom* (July–August 1989): 10–12.

McKay, Nellie Y. 1994. "Autobiography." In *Black Women in America*, edited by Darlene Clark Hine, Elsa Barkley Brown, Rosalyn Terborg-Penn, 38–48. Bloomington: Indiana University Press.

Mercer, Joyce Ann. 2008. *Girl Talk, God Talk: Why Faith Matters to Teenage Girls – and Their Parents*. San Francisco: Jossey-Bass.

Mercer, Joyce Ann. 1997. "Gender, Violence and Faith: Adolescent Girls and the Theological Anthropology of Difference." PhD diss., Emory University.

Middleton, Sue. 1993. *Educating Feminists: Life Histories and Pedagogy*. New York: Teachers College Press.

Miller, Craig Kennet, and MaryJane Pierce Norton. 2003. *Making God Real for a New Generation: Ministry with Millennials Born from 1982 to 1999*. Nashville: Discipleship Resources.

Miller, Dusty. 1994. *Women Who Hurt Themselves: A Book of Hope and Understanding*. New York: Basic Books.

Miller, Lisa D. 2021. *The Awakened Brain: The New Science of Spirituality and Our Quest for an Inspired Life*. New York: Random House.

Miller-McLemore, Bonnie. 1994. *Also a Mother: Work and Family as Theological Dilemma*. Nashville: Abingdon Press.

Mock, Janet. 2014 *Redefining Realness: My Path to Womanhood, Identity, Love & So Much More*. New York: Atria Books.

Mollenkott, Virginia Ramey. 1991. *The Divine Feminine: The Biblical Imagery of God as Female*. New York: Crossroad.

Moody, Linda. *Women Encounter God: Theology across the Boundaries of Difference*. Maryknoll, New York: Orbis Books, 1996.

Moore, Mary Elizabeth. *Education for Continuity and Change*. Nashville: Abingdon Press, 1983.

———. *Teaching From the Heart: Theology and Educational Method*. Minneapolis: Fortress Press, 1991.

Morton, Nelle. 1985. *The Journey Is Home*. Boston: Beacon Press.

Norris, Kathleen. 1996. *The Cloister Walk*. New York: Riverhead Books.

O'Connell, Patricia Killen and de Beer, John. 1994. *The Art of Theological Reflection*. Crossroad.

O'Gorman, Robert. 1990. "Latin American Theology and Education." In *Theological Ap- proaches to Christian Education*, edited by Jack L. Seymour and Donald E. Miller. Nashville: Abingdon Press.

Ott, Terri McDowell. 2018. Grappling with Race as a White College Chaplain. *The Christian Century*. February 5, 2018.

https://www.christiancentury.org/article/first-person/
grappling-race-white-college-chaplain?reload=1674243265795.

Parker, Evelyn L. *Trouble Don't Last Always: Emancipatory Hope among African American Adolescents.* Cleveland: Pilgrim Press, 2003.

Parker, Evelyn L. 2019. "Divine Fortitude: A Reflection on the Incarnation of the Black Female Child Soldier." In *Female Child Soldiering, Gender Violence, and Feminist Theologies,* edited by Susan Willhauck, 163–178. Cham: Palgrave Macmillan.

Paulsell, Stephanie. 2002. *Honoring the Body: Meditations on a Christian Practice.* San Francisco: Jossey-Bass.

Peck, McClain, Emily. 2018. *Arm in Arm with Adolescent Girls: Educating into the New Creation.* Eugene, OR: Wipf and Stock.

Peiss, Kathy. 1994. "Beauty Culture." In *Black Women in America: An Historical Encyclo- pedia,* ed. Darlene Clark Hine, Elsa Barkley Brown, and Rosalyn Terborg-Penn, 81–89. Bloomington: University of Indiana Press.

Percy, Rose J. *Dear Soft Black Woman.* Podcast.

Pipher, Mary. 1994. *Reviving Ophelia: Saving the Selves of Adolescent Girls.* New York: Ballantine Books.

Reed-Danahay, Deborah E. 1997. *Auto/Ethnography: Rewriting the Self and the Social.* Oxford: Berg.

Richards, Akilah. 2020. *Raising Free People: Unschooling as Liberating and Healing Work.* PM Press, 2020.

Ricoeur, Paul. 1974. *The Conflict of Interpretations: Essays in Hermeneutics.* Evanston, IL: Northwestern University Press.

Robinson, Tracy, and Jane Victoria Ward. 1991. "A Belief in the Self Far Greater than Anyone's Disbelief: Cultivating Resistance among African American Female Adolescents." In *Women, Girls, and Psychotherapy: Reframing Resistance,* edited by Carol Gilligan, Annie G. Rogers, and Deborah L. Tolman, 87–104. Binghamton, NY: Haworth Press.

Ruether, Rosemary Radford. 1975. *New Woman, New Earth: Sexist Ideologies and Human Liberation.* Minneapolis: Seabury.

———. 1985. *Women-Church: Theology and Practice of Feminist Liturgical Communi- ties.* San Francisco: Harper & Row.

———. 1986. *Sexism and God-Talk: Toward a Feminist Theology.* Boston: Beacon Press, 1986.

———. 1998. *Women and Redemption: A Theological History.* Minneapolis: Fortress Press.

Schipani, Daniel. 1988. *Religious Education Encounters Liberation Theology.* Birmingham, AL: Religious Education Press.

Schreiner, Olive. 1992. *The Story of an African Farm.* Oxford: Oxford University Press.

Schüssler-Fiorenza, Elisabeth. 1987. *In Memory of Her: A Feminist Theological Reconstruction of Christian Origins.* New York: Crossroad.

Seymour, Jack L. 1997. *Mapping Christian Education: Approaches to Congregational Learning.* Nashville: Abingdon Press.

Seymour, Jack L., Margaret Ann Crain, and Joseph V. Crockett. 1993. *Educating Christians: The Intersection of Meaning, Learning, and Vocation.* Nashville: Abingdon Press.

Shandler, Sara. 1999. *Ophelia Speaks: Adolescent Girls Write About Their Search for Self.* New York: Harper Perennial.

Shange, Ntozake. 1977. *For Colored Girls Who've Considered Suicide When the Rainbow Is Enuf.* New York: Macmillan.

Siqueira, Judith. Untitled editorial. In *In God's Image* 13, no. 4 (Winter 1994): 2–4.

Smith, Beverly Jean. 1991. "Raising a Resister." In *Women, Girls, and Psychotherapy: Reframing Resistance*, ed. Carol Gilligan, Annie G. Rogers, and Deborah L. Tolman, 137–148. Binghamton, NY: Haworth Press.

Smith, Sidonie. "Who's Talking/Who's Talking Back? The Subject of Personal Narrative." In *Signs: Journal of Women in Culture and Society* 18, no. 2 (Winter 1993): 392–407.

Soughers, Tara K. *Beyond a Binary God: A Theology for Trans Allies*. New York: Church Publishing, 2018.

Springtide Research Institute. Mental Health & Gen Z: What Educators Need to Know. 2022.

Starhawk. 1982. *Dreaming the Dark*. Boston: Beacon Press.

Steedman, Carolyn Kay. 1986. *Landscape for a Good Woman: A Story of Two Lives*. New Brunswick, NJ: Rutgers University Press.

Stephens, Darryl W., and Kate Ott, eds. 2020. *Teaching Sexuality and Religion in Higher Education: Embodied Learning, Trauma Sensitive Pedagogy, and Perspective Transformation*. New York: Routledge.

Stevens, Becca. 2008. *Find Your Way Home: Words from the Street, Wisdom from the Heart*. Nashville: Abingdon.

Stevens, Joyce West. 2002. *Smart and Sassy: The Strengths of Inner-City Black Girls*. Oxford University Press.

Tappan, Mark B., and Martin J. Packer, eds. 1991. *Narrative and Storytelling: Implications for Understanding Moral Development*. San Francisco: Jossey-Bass.

Ter Kuile, Casper. 2020. *The Power of Ritual: Turning Everyday Activities into Soulful Practices*. NY: HarperOne.

Parker, Priya. 2018. *The Art of Gathering: How We Meet and Why It Matters*. New York: Riverhead Books.

Thompson, Becky Wangsgaard. 1992. "'A Way Outa No Way': Eating Problems among African-American, Latina, and White Women." *Gender and Society* 4 (December 1992): 546–561.

Thompson, Kathleen. "Maya Angelou." In *Black Women in America: An Historical Encyclopedia*, ed. Darlene Clark Hine, Elsa Barkley

Brown, and Rosalyn Terborg-Penn, 28–30. Bloomington: Indiana University Press, 1994.

Thurman, Howard. 1986. *The Search for Common Ground: An Inquiry into the Basis of Man's Experience of Community.* Richmond, IN: Friends United Press.

Tigert, Leanne McCall, and Timothy Brown. 2001. *Coming Out Young and Faithful.* Cleveland: Pilgrim Press.

Torney-Purta, Judith. 1990. "Youth in Relation to Social Institutions." In *At the Thresh- old: The Developing Adolescent,* ed. S. Shirley Feldman and Glen R. Elliott. Cambridge, MA: Harvard University Press.

Townes, Emilie. 1994. "Voices of the Spirit: Womanist Methodologies in Theological Disciplines." *Womanist* 1 (Summer 1994): 1–2.

Underwood, Marion K. 2003. *Social Aggression Among Girls.* New York: Guilford Press.

Unks, Gerald. 1995. *The Gay Teen: Educational Practice and Theory for Lesbian, Gay, and Bisexual Adolescents.* New York: Routledge.

Uwan, Ekemini, Christina Edmonson, and Michelle Higgins. *Truth's Table: Black Women's Musings on Life, Love and Liberation.* New York: Penguin, 2022.

Van der Kolk, Bessel A. 2014. *The Body Keeps Score: Brain, Mind, and Body in the Healing of Trauma.* New York: Penguin.

Visweswaran, Kamala. 1994. *Fictions of Feminist Ethnography.* Minneapolis: University of Minnesota.

Vitz, Paul C. 1990. "The Use of Stories in Moral Development: New Psychological Reasons for an Old Educational Model." *American Psychologist* 45, no. 6 (June 1990): 709–20.

Vogel, Dwight D., and Linda J. Vogel. 1999. *Sacramental Living: Falling Stars & Coloring Outside the Lines.* Nashville: Upper Room Books.

Walker, Alice. 1982. *The Color Purple.* New York: Washington Square Press, 1982.

———. *In Search of Our Mothers' Gardens.* 1983. San Diego: Harcourt Brace Jovanovich.

Walker-Barnes, Chanequa. 2014. *Too Heavy a Yoke: Black Women and the Burden of Strength.* Eugene, OR: Cascade.

Walsh, Barrant W., and Paul M. Rosin. 1988. *Self-Mutilation: Theory, Research and Treatment.* London: Guilford Press.

Ward, Jane Victoria. 1993. "High Self-Esteem/Low Achievement: The AAUW Findings on Black Girls Growing Up." Paper presented at a symposium on the psychology of girls and the culture of schools, Temple University, Philadelphia.

Warren, Michael. 1987. *Youth, Gospel, Liberation.* San Francisco: Harper & Row.

Weiler, Katherine. 1988. *Women Teaching for Change.* Boston: Bergin and Garvey.

Weinstein, Emily, and Carrie James. 2022. *Behind Their Screens: What Teens are Facing (and Adults are Missing).* New York: Penguin.

Welch, Sharon D. 1985. *Communities of Resistance and Solidarity: A Feminist Theology of Liberation.* Maryknoll, NY: Orbis Books.

———. 1990. *A Feminist Ethic of Risk.* Minneapolis: Fortress Press.

Werblowsky, R. J. Zwi, and Geoffrey Wigoder, eds. 1997. *The Oxford Dictionary of the Jewish Religion.* New York: Oxford University Press.

Westfield, Lynne N. 2001. *Dear Sisters: A Womanist Practice of Hospitality.* Cleveland: Pilgrim Press.

Willhauck, Susan, and Jacqulyn Thorpe. 2001. *The Web of Women's Leadership: Recasting Congregational Ministry.* Nashville: Abingdon.

Williams, Delores. 1995. *Sisters in the Wilderness: The Challenge of Womanist God-Talk.* Maryknoll, NY: Orbis.

Wimberly, Anne Streaty. 1994. *Soul Stories: African American Christian Education*. Nashville: Abingdon Press.

Winnicott, D. W. 2005. *Playing and Reality*, second edition. New York: Routledge.

Wolf, Diane L., ed. 1996. *Feminist Dilemmas in Fieldwork*, Boulder, CO: Westview Press.

Wright, Wendy M. 1987. "Wreathed in Flesh and Warm." *Weavings* 12, no. 1 (January– February 1987): 18–27.

Zemsky, Beth. "Coming Out against All Odds: Resistance in the Life of a Young Lesbian." In *Women, Girls, and Psychotherapy: Reframing Resistance*, ed. Carol Gilligan, Annie G. Rogers, and Deborah L. Tolman, 185–200. Binghamton, NY: Haworth Press.

APPENDICES

An invitation to tell your story. This template can be adapted to recruit storytellers for your sessions of Girl/Friend Theology.

An invitation to tell your story:

Hi! I am inviting you to write a one- or two-page **story** about an event in your life that you would not mind sharing. Sometimes, the first story that pops into your head is the one you need to tell. We will be using these stories in a small group process that will send us looking for meaning, help us find liberatory images for God / Spirit / Creator, and engage us in the collective work of uprooting harmful images that are no longer helpful.

The story can be about **almost anything and does not need to be particularly "spiritual":** a special adventure with a friend, a close call with danger, an incredible gift you received, a loss you grieved, a spoiled birthday, or just a memory that won't let you go.

It **does** need to be in writing and sent to me, [YOUR NAME], at [YOUR EMAIL], in advance of the scheduled podcast recording.

The story:

should not be one you have told repeatedly in a small group or therapeutic setting

should not include your spiritual interpretation or lots of religious language (we will surface these in the conversation that ensues)

should not be a story that is too painful or too fresh to feel comfortable sharing

Please use your most creative voice to tell an engaging slice-of life-story that will help listeners experience what the moment felt like, smelled like, etc. Think *The Moth Radio* Hour or *Storycorps*, only shorter and not too fancy. Thanks for considering this request!

APPENDIX 2
THE LIVE METHOD FOR GIRL/FRIEND THEOLOGY
(SEE ALSO THE LIVE GRAPHIC)

Listen to the Story

Light a candle. Breathe and Center

Listen as if you are listening to scripture, as if you expect the Holy to show up.

Listen deeply, without an agenda, paying attention to the feelings the story stirs in you.

Immerse Yourself in the Feelings

Share the full range of emotions you felt as you listened.

Surface feelings that showed up in your body: tense shoulders, change of breathing, tears, etc.

Share briefly any stories from your own life that this story called to mind.

View it Wider

Let the story speak to the Stories you know by heart.

Where does Scripture, your faith tradition, or another faith tradition show up in this story?

How might this story unearth a new interpretation or invert a familiar passage for you?

Whose voice is missing from the story or from our conversation around it?

Where does power, inequity, or systemic evil show up in the story?

Explore "aha" moments

What surfaced for you that you might keep pondering?

What idea had heat or energy for you?

What do you want to say out loud so we can help each other hold onto it?

What Next Most Faithful Step is emerging for you here?

APPENDIX 3
FREQUENTLY ASKED QUESTIONS

1. Can I start a girl/friend theology group of my own? What skills does the facilitator need?

Yes! To help launch new groups, I've created a podcast called *Live to Tell*. Each thirty-minute episode engages a storyteller (who is under thirty) with a conversation partner who is an older friend or mentor. We experience the entire method together. This podcast is a good way to introduce a group to the idea of practicing the method; and it is also a good way for the facilitator to become comfortable leading. You can find *Live to Tell* wherever you get your podcasts, or by going to my website, www.doribaker.com.

The facilitator should be someone who embraces a feminist and/or liberatory theology and is able to hold space that is safe enough for everyone's participation (see Creating Hospitable Space below)

They must be someone who has a nonjudgmental approach to conversations about spirituality and is a calm, non-anxious presence. Levels of comfort in leading small groups vary, as does ease in holding space for diversity opinions. The best facilitators will be someone who is comfortable in a supportive rather than central role, who is able to interject their own thoughts when helpful to the group, and who is able to make sure the group abides by its agreed-upon norms.

It may be helpful to have sacred texts on hand. Sometimes a participant will think of a story from scripture, but they might not remember the details. If the details are important to making the theological connections, the facilitator may pause to consult the text.

When facilitating a group, I take notes on the conversation. If people stray too far from the four-step method, I gently point it out and circle back. For example, people are quick to move beyond their feelings into thoughts and analysis. If we have not dwelt long in feelings, I might say, "Tracy, you've introduced an important image here. Can I ask you to hold on to that for a minute while we remember to listen to our feelings? What were we feeling while we listened?" This creates habits in the group if practicing the method over time.

Similarly, participants are sometimes reticent to share theological imagery, staying in a more literary mode. The facilitator might remind them to look for images of God / Creator / Spirit by repeating one of the questions from the handout, such as "Where is God in the story? What stories or images from the Bible or another sacred text does it call to mind?"

On occasion, I have encountered stories that reveal stark evil. On those occasions, it is hard to find traces of God. It is important, in this instance, for the facilitator not to push persons to find God or good where there is none. It is appropriate to acknowledge the reality of evil, while remaining in supportive community. Ending such a session with a breathing exercise, a movement meditation, or a song may be appropriate.

It is also important that the facilitator and other adults refrain from the impulse to "fix" an interpretation that surfaces. Emerging voices are sometimes tender. It is important to gently welcome ideas, while also offering compelling alternatives to patriarchal, colonizing versions of God.

When starting a new group, I usually invite someone who has already experienced the method to be the first storyteller. This takes pressure off the new participants and allows the seasoned participant to practice what she's learned from prior experiences.

2. Does the storyteller take part in the conversation? Does the facilitator?

Yes. Both the storyteller and the facilitator are active participants, but it is best for the storyteller to listen first, share later. Additionally, the storyteller should abstain from adding content to the story itself, once it has been read. I like to say "Once the story has been shared, it no longer belongs to the storyteller. She has shared it, and it has become our communal story for the purposes of our collective meaning-making here and now. The story, as given, has a beginning, middle, and end."

It is distracting to ask the storyteller, "What happened next?" It is sometimes necessary, however, to ask a question for clarification around a confusing or unclear element of the story.

The storyteller's entry into the back-and-forth conversation is critical. The facilitator, too, should participate. Occasionally, a participant stretches to articulate a meaning that seems new or unfamiliar. This is when the facilitator draws on her usable past of history, tradition, and theological interpretation to add to the new image, acting as a midwife to its emergence. This is the teachable moment.

3. How might this method be adapted? Is this Bible Study? Does it work as a way to help youth workers examine the beliefs and practices that inform their caregiving? Could it be used as an ongoing small-group curriculum for high school youth groups or campus ministries?

Yes, it adapts easily to different contexts.

I have used this method effectively with adults who volunteer as youth counselors: it helps them learn and practice thinking theologically and is a way for them to build community. In advance, I solicited stories from each of my ten volunteers. We met monthly for shared meals. I set aside forty minutes of our time together to do girl/friend theology. At first, I chose stories that did not call for a lot of self-disclosure. As the group bonded and grew more trusting, I used the stories that called forth deeper levels of engagement. This prepared the adult volunteers to lead the method with young people.

Even though I have not used the method this way for over twenty years, I still remember images that surfaced through this time together. It was a meaningful way for these dedicated adults to support one another's spiritual growth and reflect on their ministry with youth. Over time they reported to me that girl/friend theology helped them begin to think theologically more often in the course of everyday life.

It could be used as a small-group curriculum for a youth group. Among young people who are not steeped in a religious tradition or who have suffered church harm, this method can be a gentle first step toward fostering a hunger for deeper engagement with the stories of a faith tradition.

In my work with Christian congregations, I have found that the practice of girl/friend theology creates an appetite for Bible reading. When someone comes to an "aha" moment in which a Bible story seems incredibly relevant to their life story, they sometimes uncover a desire to know more about the Bible, its origins, meanings, and history. This Bible study "from the bottom up" begins with life experience and moves toward the Bible, as opposed to traditional Bible studies that begin with the text and move toward life application.

4. What size should a group be? How often should it meet? For what duration?

The ideal size for a group is from eight to ten people. When a mixed-age group is new, it is best to have two adults for every six to eight young people so that younger voices are not overpowered by adults. Additional adults could be added as the young people gain confidence in their voice and ability. In this way, the method could become an intergenerational curriculum—a way for young people to engage purposefully with adults in an organization or congregation.

I have used several formats, such as an eight-week session, a retreat weekend, and monthly meetings. The important step is to begin with an hour of introduction, explaining the method, using the handouts below, and trying to reduce the expectation that the story needs to be a finely crafted work of art. (For more on getting stories, see below.)

On the initial meeting, I suggest walking through the method with a sample story. This allows participants to get a feel for the method immediately, reinforcing the steps by actually engaging in them. It can be helpful to begin with the story of an adult co-facilitator in order to take the pressure off young people who may be unsure of how to go about choosing or writing a story.

I allow thirty minutes to one hour for each story session, but this varies greatly from group to group. Groups who know each other well, or who have regularly immersed themselves in theological conversation, usually enjoy a more relaxed pace and can take up to seventy-five minutes. When I am facilitating, I progress toward the next step in the method when everyone who wants to speak has spoken. I move on to step four and toward closure when I feel that the energy around a story seems to have peaked.

5. How do you go about getting stories? What makes for a good story?

I send out the "invitation to tell your story" at least a week in advance, with a deadline for returning the story to me. Then, if the stories, haven't flooded in, I gently nudge with email reminders. If, as the event approaches, I still haven't gotten a handful of stories, I will reach out directly to a few known members of the group, offering to talk with them about choosing a story, or asking if they'd like to send me a voice memo of the story. Sometimes the act of writing it down can be an obstacle and talking it out or recording the story can be very helpful. I still transcribe the story so a written copy is available to listeners after the story is told out loud.

I always ask that stories be provided to me a few days in advance. This is so I can choose a story best suited for the context. This also allows me to prevent the sharing of a story that would be re-trauma-tizing or otherwise unhelpful to the group. On a few occasions when a very traumatic story surfaces in this process, I decide that pastoral care or mental health referral is necessary. I then make sure I get a story from a different member of the group,

I ask that people try to leave the word "God" out of the story. We will be looking for meaning, purpose, and symbols in the story to-gether—so I ask them to leave the interpretations to the group time. Sometimes this means gently coaching the storyteller to leave out summary statements at the end of the story or other comments that interpret—rather than tell—the story.

There are a few things the story **should not** be about. It should not be about a moment of religious conversion: extremely overt refer-ences don't leave us enough room to play. It also **should not** be a sto-ry you have told repeatedly in a small group or therapeutic setting or one you are still in the middle of living through. For certain groups, stories about suicide or self-harm are not appropriate. However, when those stories surface—and they will—I try to hold carefully the need for people to talk about mental health struggles. The story in chapter 3 "Will You Be My Friend?" is about a suicide, and it led to a rich experience for participants. Please, always err on the side of having extra support on hand for stories like this.

Here are some brief descriptions of stories that have worked well in the past:

- A woman's story about a glistening spring day when, as a teenager, she gathered with her brothers on a tree branch for a family portrait.
- A boy's story about taking a walk to the cemetery with an elderly neighbor whose husband had died six months before.
- A woman's story about a dream that came to her the summer after her twin sister died of leukemia.
- A teenage girl's story about a day she went swimming with a friend and all was right with the world.
- A young woman's story about getting a snake tattoo and the way she navigated this with her parents.

When leading a group of adults engaged in youth ministry, I ask them to think of a story from their own adolescence. In general, I will get people thinking about the story they might tell by asking them to reflect upon a time in the last six months that they have felt the presence of Spirit or Source, a time when they survived a difficulty, stood on holy ground, or experienced an event that still seems to be at work in them.

I select stories that have especially evocative imagery. Sometimes participants choose to submit a second story after they have experienced the method.

APPENDIX 4

Covenants for Creating Hospitable Space

The practice of girl/friend theology requires space where people can bring their whole selves into collective meaning-making. While this is clearly not a therapeutic intervention, these kinds of groups can support healing emotional and spiritual trauma, if we establish a trauma-sensitive environment with clear boundaries.

When starting a new group that is not part of an already existing community of practice, I begin by establishing group norms called

"Covenants of Presence."[1] Your group covenants might include such agreements as:
Be present
Presume welcome
Turn to wonder
We come as equals
Think twice before speaking more than once

In addition to Covenants of Presence, gentle warnings about what to expect can help create hospitable space. If a given story holds potential to raise intense emotions around past trauma, be sure to inform participants in advance. Welcome them to gather whatever might be supportive to them. This may include materials for self-expression through art, journaling, dancing or meditation or talking to a friend, therapist, or counsellor. [2]

APPENDIX 5
BRUSHSTROKES

When I facilitate girl/friend theology for the first time, I begin with this handout. I call it "brushstrokes" because, like a Claude Monet painting, it gives a general impression of the scene. These one-sentence descriptions allow participants to get an overview of what they are about to experience. I invite participants in the circle to take turns reading one of the sentences in bold face, pausing after each one to allow for comments. I am mindful that some people are not comfortable speaking out loud in front of a group. This

---

1 Created by the Forum for Theological Exploration and based on work from the Center for Courage and Renewal, these norms can be found in ongoing iterations via a quick internet search.

2 For more on creating trauma-sensitive learning environments, see Kate Ott and Darryl W. Stephens, editors, Teaching Sexuality and Religion in Higher Education: Embodied Learning, Trauma Sensitive Pedagogy, and Perspective Training, (Rougtledge, 2020)

non-threatening first step of reading a sentence is a way to ease the quieter voices into participation and allows the facilitator to hear each spoken voice. After each sentence, I interject an explanatory remark as follows:

Girl/friend theology is adults listening to young people; young people listening to each other; all listening for the presence of Source/Creator/Spirit.

It's important to remember that in intergenerational groups, we may on occasion mindfully prioritize the youngest voices. Sometimes, right after the story has been read or in the middle of the conversation, there will be a bit of silence. Relax into the silence. Remember, some say "silence is God's first language."

Girl/friend theology is a way to create community out of diversity.

I once thought "community" meant a bunch of people like me sitting around enjoying our similarities. Then I tasted a kind of community that emerges when people from different life experiences invite one another into their stories at a heartfelt level. We foster that kind of deep community when we begin with our stories—which are more easily entered into than our politics, our dogmas, or our beliefs.

Girl/friend theology invites the practice of testimony—as we seek to tell the truths of our lives out loud to one another.

When we share our stories and memories, we enter into the ancient practice Christians call testimony. We hear one another's stories and help weave them together into a tapestry that gives life meaning. It's not just the big stories of life that deserve our testimony. Sometimes it is the little stories, the quiet, almost-forgotten moments where glimpses of holy are hiding.

Girl/friend theology never happens the same way twice.

Sometimes the meanings we find here offer amazing windows to freedom and liberation from mental or spiritual models that held us in bondage . Sometimes they are simple or mundane. Trust the process. Accept what happens as what was supposed to happen with these people, on this day, given this story.

Girl/friend theology is risky.

It asks us to be vulnerable, to share thoughts and feelings that we sometimes keep safely locked away. Share only what you feel comfortable sharing, especially until the group has developed a level of trust. Likewise, try to honor the feelings of others. If you share some- thing that you would like the group to keep confidential, by all means, let us know.

DORI BAKER

1. LISTEN

Light a candle. Breathe and center down.

- Listen deeply as the story is read aloud
- Listen with the ears of God / Spirit / Creator / Source
- Listen with your whole body, without an agenda, paying attention to the feelings the story stirs in you

4. EXPLORE/ENACT

Explore an action you might take in the world because of our time in this story together.

- Is there an Aha-moment, an idea or phrase that holds energy for you?
- What common or recurrent themes are resounding from this conversation?
- What do you want to say out loud so we can help each other hold onto it?

L.I.V.E.
Four Steps for
Story Sharing

2. IMMERSE

Immerse yourself in the feelings that emerge.

- Share out loud the full range of emotions the story surfaces in you
- What feelings showed up in your body, for example tense shoulders, change of breathing, tears
- Share briefly any stories from your own life that this story calls to mind

3. VIEW

View it wider, opening to stories of faith, culture, and worldviews you know.

- How does this story reflect or challenge a view you hold of God / Creator / Spirit ?
- What sacred text or practice (such as prayer, grieving, pilgrimage, etc.) does this story touch on?
- Whose voice is missing from the story or from our conversation around it?

DoriBaker.com

APPENDIX 6

After walking through Brushstrokes, I distribute the above graphic describing the four steps of the method. The following comments are ones I use to guide facilitators using this method with a group of participants who are new to it.

Step One: Listen

I will set a simple center table with a cloth, a candle, and a piece of local nature such as a flower, leaf, rock, or seashell. I will light the candle just before the storyteller begins, to signal that we are entering sacred time.

I say: *I will hand out a copy of the story before it is told, but please keep it turned over while the story is being read. Don't be tempted to read ahead. Focus on the storyteller while they are reading. When they finish, if you need to refresh your memory of some detail, you can turn the story over and consult the written version.*

Step Two: Immerse

I always place my hand over my heart as I introduce this step, to remind us that it begins with our bodies. I encourage you to pay attention to what you are feeling in your body, such as increased heart rate, changes in breathing, tearfulness, heavy sighs, etc. These are sometimes our best clues to articulating feelings. Points of identification refer to times when you might say something like, "I identified with the part of your story where you got in the car and started driving."

I say: *This step is like playing with a beach ball—we bounce words and ideas back and forth, reminding each other of feelings we experienced during the story. This is not a time to censor yourself. The goal is to get the entire range of feelings out on the table.*

I might also compare this step to making seafood gumbo. We are putting a lot of different ingredients into the pot and letting them simmer together. Out of this simmering pot will arise the images, symbols, and motifs that lead us to the next step. Use your own culture's artifacts as analogy here!

Step Three: View it Wider

This is the heart of the method.

I may say: *I'll ask you to imagine the Bible you carry around in your head—your canon within the canon. Where does the story, its images, or symbols touch part of scripture? Does it remind you of Moses and the burning bush? The woman caught in adultery? Ruth and Naomi as they charted the next stage of their journey? Again, share what comes to mind without too much censoring. Someone else will probably pick up on your idea and expand it. It's okay to gently interrupt each other: that happens in the process of communal meaning-making. It's also okay to acknowledge when someone seems to be entering into a prophetic moment of speaking the truth of her life out loud for the first time, or with heightened passion. The group usually becomes silent and makes room for these moments when they happen.*

In addition to biblical images, I also invite images from epic cultural stories (e.g., *The Lord of the Rings* or *Star Wars*) and stories from other religious traditions. This is a way of welcoming "seek- ers" or others who have not been steeped in any one religious tradition.

Also, if using the method with a multifaith group, I would add specific references to the holy texts of the groups represented. In this step, I ask questions such as: Does this story remind you of a theological term that it seems to redefine or to which it gives new meaning? What title would you give this story? And finally, at some point during this step, I ask: Where is God in this story? What does

God look like here? I may keep bringing this up if it seems as though we want to avoid it.

Step Four: Enact/Explore

This is the "so what" part of the method. Is there anything we've talked about here that you want to underline? Did you have an "aha" moment? Is there something you want to continue thinking about, or something that will change the way you act in the future? I usually refer to the story about Emma's friend Rachel I recounted in chapter 3. In step four, these girls made a commitment to one another never to end their lives by suicide. They acknowledged that the story of Rachel's suicide heightened their awareness of the risks of mental illness and the importance of seeking treatment. The story session helped them determine future action. This is a stark example: usually it is more subtle. I remember statements such as, "I will always think of that little girl climbing up into your lap whenever I hear the word 'grace.'" I will remind you that we don't all come to the same conclusions. Don't try to force anyone into seeing the story your way. Once the storyteller has told her story, it becomes all of our stories. We are each free to draw our own conclusions from the conversation that follows.

ACKNOWLEDGMENTS

"For me, writing is an act of reciprocity with the world;
it is what I can give back in return for everything
that has been given me."
—Robin Wall Kimmerer, *Braiding Sweetgrass*, p. 152

God only knows where I'd be without you: you, the dear ones who accompanied my journey over the past few decades. Your wisdom lies between the lines of every page of this book. I have tried mightily to cite you, reference you, and shout you out. Truly I am because we are.

To the community of sages and saints (and you who would shy from those descriptors) who walked with me at discernment events, campus ministry gatherings, leadership forums and other places that nurture the next generation of mystics, spiritual misfits, and prophets: Thank you for challenging my thoughts when they were shallow and white and privileged. You cause me to center and recenter on those whom Jesus would call the least among us; and you show me, through love and friendship, what it will take to turn this world around. I'm not there yet, but God only knows where I'd be without you. It is my life's deepest privilege to have worked, laughed, and played among you. Special thanks to Stephen Lewis at The Forum for Theological Exploration (FTE) for the acronym LIVE and Darlene Hutto, for reminding me regularly of the joy of co-creating on a front porch at Haley Farm. Patrick Reyes, your encouragement to keep Girl/Friend Theology alive and the aspiration to become a good ancestor mean the world. Matthew Williams, your voice in my head is my barometer, daily. So much gratitude flows toward the colleagues and friends collected through FTE and related communities along the way: Rimes McElveen, Tyler Sit, Jennifer Bailey, Rich Havard, Lakisha Lockhart, Erica Littlewolf, Erik Samuelson, Earle Fisher, Emily McGinley, Linda Kay Klein, Shannon Hopkins, Ross Lockhart, Brother Lawrence Whitney, Elizabeth Mitchell Clement, Heather Wallace, Elsie Barnhart, Fran Harrison, Jodi Porter, the Wise Women and those whose names I will add to this list the moment I hit send! It was a joy to gather up the wisdom collected in one thousand spaces where our dreams danced together.

A community of scholars surrounded this work from its inception and helped it blossom into a renewable resource: Wanda Deifelt, thank you for relentlessly reminding me that college students need an update, for providing feedback on this revision, and for using it in when you teach about God and gender. Joyce Mercer, Reginald Blount, David White, Leah Gunning Francis, and Tobin Belzer. Over coffee, zoom calls, and walk-and-talks, we seek the words and images to describe holy mystery. What a gift! Extra thanks to Emily Peck, Mary Hess, Evelyn Parker for taking the time to provide brilliant feedback on this edition and Nancy Bryan, for your careful editing.

Eleiza Braun, I thank Goddess for your presence in my life! From those early retreats on your family's deck in Evanston for the first edition of this book, to our current work on *Our Own Deep Wells*, we've shared almost three decades now of putting soulful practice to work as good medicine for mental health.

For all the people who flew me out to lead retreats—from Vancouver, BC to Savannah, GA and points in between—I always thrill at the way even skeptics come out to play as a story unfolds and synapses begin to spark across the room! For new friends Rose J. Percy and Marthame Sanders, thank you for helping me transform the magic of the LIVE method to the world of podcasting through LIVE to Tell.

To my circle of friends in Lynchburg, VA: Founding a CDF Freedom School kept me awake to the challenges of finding better metaphors of source and soul by which to live. Thank you. Nick George, Nakesha Renee Moore, Tasha Gillum, Rox Cruz, Jerry Griffin. You are my people. Curt, Dave, and Steph: we feed each other in body and spirit through all the ups and downs and you are the best! To the late Rev. Diane Vie: I miss the holy sisterhood of our long walks and longer happy hours through which you helped me untangle all the inner wrestlings of my vocation.

To my white-bodied siblings across the country dedicated to dismantling whiteness: thank you for reading books on white supremacy and keeping up the long work.

To my spiritual direction groups: mornings with you ground me for the work and the play. I am grateful, Laurel Andrews Stavers, Katie Hart, Mary Anne Lippincott, and Susan Williams. Anne Gibbons, you are one of the first fans of girl/friend theology, and your shared vision made it stronger.

Lastly to my family: Girls, you did without momma on nights you coulda used her. You learned and you stretched well beyond the confines of the southern Virginia town that sought to confine your imaginations and to oppress the ones you call Lover, Friend, Partner. I am ever amazed by your courage, Erin and Olivia. The village—a global one spanning all the continents via real people, books, Zoom calls, and Instagram posts—continues *our* educations daily.

Through Erin and Olivia, I met and shared this work with Kinaya Pettiford and Emmaline Herring; both of you sharpened my thinking immensely. I'm particularly gifted by daughters and their friends who become my mentors.

Lincoln, dude, you have put up with a lot. Muchas gracias, señor. As we head into the sunset of our days, may they be filled with laughter and love and continued solidarity with the friends whom Spirit blesses at the crossroads of our lives (Jeremiah 6:8).

INDEX